Investigating
Gunpowder plot

Investigating Gunpowder plot

Mark Nicholls

Manchester University Press

Manchester and New York

Distributed exclusively in the USA and Canada by St. Martin's Press

Published by Manchester University Press
Oxford Road, Manchester M13 9PL, England
and Room 400, 175 Fifth Avenue, New York, NY 10010, USA

Distributed exclusively in the USA and Canada
by St. Martin's Press, Inc., 175 Fifth Avenue, New York,
NY 10010, USA

British Library cataloguing in publication data
Nicholls, Mark
    Investigating Gunpowder Plot.
    1. England. Gunpowder Plot
    I. Title
    942.061

Library of Congress cataloging in publication data
Nicholls, Mark, 1959–
        Investigating Gunpowder Plot / Mark Nicholls.
            p. cm.
        Includes bibliographical references and index.
        ISBN 0–7190–3225–3
        1. Gunpowder Plot, 1605.   2. Great Britain—History—James I.
    1603–1625.   I. Title.
    DA392.N53   1991
    941.06′1—dc20   90–20286

ISBN 0 7190 3225 3 *hardback*

Typeset in Linotron Sabon
by Northern Phototypesetting Co. Ltd., Bolton

Printed in Great Britain
by Biddles Ltd., Guildford & King's Lynn.

Contents

Acknowledgements and note on the text

A word of appreciation is very much due to all those who have, at various stages, helped push this book towards completion. In particular, I must thank Dr John Hatcher for the initial idea, Mr Colin Shrimpton, archivist at Alnwick Castle, for his friendly and ready assistance, Professor Sir Geoffrey Elton for his unfailing guidance to a sometimes floundering research student, Professor Gordon Batho, and Father Francis Edwards SJ. I am grateful to the late duke of Northumberland, and to the present duke, to the Marquess of Salisbury and to Viscount De L'Isle for their permission to consult and publish documents from their archives. My thanks are similarly due to the Bodleian Library, Oxford, Cheshire Libraries, Arts and Archives, the Yorkshire Archaeological Society, the Henry E. Huntington Library, California, the Archivo General de Simancas, and to the Folger Shakespeare Library, Washington DC. *The Historical Journal* has allowed me to draw upon material in my communication 'The Wizard Earl in Star Chamber'. Many other archivists and librarians have provided invaluable help, particularly Mrs Gill and Mrs McCann at Chichester, Mr Harcourt Williams at Hatfield and Dr Robertson at the Huntington Library. My colleagues at the National Army Museum have also given every encouragement. I hope all those whom I have failed to acknowledge by name will accept a general expression of thanks. Above all, I am deeply grateful to my wife Linda for her help, advice, and great patience. This book is very much for her.

While contractions have been expanded, all quotes from manuscript sources are given in the original spelling. Alterations in punctuation, made for the sake of clarity, have been kept to a minimum, although the use of capitals has been modernised. No such liberties have been taken with published sources. Except where otherwise stated, all dates are given according to the old calendar, although years have been taken to begin on 1 January. James I's reign saw the creation of several new peers and the promotion of existing noblemen. I have used the titles appropriate to the time under consideration and apologise in advance for any irritation caused in referring to one man by more than one name. The only exception to this rule has been the suppression of the title Viscount Cranborne in any *direct* reference to Sir Robert Cecil, later first earl of Salisbury.

Abbreviations

APC	*Acts of the Privy Council of England* New Series, eds J R Dasent and others, 46 vols, London, 1890–1964
Alnwick MSS	Manuscripts of the duke of Northumberland at Alnwick Castle
BL	British Library
C	Chancery documents at the Public Record Office
CRO	County Record Office
Calendar SP . . .	*Calendar of State Papers, . . .*
E	Exchequer documents at the Public Record Office
HMC	Royal Commission on Historical Manuscripts
Hatfield MSS	Manuscripts of the marquess of Salisbury at Hatfield House: Salisbury (Cecil) manuscripts
PEA	Papiers d'Etat et de l'Audience at Brussels
PRO	Public Record Office
PROB	Prerogative Court of Canterbury probate materials at the Public Record Office
SP	State Papers at the Public Record Office
STAC	Court of Star Chamber records at the Public Record Office
Simancas E	Archivo General de Simancas, Sección de Estado
Syon MSS	Manuscripts of the duke of Northumberland, originally held at Syon House, now transferred to Alnwick Castle
YAS	Yorkshire Archaeological Society, Leeds

Descriptions of certain accounting papers in Syon MSS Class U have also been abbreviated. Thus 'Robert Delaval, declaration, 1 Apr 1603–25 Mar 1604' refers to the auditor's declaration of the account of Robert Delaval for the household accounting period 1 April 1603 to 25 March 1604.

Part I

The treason: investigating Gunpowder plot

The greater the offences are, the more hydden they lye

Earl of Salisbury, June 1606

I

Discovery

On 6 November 1605, Robert Cecil, earl of Salisbury, principal Secretary and chief minister to James I, wrote jubilantly to the English ambassador in France, Sir Thomas Parry, that it had 'pleased Almighty God, out of his singuler goodness, to bring to light the most cruell and detestable practise, against the person of his majesty and the whole estate of the realme that euer was conceaued by the hart of man, at any tyme, or in any place whatsoeuer'.[1] But the author more than any other man in England was fully aware that, though the Lord might indeed have revealed the bare existence of a Gunpowder plot, it would be the lot of mortals to discover the details and ramifications of a complex treason that had been long in the planning. Our brief here is to examine the ways in which an early-modern government set about this imposing task, for such a study of the authorities' response to an unforeseen crisis tells us a good deal, not only about problem-management by an early-Stuart administration, but also about the way in which the privy council and its agents ran the country. This is a tale of political co-operation, practical weaknesses, yet of considerable efficiency at the administrative heart of Stuart England. It is also a tale of political opportunities taken and missed, a story of frustration and of a genuine lingering uncertainty – perhaps inevitable – that remained when most of the known plotters had gone, with their secrets, to the grave.

If we are to consider these investigations as an administrative problem, we must at the outset face up to an issue that has clogged so much of the literature on this Gunpowder treason down the years: we must assume that the plot came as a genuine surprise to the authorities. Despite the multitude of doubting voices who have suggested that the fell hand of Salisbury lay behind everything this is not too improbable an assumption to make. When Joel Hurstfield remarked wearily that attempts to prove the plot to have been 'a fabrication' had 'become a game, like dating Shakespeare's sonnets: a pleasant way to pass a wet afternoon, but hardly a challenging occupation for adult men and women', he reflected the views of many other historians.[2] It is now nearly a century since S R Gardiner produced a characteristically considered, magisterial answer to the Jesuit Father John Gerard's question *What Was the Gunpowder Plot?*,[3] and discoveries made since have only confirmed that suspicions of foreknowledge or manipulation of the treason by Salisbury and the council were in large part born of ignorance and an over-reliance upon the gossip and rumour which surround all such actions.[4]

Gardiner, however, wrote in great haste; his *What Gunpowder Plot Was* was published a matter of months after Gerard's book, and by choosing to fight Gerard on the Jesuit's own ground he did not, after a promising start, develop the 'secular' dimension of, and the investigations into the plot, as much as an historian so expert in and mindful of the forms and development of seventeenth-century politics might otherwise have done. That we can still read and be half-convinced by books on the plot from proponents of the 'conspiracy theory' shows how neglected is the study of the first ten years of the Stuart dynasty. The most effective way to counter such views is to look in some detail at the investigations themselves, for there is no better testimony to the ignorance in which Salisbury and his colleagues first worked.

'Early modern administration', we are told, 'was characterized by the co-existence of private-regarding behaviour and the pursuit of the public interest', nepotism and patronage, bribery and favour were endemic in English government.[5] Yet it has also become more and more apparent that the governance of late-Tudor and early-Jacobean England was, for all its faults, surprisingly efficient, and that the governors were in large measure men convinced that they acted in the best interests of the country at large. Who, though, were these governors, these men whose efficiency was now, with the discovery of Gunpowder plot, to be put to the test? In order to rule her realm, Elizabeth I relied first of all upon the labours of an increasingly small and select body – her privy council. After more than forty years marked by a royal reluctance to be over-generous with honours, and by the inevitable ravages of time on the generation that had brought her to power, the queen's once-large council comprised just fourteen men in 1603.[6] However, as its size decreased, so its prestige grew – and upon its ability to manipulate the authority of central power rested the success of any early-modern government, limited by the small professional staff at its disposal and reliant to a high degree upon the goodwill and co-operation of the influential men of the shires.[7]

'So wide were its interests, so all-embracing its activities, that the history of the privy council during the sixteenth and seventeenth centuries is really little less than a history of England during that period.' This observation of seventy years ago has stood the test of time.[8] Well before 1603, the privy council had become the true heart of English government. Parliament met but intermittently, while the council – theoretically in constant attendance upon the monarch – sat on a regular basis to decide matters of near-infinite variety, embracing almost every aspect both of central and local administration: appointing sheriffs and local officials, controlling abuses of customs and statutes of all kinds, enforcing financial regulations, arbitrating in disputes among county officials, authorising licences for tradesmen, sanctioning foreign travel – and, of course, investigating conspiracies. There were no set days for its meetings; responding to the dictates of state affairs these took place where and when sufficient councillors were assembled. Only during law terms did the council come together on two regular days a week to exercise its legal functions as a court sitting in star chamber.[9]

Unfortunately, we have few council records detailing the investigation into Gunpowder plot, for the regular series of registers kept by the council's clerks – which chronicles its decisions – breaks off early in 1602, and does not resume until 1613. The destruction of registers for the intervening years in a fire at Whitehall in 1619[10] has long hindered the efficient study of early-Stuart administration, for although we have some sources to lessen their loss[11] it is very difficult to reconstruct the business of the council during these missing years with any degree of detail. Fortunately, since letters from the council were important documents, recipients tended to keep them and care for them. It is therefore possible to reconstruct the registers from the surviving archives of these recipients, and while this cannot, of course, ever replace the entire register and must bias our picture of the council's activity towards the better kept and often the more bureaucratic archives, it nevertheless permits us to go some way towards remedying the loss. It has been suggested that the loss of the registers also helps exaggerate Salisbury's role in government over these years, and although this is at least arguable, the survival of the Hatfield archives as one of our principal and most thoroughly examined sources for the history of the period inevitably means that the statement carries with it an element of truth.[12]

This book sets out to look at the way in which James and his privy council approached the investigations into the plot – first of all in broad terms and subsequently through an individual case study of the way in which charges were fashioned against Henry Percy, ninth earl of Northumberland. Since, however, discovery precedes investigation we must first examine the events which prompted Salisbury's exultant letter. Gunpowder plot came to light through a rather fortuitous series of events, which itself sheds no very clear light on the nature of the conspiracy, serving rather to confuse than to enlighten. On 26 October the Catholic peer Lord Monteagle visited his house at Hoxton for the first time in several weeks. During dinner, an unknown man of 'reasonable tall' stature, his features obscured in the twilight, delivered a letter to one of the household servants who happened to be taking a breath of evening air at the entrance to the dwelling. On receiving it, Monteagle passed the letter to another of his servants, asking the man to read it aloud for him while he ate. The message ran as follows:

My lord, out of the loue i beare to some of youere frends I haue a caer of youer preseruacion, therefor I wowld aduyse yowe as yowe tender youer lyf to deuyse some exscuse to shift of youer attendance at this parleament, for God and man hathe concurred to punishe the wickednes of this tyme, and thinke not slightlye of this aduertisment but retyere youre self into youre contri wheare yowe maye expect the event in safti, for thowghe theare be no apparance of anni stir yet i saye they shall receyue a terrible blowe this parleament and yet they shall not seie who hurts them, this cowncel is not to be contemned because it maye do yowe good and can do yowe no harme for the dangere is passed as soon as yowe have burnt the letter and i hope God will giue yowe the grace to mak good use of it, to whose holy proteccion i commend yowe.[13]

Driven perhaps by his own uncomfortably treasonous past, in which he had consorted with those involved in the rebellion of the earl of Essex as well as with Jesuit priests and their supporters, Monteagle lost no time in taking the strange letter to court at Whitehall, where he found the earls of Salisbury, Suffolk, Worcester, and Northampton, all on the point of sitting down to supper.

Requesting a private word with the Secretary, Monteagle took him aside and explained what had happened.

Salisbury's first reaction was one of some scepticism, although he praised Monteagle for not concealing 'a matter of such a nature, whatever the consequence might prove'. There was already talk of treason in the air: principally in the form of rumours out of France that Catholic priests were hatching some kind of plot to coincide with the opening of parliament. When the authorities looked back to the summer of 1603, they would remember that William Watson and other principal Bye plotters had planned to kidnap the new king, while telling their less-committed supporters that the plan was simply to present just such a petition as that supposedly intended by the priests in 1605. The natural reaction would be to suppose that the discovered treason and the 'petition plot' were in some way linked, to imagine that Watson's scheme had been resurrected. As the *King's Book* – the official contemporary account of Gunpowder plot – later explained, the council felt that such petitioners would at best be 'sturdie beggars, crauing almes with one open hand, but carrying a stone in the other'. While never completely trusting the man, Salisbury continued to make use of his informer among the secular priests, George Southwick, whose reports on their activities, although increasingly valueless, continued into 1606.[14]

Nor was that the only plot afoot. Although it is not clear whether the document had ever come before the Secretary, he had also been advised by William Turner, an informant based in Brussels, that wilder spirits among the Catholic *émigrés* there, particularly Hugh Owen, the pro-Jesuit agent-intelligencer – were hatching a plot to invade England. Having taken pains to try Turner's sincerity, Owen had apparently told him in private of imminent arrangements for a spearhead force of 1,500 Spaniards – backed by 300 English cavalry confidently expected to join their ranks once news of the invasion spread in England – to strike out rapidly from Dover to Rochester where they could seize the bridge over the Medway, immobilise the fleet, and hold London at their mercy.

One of Salisbury's more reliable informants, Turner had been sending reports to London for at least seven years, but on this occasion he made the mistake of entrusting his information to Sir Thomas Edmondes, English ambassador to Flanders. Edmondes thought Turner a rogue, describing him as a man of 'light and dissolute life' in a letter to Salisbury on 27 September, and he probably accorded little credit to these disclosures.[15] There was in any case no talk of home-grown treason in Turner's information, but again the letter to Monteagle might have seemed like nothing more than another manifestation of the same rumour.

On the other hand, there was no sense in taking chances, even if the letter were some practical joke or the work of a madman. That same night, it was shown to other members of the council then at court and a decision was taken to do nothing until the king returned from a spell of hunting at Royston.

James was in London again on 31 October, and he was told of Monteagle's little adventure on the following day. According to the later official version of events he immediately perceived that the letter predicted an attempt to blow up the parliament house, Salisbury and the council tactfully concealing the fact that, although not guided by the same divine providence attendant upon a king, they had already guessed as much. But then as now it was not uncommon for the government to receive such anonymous, apocalyptic warnings,[16] and it was important that, while the letter was taken seriously, it should not be allowed to alter plans unduly. To avoid an overreaction would also be the wise course if after all the warning proved genuine: 'nothing should be done to interrupt any purpose of theirs that had any such devilish practice, but rather to suffer them to go on to the end of the day'. So it was that no further steps were taken until the afternoon of 4 November, the day before parliament was due to meet, when the earl of Suffolk – who as lord chamberlain was responsible for ensuring that all the arrangements for the new session were complete – went on a tour of inspection. Monteagle, who had expressed a wish to accompany him, was also present.

The buildings forming the old palace of Westminster were very different to those occupying that site today, with public chambers, private dwellings, and commercial premises old and new all jumbled together in a confined space. After visiting the lords' chamber itself the party descended to inspect the ground-floor vaults which ran the length of the building.[17] They noticed that there was an uncommonly large store of firewood laid up in one of these cellars, and asked a serving man, whom Suffolk later described as 'a very tall and desperate fellow', whose fuel this was. They were told that it belonged to the man's master, Thomas Percy, a gentleman pensioner or member of the king's official bodyguard, who had rented the cellar for some months. Eager not to arouse the attendant's suspicions, Suffolk moved hastily on, returning to court soon after. On the way Monteagle, an old friend of Percy, expressed surprise at the servant's words, since he had not been aware that Percy rented a property in Westminster. He also mentioned that Percy was a Catholic.

This was quite enough to excite the king's suspicions. When he heard Suffolk's report, James ordered a thorough search of the vaults which, still with an eye to keeping matters low-key until the last possible moment, was to be carried out ostensibly to trace some 'stuff' and hangings belonging to the king's wardrobe. A Westminster magistrate and gentleman of the privy chamber, Sir Thomas Knyvett,[18] was appointed to oversee operations.

Accounts of the subsequent search vary slightly in the precise sequence and timing of events, but no more than one would expect given the scope for rumour and embellishment in such a tale.[19] Around midnight, Knyvett led his party in a surprise raid on the cellar. Upon arrival they met the attendant who had spoken to Suffolk that afternoon emerging from the room, booted and spurred. Thinking him strangely attired for the time of night, Knyvett ordered his arrest[20] and began to probe among the piles of firewood. Within minutes it was clear that the fuel store held a sinister secret – the wood had been merely a screen concealing thirty-six barrels of gunpowder. The attendant was searched, and a watch, matches, and touchwood found about his person. He was bound securely while Knyvett hastened off to inform the court. Members of the privy council close at hand were roused from their sleep and, an extra guard having been set, they assembled in the king's bedchamber where the prisoner was brought before them for questioning.

For two days following this dramatic discovery, however, the council had little further evidence on which to work. Their sole prisoner, who gave his name as John Johnson, though interrogated three times at least before the evening of the sixth, would admit nothing beyond the inescapable fact that he worked for the lessee of the Westminster property, Thomas Percy, and had intended – had he not been prevented – to have 'blowen vpp the vpper howse, when the king, lords, bishops, and others hadd ben there'. Referring, apparently, to the anonymous letter sent to Monteagle, he remarked laconically that 'the giuing warning to one ouer threw us all' and according to tradition he was quick to tell the horrified king that he would have blown both James and his Scottish courtiers back to their northern mountains. But though faced with a multitude of probing and leading questions, some of them drafted by James himself, he gave away very little else, muttering defiantly: 'you would haue me discouer my frendes'.[21] Percy was nowhere to be found, and there remained a very real possibility that this pair of desperadoes had allies equally resolute and still at large. For a government waking to the fact that it had escaped fiery destruction by a matter of hours this was a sobering thought.

All possible leads were, of course, followed. A proclamation for Thomas Percy's arrest was issued without delay. Enough people at court were acquainted with the fugitive to provide an accurate personal description: 'The sayde Percy is a tall man, with a great broad beard, a good face, the colour of his beard and head mingled with white haires, but the head more white then the beard, he stoupeth somewhat in the shoulders, well coloured in the face, long footed, small legged.'[22] In addition, the ports were closed, probably after an emergency meeting of the privy council on the morning of 5 November, and a guard was prudently set on the residence of the Spanish ambassador to pre-empt any trouble from the London mob.[23] The council meeting also had an internal matter to resolve, for one of its own number, the earl of Northumberland, was both cousin to and patron of the traitor Percy. After what seems to have been a tense, confused exchange, Northumberland departed under the impression that, while the other lords had 'willed or advised' him to stay in his house, he yet remained free to come and go as he pleased. His colleagues, however, apparently felt that their wishes should have bound him implicitly if not explicitly.[24] Meanwhile, Percy's lodging was searched – with minimal results[25] – and the lord chief justice Sir John Popham, a councillor who maintained a number of contacts among the priestly 'underground' in the capital, set to work ferreting out information on possible suspects.[26] Parliament met briefly in the afternoon, but was at once prorogued until the following Saturday.[27]

Popham's efforts were naturally assisted by information volunteered from London landladies and others who had encountered anyone behaving suspiciously in recent weeks.[28] By its very nature, though, such evidence, while containing some more-than-useful nuggets, had to be sifted carefully; the number of false trails started in this way was large. A rash of reports on 5 November had the fugitive Percy escaping from the capital in almost every direction possible.[29] Upon command from the council a groom of the privy chamber, John Lepton, set off early that morning to follow the most likely lead. Percy was known – Northumberland would hardly have concealed the matter – to have been escorting his master's Michaelmas rents from Northumberland, Cumberland, and Yorkshire up to London shortly before the treason was discovered. It was clearly possible that the traitor had either sought refuge in the country he knew best, or that he might even then be employing the money to some mischievous end. But Lepton missed his man, and his epic ride took him to Scotland before he realised that the trail had grown cold.[30] The owner and former tenant of the traitor's Westminster dwelling were soon questioned, but beyond casting suspicion on some of Northumberland's household officials who had helped Percy acquire the leases this accomplished little.[31]

There was some progress amid the frustration. By the evening of 6 November, Popham's enthusiastic enquiries had produced a list of possible suspects which, as it turned out, included many though by no means all the conspirators. This list, however, apparently consisted principally of known Catholics who had suddenly gone missing from their lodgings and accustomed haunts around London. 'By examynacions taken by me this after noone,' Popham wrote to Salisbury, 'ther ys pregnant suspycion to be hadd off . . . Robert Catesby, Ambrose Rockwood, one Keyes, Thomas Wynter, John Wryght and Chrystoffer Wryght and some suspicion of one Grant.'[32]

These names cause no great surprise, several are of men that Popham would have known personally in the small world of Jacobean London. Robert Catesby came of an old midlands family. His ancestor Sir William Catesby, the 'Cat' of the old rhyme, had been speaker of the House of Commons and chancellor of the exchequer in a successful public career under Richard III, brought to a premature end after Bosworth. His father was loyal to the Catholic faith and suffered the heavy financial penalties of that age, but Robert, born in 1573, seems initially to have conformed to the state religion. He attended Gloucester Hall, Oxford, in 1586, and married at nineteen Catherine Leigh, a girl from a protestant family. A few years later, however, the death of his eldest son was followed shortly after by that of his young wife, personal tragedies compounded by the loss of his father in 1598. It may have been at this time of grief that

Catesby again found solace in his old family faith. Loyalty to a
personal patron perhaps explains his involvement in the Essex
rebellion, an indiscretion which cost him a fine of £3,000, but there
seems little doubt that a streak of wildness in his nature burned
brightly at times, a recklessness made all the more dangerous by his
undoubted personal attractions. The Jesuit Father Oswald
Tesimond, who knew him perhaps as well as anyone, describes
Catesby as being over six feet tall, with noble and expressive
countenance and manners, one whose dignity impressed all those
who associated with him. Tesimond's character sketches are often
flattering, but in Catesby's case, there is good reason to believe
him.[33]

Ambrose Rookwood too came from an old recusant family, with
its seat at Coldham Hall, Stanningfield, Suffolk. According to
Tesimond, he was around twenty-six years old in 1605, 'well-built
and handsome, if somewhat short', a genial man, and one 'well-
lettered', having 'spent his youth acquiring the humanities in Flanders' before inheriting the wealthy Stanningfield estate in 1600. He
had married into another prominent recusant family, the Tyrwhitts
of Lincolnshire, and was known for the fine horses which he kept.[34]
Thomas Winter is described by Tesimond as 'a young man of considerable ability and great courage'. He is said to have been aged
thirty-four at the time of Gunpowder plot and while his family
background is obscure the Winters were apparently related by
marriage to the Throckmortons of Coughton, making them cousins
of Catesby whose mother was a Throckmorton. One authority
maintains that Winter fought against the Spanish troops in Flanders
during the 1590s, converting to Catholicism around the turn of the
century, but the source of his information remains hidden. We do
know, however, that Winter participated in Essex's rising, and this,
combined with his religious profession, would have been quite
enough to excite Popham's suspicion. He was also closely tied to
Monteagle, having served him as some sort of secretary in recent
years.[35]

The brothers John and Christopher Wright, descended from the
Wrights of Plowland Hall in Holderness, Yorkshire, were again
participants in the rebellion of 1601. Along with Catesby they had
been placed under arrest at the time of the queen's death, the
chronicler William Camden describing them contemptuously as men
'hunger-starved for innovation'. Although Popham may not yet have

known it, they were brothers-in-law of Thomas Percy, and were cousins of Thomas Winter. John Wright was said to have been an excellent swordsman, a taciturn man, loyal to his few close friends. Tesimond concedes that – before his conversion to Catholicism – he had been 'prone to quarrelling, but after he was reconciled to the church he became a man of exemplary life'.[36]

Another in this 'family group' of suspects was John Grant, a Warwickshire gentleman who had married Thomas Winter's sister Dorothy. The owner of Norbrooks, a strongly walled and strategically important Warwickshire mansion, Grant had been yet another participant in the Essex rebellion.[37] There was little to recommend Robert Keyes as a suspect beyond his resolute nature and his apparent poverty – a combination serving as dry tinder to a revolutionary spark. The son of a protestant rector and a daughter of the Tyrwhitts, Keyes and his wife had for some years been close dependants of the Catholic peer Lord Mordaunt.[38]

As yet the accusations made against these men rested on nothing more than 'pregnant suspicion'. Popham did not know their whereabouts, he could only give the Secretary the names of their family homes, expressing at the same time his fears, based on some unidentified and groundless information, that Percy and Christopher Wright had – or soon would – escape by boat down the Thames. Jubilation had thus to be mixed with caution. On 5 November the inhabitants of London were encouraged to celebrate the deliverance of king and state with bonfires – so long as 'this testemonye of ioy be carefull done without any danger or disorder' – and that night the city witnessed, in the words of one observer, 'great ringing and as great store of bonfires as ever I thincke was seene'.[39] But the authorities, while avoiding panic, could not afford to relax their efforts. As fires lit the November sky the council was trying to find a priest willing to persuade Johnson that he was morally bound to disclose the names of his confederates[40] and even resorting to the astrologer Simon Foreman in their efforts to track Percy down.[41] Anxiety sharpened fears and shortened patience. In preparing his own list of questions for the prisoner, James encouraged his ministers to use torture, starting with 'the gentler tortures' and working up, if that was what it took to make him talk.[42]

The king's reaction was understandable; it was essential to discover the whereabouts of Johnson's confederates. The prisoner, in the event, showed no reluctance to supply information at this stage,

although the facility of his replies perhaps gave the examiners more
than slight cause to doubt that he was speaking the truth. Many of
James's own questions set out to establish just what sort of man
could have conceived such a treason against himself and his family.
Answering the king, Johnson maintained that he had been born in
Yorkshire, 'in Netherdale', that his father had been called Thomas,
and that his mother's maiden name had been Edith Jackson. He
claimed to be thirty-six years old, to have had a living from a 'farme
of 30*li* per annum', and to have acquired the scars which marked his
body 'by the healinge of a pluracye'. He denied having used any
intermediary to enter Percy's service, denied too that he had ever
served another master. The house, he said, had been hired around
midsummer 1604, and they had begun to bring in gunpowder some
six months later. A letter had been found on the prisoner's person
addressed to 'Fauks', and in answer to the king's obvious question,
he explained ingenuously that he had used that name as an alias. He
insisted that he had been brought up a Catholic by his parents, and
that consequently he had never been converted to the religion.[43]

The truth began to emerge only on 7 November. That day, in the
face of repeated questioning and having had time to reflect on the
hopelessness of his position, the captive's 'Roman' resolution began
at last to slip. He confessed that his real name was Guy Fawkes,
confessed too that he and his colleagues had at the start been five in
number, and that 'some five or six more' had subsequently shared in
at least part of the secret. It had, he claimed, also been their intention
to seek help from Sir Walter Ralegh and other prisoners in the Tower
of London once the explosion had taken place, for they had resolved
to 'have made vse of all the discontented people of England'. Here
was another link with the troubles of 1603 for the council to ponder,
since Ralegh had been condemned in that year for plotting the death
of James and his family in the so-called Main conspiracy. Only now
did Fawkes express some regret for what had been planned, saying
that 'yt was past, and he is nowe sorry for yt, for that he nowe
perceyveth that God did not concurre with yt', yet he still refused to
name his colleagues, stubbornly holding to an oath of secrecy which
had been taken by them all.[44]

For the first time, then, the investigators came to know the history
of the man they were dealing with, discovering that the story which
had emerged in response to the king's questions, while misleading,
had not been totally false. He was the son of Edward Fawkes,

proctor and later advocate in the consistory court of York, a staunch protestant. Born in the Stonegate district of the city, Guy had been baptised at St Michael-le-Belfry in 1570 and had entered St Peter's School in 1578, where his schoolmates had included John and Christopher Wright. Edward Fawkes had died a year later, and Guy's mother Edith had remarried into the Catholic Bainbridge family resident in Scotton. It may have been the influence of his stepfather that had first inclined the young man to Catholicism, or he may have fallen under the spell of John Pullen, headmaster of St Peter's, who was subsequently named as a suspected Jesuit. Whatever the prompting, there is evidence to show that, when he reached the age of twenty-one, Fawkes had sold his inheritance, and had set out to join the Catholic forces in the Low Countries. Subsequently, for upwards of a dozen years, he had pursued a military career in the seemingly unending wars between the protestant United Provinces of the Netherlands and the southern parts of Flanders which had remained loyal to both their Catholic faith and their Spanish king.[45]

Fawkes's information was supplemented throughout that day by messages from the midlands. Word was reaching London that the country was beset by rebellion. The stable of Warwick Castle was reported to have been raided by John Grant and others on the Tuesday night,[46] and the sheriff of Warwickshire, having examined captured servants of Robert Winter and Ambrose Rookwood, had reason to believe that as many as one hundred men were up in arms.[47] He named four country gentlemen, Robert Acton, Robert Catesby, John Grant, and Ambrose Rookwood, as leaders of the unrest. Their purpose remained unclear, but Fawkes had already confessed that the plotters had hoped to proclaim as queen James's ten-years-old daughter Elizabeth, then living with John Lord Harington at Combe, near Coventry.[48] The council must have been relieved to learn soon afterwards that Harington, on hearing of the raid on Warwick Castle, had moved his charge to the apparent safety of Coventry.[49] With the scale of the rising still uncertain, Charles Blount, earl of Devonshire, younger and more experienced than most other members of the council in military affairs after his years in Ireland putting down Tyrone's rebellion, was entrusted with organising and commanding an army for its suppression. It is ironic, but a reflection on the extent of official knowledge at this stage, that one of Devonshire's volunteers was Francis Tresham, subsequently revealed to have himself been involved in the treason.[50]

Notes

1 PRO SP 78/52, fol 338. Although this draft is dated 6 November, the letter was probably sent to Parry on 9 November along with similar letters to the ambassadors of Holland and Spain

2 Hurstfield, 'Gunpowder Plot and the Politics of Dissent', pp 340–1. See Nicholls, 'Investigating Gunpowder Plot', p 124

3 Gerard, *What Was the Gunpowder Plot?*; Gardiner, *What Gunpowder Plot Was*

4 For example, see Roger, 'Ordnance Records and the Gunpowder Plot', pp 124–5. See also below, pp 214–18

5 Peck, 'Problems in Jacobean Administration', p 831; see Peck's 'Corruption at the Court of James I', G E Aylmer's *The King's Servants: The Civil Servants of Charles I, 1625–42*, New York, 1961, and Hurstfield's 'Political Corruption in Modern England: The Historian's Problem', *History*, LII, 1967 on the problems of establishing standards by which to judge 'corruption' in early-modern England

6 On the composition of the council in 1603 see appendix 3

7 The staff of the council was at all times limited, both in numbers and in ability (Jensen, 'Staff of the Jacobean Privy Council', esp pp 17–28, 33–9, 41)

8 Adair, *Sources for the History of the Council*, p 7

9 The variety of its business can be seen from a glance at the pages or index of any volume of the published *Register*; Cheyney, 'Court of Star Chamber', pp 728–9. For the irregularity of council meetings see Hill, 'Sir Julius Caesar's Journal', pp 315–27

10 *APC 1613–14*, pp v–ix

11 In particular, the volume of extracts from the registers compiled by Ralph Starkey which covers the period 1550–1610, and which includes summary details of some contents of lost registers (BL Additional MS 11402)

12 See appendix 3

13 PRO SP 14/216/2

14 PRO SP 14/3/16; The *King's Book* is the popular name for *His Maiesties Speach in this last Session of Parliament . . .*, London, 1605. Sometimes the name is used to describe a later pamphlet which incorporates *A True and Perfect Relation* of the trials of the plotters, published in 1606; *His Majesties Speach*, sig F2; PRO SP 14/216/16. See also Dodd, 'Spanish Treason, Gunpowder Plot and Catholic Refugees', pp 643–6; PRO SP 78/52 fols 244, 272, 292; Birch, *Historical View*, pp 233–4

15 Anstruther, 'Powder Treason', pp 452–6

16 Early in December 1605 Salisbury received a 'death threat', ostensibly from a Catholic group, which at the same time professed total loyalty to a king misled by his minister's evil counsel (Hatfield MS 113/76). In preparing questions for Fawkes soon after the discovery, James mentioned a 'pasquil' that had foretold his death (PRO SP 14/216/17). See

also SP 14/19/6; 14/216/199; Hatfield MS 206/22, for other threats of this nature

17 For the topography of early-seventeenth-century Westminster see Gardiner, *What Gunpowder Plot Was*, pp 77–113

18 Knyvett was 'Keeper of the Palace at Westminster', see Edwards, *Greenway Narrative*, p 113n

19 The difficulties in the official tale raised by Gerard in *What Was the Gunpowder Plot?* are effectively demolished by Gardiner in *What Gunpowder Plot Was*, pp 114–37

20 Some accounts put the arrest later, in a chamber of the rented lodging

21 PRO SP 14/216/6, 16A, 19; Birch, *Court and Times of James I*, i, p 37

22 Larkin and Hughes, *Stuart Royal Proclamations*, i, p 123

23 East Sussex CRO MS Rye 47/69/2; Hatfield MS 112/162

24 Alnwick MS 101, fol 14

25 PRO SP 14/216/15; 14/16/9, Justice Grange to Salisbury, 5 Nov 1605, with information from papers found there

26 PRO SP 14/216/10

27 *Lords' Journals*, ii, pp 355–6

28 PRO SP 14/16/11–17

29 PRO SP 14/216/7, 9, 14, 234

30 PRO SP 14/216/36; Hatfield MS 113/54

31 PRO SP 14/216/24, 39, examinations of Ellen Bright and Roger Neck, 6 Nov 1605, and of Susan Whynniard, 7 Nov 1605

32 PRO SP 14/216/20, 20A. See also Sir Edward Coke's painstaking list of 'proofes against Thomas Percey', probably compiled on 6 November and based upon Fawkes's confessions up to that time (SP 14/16/18)

33 Edwards, *Greenway Narrative*, pp 54–5; Jardine, *Narrative of Gunpowder Plot*, pp 28–32

34 Edwards, *Greenway Narrative*, pp 99–100; Jardine, *Narrative of Gunpowder Plot*, p 64

35 Sidney, *A History of the Gunpowder Plot*, p 34; Edwards, *Greenway Narrative*, pp 55–6; Jardine, *Narrative of Gunpowder Plot*, pp 33–4

36 *Camdeni Epistolae*, pp 347–8; Edwards, *Greenway Narrative*, pp 63–4n

37 Jardine, *Narrative of Gunpowder Plot*, pp 51–2

38 *ibid*, p 43; PRO SP 14/216/182

39 Guildhall, City of London Record Office, Journal of Common Council vol 27, fol 4; McClure, *Letters of Chamberlain*, i, p 213; Stow, *Annales*, p 880

40 See *The Advocate of Conscience Liberty*, p 227. This was probably the reason why Ben Jonson, at that time still a Catholic, was then asked by the privy council to find a priest willing to perform some undisclosed but dangerous service. Jonson was soon forced to admit that all his priestly contacts were too scared to come out of hiding (see De Luna, *Jonson's Romish Plot*, pp 115–43)

41 Thomas, *Religion and the Decline of Magic*, p 312

42 PRO SP 14/216/17

43 PRO SP 14/216/19

44 PRO SP 14/216/37
45 See Simons, *Devil of the Vault*; Garnett, *Portrait of Guy Fawkes*; Toyne, 'Guy Fawkes and Powder Plot', pp 22–4
46 PRO SP 14/216/22
47 PRO SP 14/216/35
48 PRO SP 14/216/37
49 PRO SP 14/216/23, Harington to Salisbury, 6 Nov 1605
50 Stow, *Annales*, p 880. Stow (pp 879–80) gives a graphic description of the general uncertainty which prevailed at all levels of London society before news that the rebellion had been suppressed was received

II

Rebellion and ruin

This ominous news from the midlands produced or coincided with a flurry of activity in London. Since nothing had lessened the preliminary suspicions against Northumberland, and since when writing to his estate officers in the north he had showed as much concern for his rents as for the capture of his kinsman, the earl was confined to Lambeth Palace in the charge of his fellow-councillor the archbishop of Canterbury.[1] In direct response to the Warwick incident, a second proclamation appeared naming those suspects who had betrayed themselves by flight: Percy, Catesby, Rookwood, Thomas Winter, Grant, John and Christopher Wright. This list, however is perhaps most revealing in the names which are not mentioned – among them Robert Keyes, who had been on Popham's list but who had played no part in the rebellion. Moreover, John Grant is rechristened Edward, and 'Robert Ashfield, servant to Robert Catesby Esquire' is included in the proclamation, just possibly in mistake for Thomas Bate, a loyal servant who followed Catesby almost to the end.[2]

The midlands rebellion, though, was a short-lived affair; even while the council took steps to deal with it the revolt was fizzling out. Lacking any real purpose or plan of action, the rebels spent 6 and 7 November meandering from one Catholic house to another across Warwickshire and Worcestershire; from Norbrooks to Huddington, from there to Lord Windsor's house, Hewell Grange, pathetically dragging with them on the Thursday a cart laden with sufficient weapons and armour to equip a force three or four times their size. The ringleaders kept a constant watch, not just for the forces of the counties through which they were passing, but also for deserters from their own ranks as first enthusiasms wore off and their servants and retainers began to grasp the inevitable consequences of their actions. Hopes that the situation could be retrieved were never high, and reading depositions and examinations taken later one can sense the will to resist draining away. John Winter, who had joined his brothers Thomas and Robert in their enterprise, initially asserted boldly that he and his colleagues would make for Ireland while others thought that they might find sympathisers in Wales, but these apparent refuges were only mirages on a fast-receding horizon.[3] At Hewell, when plundering still more weapons, they tried to recruit bystanders announcing that they were 'for god and the countrie, whervppon one [of] the countrimen sett his backe to the wall and sett his staff before him saying he was for King James for whome he would live and die and would not goe against him'.[4] Another disillusioned rebel, Sir Everard Digby, later confessed that 'they in the whole when they had most were not aboue fiftie horse. And that not one man cam in to take there parte thoughe they expected for verie many.'[5]

A mass desertion at Holbeach, Stephen Littleton's house in Staffordshire where they rested on the night of 7 November, together with the accidental explosion of some gunpowder which they were drying before a fire, finally broke the fugitives' spirits. What more conclusive proof could there possibly be that God Himself was against them in their proceedings?[6] When Sir Richard Walsh, the sheriff of Worcestershire, attacked the house on the following morning his men encountered very little resistance. Catesby and Percy, fighting back to back, were mortally wounded by a single shot fired by one John Street of Worcester; the brothers Wright also fell dying. Rookwood and Thomas Winter were wounded, indeed Winter seems to have owed his life to a responsible member of the posse who deflected a pike thrust which might otherwise have lost the authorities another vital witness. As it was, the 'baser sort' among the sheriff's force apparently so ill-treated or neglected the severely wounded traitors that all four soon died without making any recorded statement.[7] Robert Winter, Digby, and Bate having already escaped, Rookwood, Thomas Winter, and the rest – only some eight in number – were seized and taken first to Stourbridge, then on to Worcester the following day. Of those rebels still at large, Digby and Bate were captured soon after.[8]

On 9 November reports that the insurrection had been

supressed reached London, rendering superfluous not only a third proclamation, issued on 8 November, which had attempted to set rebel against rebel by singling out Percy for particular opprobrium and by offering a handsome reward to his captor,[9] but also Fawkes's most recent confessions in which he had both described how the treason had developed and had disclosed the names of his associates for the first time.[10] The news from Staffordshire must have been received by the council with decidedly mixed feelings, however, for according to Fawkes's statement Robert Catesby, Thomas Percy, and John Wright had all been involved in the conspiracy from its inception.[11]

Until the arrival of Thomas Winter and the other rebels in London, therefore, the authorities' knowledge of the plot rested on what Fawkes had told them in his confessions of 7, 8, and 9 November, particularly that made on the eighth.[12] It seems almost certain that torture was used to extract statements at some point, although the prisoner's resolve, already cracking on the morning of 7 November,[13] may have weakened further as the day wore on without recourse to such 'encouragement'. Fawkes disclosed then that he had been recruited by Thomas Winter in the spring of 1604, whilst serving in Flanders with the Catholic forces, and that he had returned with Winter to England where, having sworn an oath of secrecy, he had been made privy to the details of the conspiracy. He confessed that he and his accomplices had first tried to drive a mine under the House of Lords during the winter of 1604–5 and that they had been finding the work very heavy going before, providentially, the lease of the vault had fallen vacant in early spring. He confessed further that he had returned to Flanders the following Easter, not, as he had said on 5 November 'to see the countrey and to passe away the time',[14] but rather to keep out of London until nearer the day appointed for the opening of parliament.

To this extent Fawkes hardly proved reticent, but on other issues, above all on the plotters' plan of action after the hoped-for success of their scheme, he still would or could say little. He admitted only that they had prepared a proclamation on behalf of Princess Elizabeth which had prudently made no mention of their wish to alter the established religion – that was something which could be 'explained' later. The princess would, of course, have been brought up as a Catholic and would eventually have been married to a suitable candidate of the same faith. They had considered making an attempt to capture Prince Charles, but lacking any military strength near London they had realised that the capture of Elizabeth should take priority. James's eldest son Prince Henry would, they had assumed, have accompanied his father to parliament and so shared the king's fate.[15] Fawkes was silent on the question of a protector for the young princess once she had fallen into their hands, nor did he at any time suggest that the plotters had expected or solicited foreign support for their enterprise; indeed his xenophobia was never concealed. His continued evasiveness on these matters of great moment obviously irritated the examiners, and he was interrogated on them once again on 16 November. Still he had nothing very incriminating to say.[16]

Soon after the discovery, although it is not certain just how soon, the task of investigating the conspiracy was entrusted by the king to a commission comprising the attorney-general, Sir Edward Coke, and seven privy councillors: Popham and the earls of Salisbury, Nottingham, Suffolk, Northampton, Devonshire, and Mar. It is probable that this informal commission also included a second Scottish peer, the earl of Dunbar, since he witnessed several subsequent examinations.[17] The commission was for the time being itself an adequate response to the task in hand, for with only Fawkes to question these noblemen, busy though many of them were with state affairs and the demands of court life, were quite capable of handling the matter on their own. Occasionally their powers were already being delegated, but although Fawkes's confession of 9 November was taken by Coke, the lieutenant of the Tower Sir William Waad, and the Tower official Edward Forsett, it was duly acknowledged by the prisoner before the lords commissioners on the following day.[18]

One other immediate lead had to be pursued. In his confession of 9 November, Fawkes named Francis Tresham as a fellow-conspirator. Tresham, another scion of an old Catholic family and still another former participant in Essex's rising, had only recently inherited extensive estates in Northamptonshire on the death of his father Sir Thomas in September 1605.[19] He had been in London since 5 November. Needless to say, Tresham was soon arrested and faced interrogation on 12 November. He denied any treasonable part in the affair, however, and in a voluntary confession written on the following day he insisted that, although Catesby had caught him off-guard the month before and had indeed told him of the plot – principally, it seems, to raise cash for the enterprise – he had ever since done all in his power to persuade his unwanted colleagues that they should abandon their plans.[20] Whether or not he was telling the truth, it was obvious that Tresham had been admitted to the conspiracy at a late stage and had little notion of the original plotters' intentions. Compared with Fawkes he was clearly small-fry, and the commissioners knew it.

While the fight at Holbeach had robbed the investigators of potentially vital witnesses, it had at least won them a number of important prisoners. But their natural enthusiasm to question these men had to be tempered by the fact that the culprits were in Worcestershire, over 100 miles from London. Initially the commissioners ordered Walsh to examine the gentlemen among his prisoners on set questions supplied from the capital.[21] The questions, as one might expect, were wide-ranging and clearly designed to probe for almost any kind of information that the captives might be able to supply. Only half the original list of 'interrogatories' survives, but there is no shadow of a doubt that the questioners' first concern was to discover whether some great nobleman had been behind the plot. Thus the prisoners were asked: 'whome dyd yow account the princypallest person off qualyte to depend vpon in any Chatholic Cause and vpon what grownd or reason?' 'Dyd yow not', they were pressed, 'account yt very requysit in this accion to haue hadd care for the preservacion of some noble persons and what were they?' They were also required to say whether they had heard at any time 'that some noble persons hadd vndertaken to haue joyned vpon any occasyon offered with the Chatholic partie', whether they had discussed 'who shold be the hedd of your faccion in your procedyng after', and if so 'who should it haue ben?'[22] When Walsh put these questions to Thomas and John Winter, John Grant and Grant's over-loyal friend and dependant Henry Morgan on 12 November, however, three said nothing, claiming that they knew nothing of any plot. Thomas Winter alone volunteered significant information, saying that they had expected neither foreign assistance nor help from any other Englishmen apart from 'such as weare of the same necessitie for religion'. He denied any knowledge of a 'generall head', saying disingenuously that 'of theire owne companie eyther Robert Catesbie or Thomas Percie should be the chiefes of them'.[23]

Upon reflection, the commissioners seem to have anticipated that such indirect methods – without the immediate means to follow up leads using knowledge gained from Fawkes – would serve little purpose. Even before Walsh could send them the meagre results of his labours he received another letter from their lordships dated 11 November, requiring that 'suche of the treators as may convenientlye without hassard of theyr lyves shold bee presentlye sent upp'.[24] Walsh's friend and kinsman Sir Henry Bromley at once volunteered to escort them to London,[25] while Walsh himself embarked on a thorough search of Huddington and Grafton.[26] At about the same time, Bartholomew Hales and others brought the suspects arrested in Warwickshire – including some wives of leading conspirators – on a similar journey,[27] and on 16 November the privy council began to make arrangements to receive the influx of prisoners, spreading the load between several gaols and lodging the women with various London aldermen.[28]

After the examination of Tresham on 12 November there was of necessity a lull in the commissioners' work, since Fawkes, to all appearances, could say little more. For some days the investigators in effect marked time: they ordered the Catholic John Talbot of Grafton, heir-presumptive to the earl of Shrewsbury and a relative of some of the plotters who had, moreover, been visited by Thomas Winter and Stephen Littleton on the morning of 8 November, to come to London 'all excuses set apart'[29] and told the sheriff of Staffordshire that he was not to dispute custody of Walsh's prisoners, even though Holbeach lay just on the Staffordshire side of the county boundary.[30] Among the nobility, suspicion did not fall upon Northumberland alone. On 15 November, two of Catesby's close friends, the Lords Mordaunt and Montagu – who had both been out of London on the fifth and so clearly had never intended to be present at parliament – were sent to the Tower.[31] For the present, Northumberland remained at Lambeth, as yet unexamined by his fellow councillors, and entrusted to the care of a Northamptonshire knight, William Lane.[32] Next day, the council felt that the ports could be reopened, and on 17 November an order was sent into Staffordshire for the exhumation and quartering of those slain at Holbeach. A further proclamation was issued on 18 November for the arrest of Stephen Littleton, owner of Holbeach, and Robert Winter, one of the plotters named by Fawkes. The heads of Catesby and Percy were shortly afterwards sent to the capital where they adorned the scene of their intended crime for many years, the customary awful reminder of the perils involved in treason.[33]

Themselves keen to learn the plot's secrets, the commissioners fully realised that they had a duty to satisfy public interest in the case, both at home and abroad. In addition there was, of course, much propaganda mileage to be made from the affair, although it was not at first clear what form such propaganda might take. Ambassadors at the London court were soon given details of the plot[34] and letters based on that of Salisbury to Parry were sent to all English envoys abroad.[35] As early as the tenth, Salisbury seized upon the opportunity provided by Fawkes's confession to write to Edmondes urging the ambassador to press for the extradition of Hugh Owen.[36] While Sir Charles Cornwallis in Madrid, who had laid and then abandoned plans for a celebratory party, reported that interest there in the treason had rapidly cooled,[37] the same could hardly be said of the domestic population, but the council's imperfect knowledge of the plot was clearly reflected in the way that details were disclosed. It was not until the hasty prorogation of parliament on 9 November that something approaching a coherent narrative of the affair was set before the assembled lords and commons by the lord chancellor, Lord Ellesmere.[38]

His account of the discovery was substantially the same as that sent to Parry and his fellow ambassadors, although the king was now given full credit for interpreting the cryptic warning sent to Monteagle.[39] James made a graceful if self-congratulatory speech, comparing recent events with the Gowrie conspiracy of August 1600, for had not both these monstrous treasons been foiled on the fifth day of the month, and on a Tuesday too? Yet there were, admittedly, some differences. 'This', he exclaimed, referring to the Gunpowder plot, 'was not a crying sinne of blood, as the former, but it may well be called a roaring, nay a thundring sinne of Fire and Brimstone, from the which God hath so miraculously deliuered vs all.'[40] It is likely that Fawkes's confession made on 8 November – in which he had first given an account of the genesis and development of the conspiracy – was also read so that the knights and burgesses could carry a full story home to their counties.[41]

Much the same outline of events was set before another audience at the Paul's Cross sermon preached on the following day by the bishop of Rochester, William Barlow. Such gatherings of Londoners provided ideal opportunities for the dissemination of official information, and blessed with a particularly vivid turn of phrase, Barlow was an ideal man to put the message across. He took for his text Psalm 18, verse 50: 'Great deliverances giveth He vnto his King,

and sheweth mercy vnto his anointed David, and to his seed for ever',
proceeding to explain how the Lord had delivered James just as He
had saved the Israelite king. Barlow expounded with relish on the
evil that the plotters had intended. One could, he suggested, observe
in their conspiracy 'a cruell Execution, an inhumane crueltie, a
brutish immanitie, a diuelish brutishnes & an Hyperbolicall, yea an
hyperdiabolicall diuelishnes'. Fawkes had indeed been a very 'Diuell
of the Vault' and his wicked intentions had been unparallelled in all
the bloody chapters of classical history. 'Caligula', whispered
Barlow, 'was but a shadow to this traytor', for he had only 'wished
that all the Citizens of Rome, had but one necke, that at one blow hee
might cut it off: but this Blood-sucker, not only wished it, but
contriued it, prepared for it, and was ready to execute it.' Fawkes's
confession was read once again, perhaps along with that made on the
ninth in which he had named his colleagues. Also read were 'such
papers as concerned the confession which was then knowne, and
notes given vpon them by the Preacher' – a reference perhaps to the
outline of the discovery read to parliament.[42] Beyond this, though,
there was as yet little enough to set before the public.

The authorities decided early on that an official version of the
affair should be published as swiftly as possible. Propaganda advan-
tages thus gained were far from negligible, but there does seem to
have been real pressure to satisfy an audience eager for further
details. The publication that eventually emerged shows all the signs
of having been put together in some haste. At first, the intention
seems to have been to publish the king's speech to parliament on 9
November, together with an embellished but essentially unchanged
version of the plot's discovery and – as an effective admission of guilt
– the words of Fawkes himself taken from his confessions. On 17
November, after his re-examination on the previous day, a revised
version of his 8 November confession was prepared. This replaced
the original third-person account with a more dramatically effective
first-person narrative, incorporating the names of his confederates –
disclosed on 9 November – into his main confession.[43] Some less
significant parts of the original were omitted, for example Fawkes's
admission that he had stood close to the king at the earl of Montgomery's wedding earlier in the year. The differences between the
texts of 8 and 17 November, which so preoccupied Father Gerard,[44]
were essentially no more than alterations in style, made for the
purpose of incorporating in one publishable confession all that

Fawkes had to tell. It may be noted that Fawkes signed this amended version.

The confession as it finally appeared in print differed in only one respect from this 'draft' of 17 November. The published version has Fawkes confess that one of his purposes in travelling to Flanders in 1605 had been 'to acquaint Owen with the particulars of the plot'. This was possibly no more than editorial gloss: Fawkes clearly did not deny the fact, and as shall be seen Thomas Winter's confession which appeared in the same publication admitted that this had been the main purpose of his visit.[45] That Fawkes and Owen knew one another was quite obvious, and as the government realised it would have been all but impossible for Owen, allegedly involved that very summer in plotting some sort of military enterprise against England, to have been wholly ignorant of what was going on.

It seems clear that the publishing schedule of *King's Book* – soon adopted as a popular name for this composite publication – was very much at the mercy of events: while the authorities might have liked to see it appear at an early date, preparations were stayed when it was learnt that other principal traitors had survived the encounter at Holbeach. Further information from Worcestershire was thus eagerly awaited. On 9 November Sheriff Walsh's letter reported that Percy and the Wrights were still living, although 'verilie thoughte wounded to deathe'.[46] Walsh confirmed his gloomy forecast on 13 November, but he also had some more cheering news for the council: Thomas Winter, whom Fawkes had named among the five original plotters, was 'lyveinge, and in noe danger', recovering well from his wounds.[47] Henry Bromley, when setting out for London with his prisoners, further whetted their lordships' appetites, promising that he would deliver them 'yet a live a principall consperitor of the grande treason'.[48] At some point in mid-month the decision was taken to include a statement by Winter in the forthcoming publication, provided that what he had to say was worthy of inclusion. When the book was published, the editor, at the end of Fawkes's confession, explained frankly that

in regard that before this discourse could be readie to goe to the presse, Thomas Winter being apprehended, and brought to the Tower, made a confession in substance agreeing with this former of Fawkes, onely larger in some circumstances: I haue thought good to insert the same likewise in this place, for the further cleering of the matter, and greater benefit of the Reader.[49]

Ever since the Gerard–Gardiner debate at the end of the last century, the authenticity of Winter's confession dated 23 November – the document included in *King's Book* – has been almost constantly in question.[50] This full and detailed confession survives in one printed and two manuscript forms. The original, all apparently in Winter's hand, is at Hatfield.[51] A very slightly amended copy made by Levinus Munck, Salisbury's secretary, is in the Public Record Office.[52] A curious feature of the Hatfield document is that the signature differs from every other example of Winter's signature still extant. While the usual form is 'Tho Wintour', 'Thomas Winter' appears at the foot of the Hatfield confession. This is by far the most significant piece of evidence advanced in support of the forgery theory. Of course, as Gardiner and many others have pointed out, an expert forger, who alone could have produced so lengthy and otherwise convincing a document, would hardly have made such an elementary mistake. They have observed too that there seems little purpose to such an elaborate deception since the confession, conveniently comprehensive as it undoubtedly is, does not add a great deal to the facts of the treason revealed in other examinations. There was, besides, no pressing requirement to produce authentic handwritten confessions in the seventeenth-century courtroom. The immediate response of those who doubt, however, is to point out that, if a forger was unlikely to make such an error, it is surely much more improbable that Winter himself should have changed his signature.[53]

Gardiner could only suggest that he had adopted a form more familiar to the lords in a rather desperate attempt to curry favour and escape his doom,[54] but bearing in mind the simultaneous preparation of *King's Book* there is another, related, explanation. Before making any confession, Winter was visited in the Tower by Salisbury and – probably – by other commissioners. Having examined him and established that what Fawkes had said of him had been true, it seems that they suggested he should write – expressly for publication – his own narrative of the plot. For a time Winter's shoulder wound prevented this, but on 21 November Waad reported that his prisoner then felt able to 'write that he verbally declared to your lordship', adding anything else which came to mind in the process.[55] Winter clearly had nothing to lose. His only hope, and it was really a vain hope, lay in at least appearing to be completely frank with his captors. The document at Hatfield bears all the hallmarks of a draft.

It is extensively corrected by the author, who concludes his statement
'your honours poor and penitent prisoner Thomas Winter', *writing*
rather than signing his name in full and in its most familiar form for
publication purposes. Coke, apparently happy at the result, added
an endorsement when the confession was seen and witnessed by the
lords commissioners on 25 November, altering the date to reflect this
'authentication' and declaring that the work was entirely in Winter's
hand.

The PRO version appears to be the revised draft, having been
checked both by Salisbury and the king, the latter criticising one
passage for containing 'an unclere phrase'. It was this version,
slightly changed from the Hatfield original but like Fawkes's confession without any material alteration, which was published in *King's
Book*.[56] In both the PRO and published versions Winter's unhappy
valediction was omitted, his testimony being edited to conclude
abruptly 'yours etc'. It was no doubt felt that the desired portrayal of
Winter and his colleagues as hardened and incorrigible villains
would be obscured by the inclusion of any such expression of regret
for what had passed.

Once Winter's statement had been processed, publication of
King's Book was delayed no longer. It appeared most probably at the
end of November, incorporating Winter's confession as a fourth part
and concluding with an account of the midlands rebellion; a
patchwork composition itself bearing witness to the slow, tentative
way in which the investigators acquired their knowledge of the
plot.[57]

Notes

1   Stow (*Annales*, p 881) wrote that he was confined to his house on 7
November, and sent to Lambeth later, but the Northumberland household
accounts record that the earl's night-clothes were taken to Lambeth that day
(Batho, *Household Papers*, p 6)

2   Larkin and Hughes, *Stuart Royal Proclamations*, i, pp 124–6

3   PRO SP 14/216/144. The course of the rebellion can be pieced
together from many documents in 'Gunpowder Plot Book', a nineteenth-
century compilation of state papers relating to the treason (SP 14/216).
Among those to have done so in some detail are Jardine, *Narrative of
Gunpowder Plot*, pp 105–17 and Morgan, *Great English Treason*, ii, pp
177–250. Those fully aware of the magnitude of the disaster were from the
start far less sanguine than John Winter: Percy, for example, had few
illusions as to his fate. At his early-morning departure from the capital, he
told his servant William Tailbois that he was 'undoone'. When the puzzled

Tailbois asked him why he should say such a thing, Percy replied tersely 'let it satisfie thee that I saie so' (PRO SP 14/216/158)

4   PRO SP 14/216/119
5   PRO SP 14/216/135
6   Hatfield MS 113/54
7   PRO SP 14/216/55; Hatfield MS 113/4
8   PRO SP 14/216/55; 14/216/145, examination of Thomas Bate, 4 Dec 1605; 14/16/94, examination of Sir Everard Digby, 19 Nov 1605; PRO E134 4 James I/Trinity/6. Those captured alive at Holbeach were Winter, Grant, Rookwood, Henry Morgan gent, Thomas and Edward Okley, carpenters and servants to Robert Winter, Edmund Townsend, a servant of Grant, Nicholas Pelborough, servant of Rookwood, Richard Trewman, another servant of Robert Winter, and Stephen Littleton's servant Richard Day
9   Larkin and Hughes, *Stuart Royal Proclamations*, i, pp 127–8
10   See the postscript to Salisbury's letter to Sir Thomas Edmondes, with the altered date (BL Stowe MS 168, fol 213); PRO SP 14/216/49, 54
11   PRO SP 14/216/54
12   PRO SP 14/216/49
13   The tenor of his confession on 7 November is more frank than those which went before. See Hatfield MS 112/164, Waad to Salisbury, 7 Nov 1605
14   PRO SP 14/216/6
15   PRO SP 14/216/49, cf Hatfield MS 113/54, Thomas Winter's confession, 23 Nov 1605
16   SP 14/216/100
17   PRO SP 14/216/129; *Calendar SP Venetian 1603–7*, p 301. See Bellamy, *Tudor Law of Treason*, pp 105–6
18   PRO SP 14/216/54
19   Wake, 'Death of Francis Tresham', p 31
20   PRO SP 14/16/62, 63
21   PRO SP 14/216/87. Compare this procedure with that adopted in various sixteenth-century proceedings (Bellamy, *Tudor Law of Treason*, pp 104–5)
22   PRO SP 14/16/57
23   PRO SP 14/16/58–61
24   PRO SP 14/216/88
25   PRO SP 14/216/89
26   Hatfield MS 191/74. He discovered and secured considerable quantities of armour
27   PRO SP 14/216/90; Hatfield MSS 113/68, 115/36, 191/73
28   BL Additional MS 11402, fol 108
29   *ibid*
30   *ibid*
31   *ibid*. For Montagu's earlier efforts to explain away recent contacts with Catesby see PRO SP 14/216/48A, 74, 86
32   PRO SP 14/216/102; Hatfield MSS 97/68; 113/27, 50; 114/65–8; 191/72, letters of Sir William Lane to Salisbury

33 Hatfield MS 113/14; Larkin and Hughes, *Stuart Royal Proclamations*, i, pp 128–9. In their letter to the sheriff of Staffordshire ordering the exhumation of the traitors, the common practice of ordering the quarters displayed in 'some principall townes where they most ledd their life' was also followed (BL Additional MS 11402, fol 108). In February 1606 Ralph Dobbinson asked the privy council to settle a bill for 23s 9d which he had spent on iron work in setting up the heads that month (Hatfield MSS 113/172, 190/47). Apparently the council had planned to add Tresham's head to the others, but had been told by the judges that, since Tresham had not taken part in the open rebellion, and had not yet been indicted, his corpse could not 'be so vsed' (Hawarde, *Les Reportes*, p 257). After attainder, though, it was set up in Northampton (Wake, 'Death of Francis Tresham', p 35)

34 *Calendar SP Venetian 1603–7*, pp 295–7

35 eg Sawyer, *Winwood Memorials*, ii, p 170 (to Sir Thomas Edmondes)

36 Hatfield MS 227, p 116

37 BL Harley MS 1875, fol 301; see also Wormald, 'Gunpowder, Treason, and Scots', p 165

38 *Lords' Journals*, ii, pp 356–9

39 PRO SP 14/216/129

40 *His Majesties Speach*, sig B2

41 PRO SP 14/216/49

42 Barlow, *Sermon Preached at Paules Crosse*, sigs B, C2v, C3v, D, E. Cf McClure, *Letters of Chamberlain*, i, p 213

43 PRO SP 14/216/101

44 Gerard, *What was the Gunpowder Plot?*, pp 169–77, 268–77; Gerard, *Gunpowder Plot and the Gunpowder Plotters*, pp 7–12

45 *His Majesties Speach*, sigs H3, K2. Fawkes does not seem to have mentioned Owen in a confession until 20 January 1606 (Bodleian MS Tanner 75, fol 142). Like that confession, however, other statements made by Fawkes survive only as incomplete copies, including two made on 25 and 30 November 1605 (Abbot, *Antilogia*, pp 137, 138, 139v–140, 160, 161v; BL Harley MS 360, fols 115**v, 116v; Bodleian MS Tanner 75, fols 141v–142, 203 [in a volume of transcripts of original documents copied by Archbishop William Sancroft, c1680, possibly as preparation for a book on the plot]; Tierney, *Dodd's Church History*, iv, appendix, p lii–liv; PRO SP 14/216/175, 14/20/52. See also SP 14/19/93, Coke's list of evidence prepared for use at Garnett's trial). It is possible that these copies owe something to later 'embellishment', yet several at least were read during the trials in 1606, supplying then the same points that the surviving extracts show today. Of the above list, for example, some of Fawkes's depositions were read at Northumberland's trial

46 PRO SP 14/216/55

47 PRO SP 14/216/87; Hatfield MS 113/54

48 PRO SP 14/216/89

49 *His Majesties Speach*, sig H4v; Robert Barker, the king's printer, was responsible for publishing the work

50   Gerard, *What was the Gunpowder Plot?*, pp 167–9; Gardiner, *What Gunpowder Plot Was*, pp 54–71; Gerard, *Gunpowder Plot and Gunpowder Plotters*, pp 12–23; Gerard, *Thomas Winter's Confession and the Gunpowder Plot*; *The Athenaeum*, 3658 (4 Dec 1897), pp 785–7; 3660 (18 Dec 1897), pp 855–6; 3698 (10 Sep 1898), pp 352–3; 3700 (24 Sep 1898), p 420. See also issue no 3662 (1 Jan 1898), p 23. Most books on the plot written since then have had something to say on the matter. So too have Herbert Thurston, G and H Jenkins, Christopher Devlin, and Hugh Ross Williamson in *The Month*, cl, 1927, pp 500–10; NS iv, 1950, pp 243–51; NS vi, 1951, pp 304–6; NS vii, 1952, pp 83–8, 162–76, 231–3, 290–305. See also the exchange in the *Times Literary Supplement* for 1951, pp 691, 731, 749, 765, 785

51   Hatfield MS 113/54. There is a facsimile in Gerard, *Thomas Winter's Confession*

52   PRO SP 14/216/114

53   See especially Williamson's articles in note 50 for the development of Gerard's argument

54   *The Athenaeum*, 3658, p 786

55   Hatfield MS 113/24

56   *His Majesties Speach*, sigs I–L

57   Gardiner, *What Gunpowder Plot Was*, p 74n; see also Jardine, *Criminal Trials*, ii, p 5

III

The depths of treason

Winter's confession belongs to what one might call the second phase of investigations into Gunpowder plot, that in which the authorities, still concerned to learn more about the mechanics of the affair and to identify further conspirators, were in a position to examine all known suspects apart from Owen, Stanley, and the elusive Jesuits. There were, indeed, rather too many prisoners, and the government found itself faced with a logistical dilemma not dissimilar to that posed by the collapse of the Essex rebellion in February 1601. Besides the principals in Essex's rising, men like the earl of Southampton and Sir Christopher Blount, there had been some eighty or ninety lesser rebels, for the most part gentlemen-soldiers dependent on the earl or wild-spirited young men including, as we have seen, Catesby, Tresham, and the Wrights. It had been necessary to put basic questions to these men on the off-chance that some among them had worthwhile information.[1] In 1605, by comparison, the sheriff of Warwickshire had detained forty-six prisoners by mid-November,[2] and at least the same number were held in other counties. Most were eventually sent to London. Given the almost uniformly low social status of these men and women, it was obvious that the lords commissioners' valuable time would best be spent in examining known ringleaders, for otherwise the investigations would be prolonged interminably.

To solve this problem the commissioners drew upon recent experience. Following a precedent set in 1601, they established a subsidiary commission on 19 November composed of Sir Julius Caesar and Sir Roger Wilbraham, masters of requests, Sir Edward Phelips and Sir John Croke, serjeants-at-law, John Doddridge, Sir Francis Bacon, Sir Walter Cope, Sir George More, and Sir Henry

Montagu, under the supervision of Coke who acted as their link with the lords commissioners.[3] They were supplied with a general list of initial questions for the lesser prisoners,[4] together with the names of those suspects then held in city prisons. Seven men of gentle birth, Digby, John and Thomas Winter, Rookwood, Grant, Keyes, and Morgan were lodged in the Tower 'reserved only for the lords commissioners', as indeed were Sir John Talbot and the suspect peers, but by early December the names of more than ninety others had been left for the attention of the junior commission, the council in their original instructions requiring it to examine these suspects 'and discerne the better, both what examinacions shall be perfected and concluded by yow without further enquiry; and also which of them shalbe needfull for vs to take further knowledg of againe for any speciall respect'. They were also given power to decide what further action, if any, was required in each prisoner's case 'according as they shall appeare to be guiltie or guiltilesse'.[5] Compared with 1601, the more-complex Gunpowder investigations proved far more time-consuming,[6] but the junior commissioners set about their task with great enthusiasm, taking at least forty-three written examinations between 23 November and 30 December. Some of the most fruitful were sent complete to Coke and the lords commissioners, while others were summarised and edited to supply the salient points alone.[7] These minor examinations provided little important information, but given the length and complexity of some of the interrogations the promptness and efficiency with which this work was carried out are rather impressive.

Meanwhile, Salisbury and his colleagues were at more-significant labours. Beginning with Sir Everard Digby, who was questioned on 19 and 20 November, they spent about a fortnight examining and re-examining Northumberland, Talbot, and their 'reserved' prisoners. We know little about the process of interrogation save that when present Coke acted as scribe, taking down the suspects' incriminating words in his unmistakable hand and subsequently annotating the documents in an equally striking italic. The potential scope of their work increased on 26 November when two further suspects, Lord Stourton and Henry Huddlestone, were sent to the Tower,[8] Northumberland following them there on the following day.[9]

Like their junior commission, the lords commissioners were nothing if not thorough; Digby, Fawkes, Keyes, Rookwood, Winter, and Tresham were all examined more than once on a wide range of questions.[10] Surviving lists of interrogatories drawn up for them and for Northumberland by Coke and Popham show how the minds of the questioners were working.[11] These lists covered many topics, were full of half-formed and often unfounded suspicions, and included several lines of enquiry which ultimately led them nowhere. At the beginning of December, for instance, Coke suggested that Winter and Fawkes should be asked 'whether they meant not to employ Nevill and Dacres northwards, and what assurance they had of them and by whome' – but nothing more is heard of these disgraced and disinherited Catholic noblemen, then in exile on the continent.[12]

This question was probably suggested by a confession made by William Watson in the summer of 1603 and is a fine example of the way Coke, in preparing questions for the prisoners, frequently seems to have turned for inspiration to examinations taken in the aftermath of the Bye and Main plots. Interrogations framed for Northumberland show the influence of these earlier confessions quite clearly. In a treason otherwise devoid of suspects among the high nobility Northumberland was thought to have been the plotters' first choice as future protector of the realm, and Coke was prepared to cast his net wide to catch so choice a fish.[13]

Of course, evidence and testimony had continued to pour in from Londoners and from county officials ever since news of the plot had been made public. Generally speaking, though, they produced few worthwhile leads.[14] Indeed, one of the immediate results was to add a fresh complication to the investigators' task. Already the first of what was to become an avalanche of petitions on behalf of those who had given loyal service during the midlands rebellion were beginning to arrive at Whitehall and, armed with recommendations from their masters, some like Thomas Bannister were themselves coming to London to press their cases, bringing with them 'superstitious and popish idols' looted from the rebels, both alive and dead. Such men had to be heard, and their claims duly processed.[15]

The response of the counties to the news of Gunpowder plot shows both the inherent strengths and weaknesses of the central government. Loyalty, of course, was supremely evident. In Hampshire, for example, responding to directions from the council, gentlemen of the county met promptly at Winchester to set watches in their shire and pre-empt any trouble from recusants.[16] When Lord

Zouche, president of the council in the marches, ordered the Welsh counties to watch for strangers trying to escape from the western ports, Pembroke was swift to comply,[17] and upon first receiving the proclamation against Percy the mayor of Chester wasted no time in closing his port.[18] In Middlesex, meanwhile, Catesby's home at Moorcrofts near Hillingdon was all but taken apart by the local authorities in an enthusiastic hunt for fugitive suspects.[19] All too often, though, the discovery was used to further inter- and intra-county rivalries, neighbour informed against neighbour, and any local official – such as the sheriff of Staffordshire – who had shown sympathy towards local Catholics could almost guarantee trouble ahead from zealous colleagues. As we have seen, Holbeach House lay in Staffordshire, and its sheriff was quick to criticise Walsh's infringement of county borders, insisting that it would not have taken him long to deal with the rebels.[20] Walsh and others retorted by accusing many Staffordshire gentlemen of harbouring popish inclinations, observing that county boundaries could never be allowed to impede the pursuit of manifest traitors.[21]

Others concentrated on sending letters of encouragement to the council. Sir Francis Hastings urged Salisbury to spare nothing and nobody in getting to the bottom of so foul a treason, drawing on long protestant memory to show how the Catholics were incorrigible plotters against the well-ordered state of England.[22] The penurious dowager countess of Kent saw in the treason an escape from her hardships, writing to Salisbury to ask him if he thought it worth her while begging some part of the traitors' estates now fallen forfeit to the king.[23] Men were still turning up at court offering their services in putting down any rebellion well after the midlands rising had been finally extinguished.[24] Their enthusiasm was all very well, but once aroused it could lead to more work for the authorities rather than less.

A strong rumour that the plotters had counted on support from a regiment of English Catholics recently levied to fight for Spain in the Low Countries set the investigators off on a fresh line of enquiry.[25] After the peace with Spain, James had felt obliged to permit the raising of this force, but his feelings towards those inclined to serve in it were at all times quite clear,[26] and the government had retained control of the power to appoint the commander.[27] Edmondes, having secured the house arrest of Owen and his servant Bailly, had been rebuffed in attempts to bring about their extradition and had busied himself in discovering evidence that told against them. His discoveries had proved – at least to the ambassador's own satisfaction – that Catesby had tried to gain control of the force during the previous spring and summer, contacting Owen and others to support the appointment of his friend Sir Charles Percy, Northumberland's brother, as colonel.[28] Although that manoeuvre had fallen through, Percy's appointment having been blocked by the king, Owen's influence remained strong among the English Catholic mercenaries, and suspicion concerning his role in the plot, exacerbated by continued failure to bring him to account, grew accordingly.

In questioning Tresham and Thomas Winter, the authorities also learnt the details of a former treason in which they, together with Catesby, Monteagle, and Garnett, had negotiated for a Spanish invasion of England before the death of Elizabeth.[29] With Monteagle marked out as a saviour of the realm, with no desire to offend Spain, and with a degree of indemnity having been extended to actions before the king's accession[30] the examinations into this affair and any subsequent publication of the revelations had to proceed cautiously, but once it appeared that Fawkes had been sent from Flanders to Spain on a similar errand in the summer of 1603 and when Winter disclosed that Christopher Wright had been at the Spanish court at the same time, questions clearly had to be asked. There is some indication that at one stage the authorities had considered publishing details of the so-called 'Spanish treason' in *King's Book*, but that the sensitive elements in the story subsequently dissuaded them. Certainly, Winter was asked to write out a full account of the affair following his examinations of 25 and 26 November, and was required to add further details on points where the commissioners felt that he had been reticent, following a pattern set so recently in his account of Gunpowder plot itself.[31]

The exploration of the 'Spanish treason' led to a widening of the scope of questions posed to other prisoners in the following days.[32] With his mind still returning at times to unresolved aspects of the Main plot, Coke suggested that new evidence might come to light if Fawkes were asked 'whether he heard not in Spaine or els where of the Lord Cobhams employment into Spaine or any matter concerning Sir Walter Raleigh in that behalf'.[33] Although both Henry Brooke, Lord Cobham and Sir Walter Ralegh had been convicted of treason for their parts in that conspiracy their lives had been spared, and Ralegh's conduct at his trial had won him a good deal of sympathy, some of it at the expense of his prosecutor, Coke. Ralegh's case in particular still rankled both with the attorney-general and perhaps with others in authority, for some considerable effort was made to detect his involvement in the Gunpowder conspiracy.[34] The efforts, though, were uniformly unsuccessful.

It is not difficult to discern methods used by the examiners. Quite clearly, they worked by winning new information from one suspect and then confronting others with their discoveries in the hope of making further progress. This 'fishing' policy was a natural procedure to adopt, tried and trusted and perhaps the only obvious course, but it was slow, complicated work when there were so many leads to follow and so many prisoners to question. Even in December, after a month of investigations, Coke was reminding himself that Winter ought to 'be examined of his brother for no man els can accuse him', while the king had to remind his commissioners to ask who had received the powder at Lambeth, a question lost among so many others.[35] Clues fell into place, but bred new suspicions and suggested new connections of evidence. As late as 12 December, Waad learnt that Monteagle had owed money to Percy's wife and daughter, strengthening the suspicion that Percy had written the anonymous letter.[36] Already, the commissioners were being left with the unpleasant feeling that important facts were somehow escaping them, and they made no effort to conceal these suspicions. At more than one trial resulting from Gunpowder plot, Coke acknowledged that the interval between discovery and arraignment had been lengthy. By way of explanation he observed that 'great thinges should proceed slowlie', and that 'truth is the daughter of tyme, especiallie in this Cause wherein the greatest matters were latelie discouered'. Twenty-three days, he declared, had been spent in examinations prior to the arraignments of Fawkes, Winter and their associates.[37] Coke laboured his point and other factors did play their part, but it was a valid point nonetheless.

By the first week in December, therefore, the authorities had succeeded in putting together a comprehensive outline of the plot detailing both its development and its intentions. They knew what had happened on Winter's trip to Spain in 1602, when, if Winter himself was to be believed, Philip III had personally promised him military support the following year. They knew that while Monteagle and Tresham had abandoned further plots after the queen's death and had resolved to support the new king, Catesby had sent

Christopher Wright into Spain again to find out how the change in dynasty had altered Spanish intentions. The news had, from the plotter's viewpoint, been bad, for the Spaniards were now clearly set on peace with England, and the financial support formerly guaranteed extremist Catholics in England remained nothing more than a promise unperformed.[38]

Above all, they knew that the idea of blowing up the parliament house using gunpowder had originated with Robert Catesby early in 1604. In discussions with his friends, notably the hot-tempered Thomas Percy, he had urged patience while he thought through his scheme. Then he had revealed the plot in outline to John Wright and Thomas Winter, having sworn them both to secrecy. Catesby's reasoning for the deed was simple but in its way quite logical: 'In that place', he declared, 'haue they done vs all the mischeif, and per-chance God hath desined that place for their punishment.' According to Winter, Catesby was prepared to attempt a peaceable solution first, and with that aim in mind Winter travelled to Flanders to try to persuade the Constable of Castile to insist upon good terms for English Catholics in the forthcoming peace negotiations. But they entertained no great hopes of this initiative, for Winter's brief also extended to searching out 'some confident gentleman . . . best able for this busines' – and they already had Guy Fawkes in mind. Although the Constable proved friendly, Winter was convinced by Owen that he could expect little from that quarter, and told Owen that 'ther were many gentlemen in England who would nott forsake their country vntill they had tried the vttermost, and rather venter their lives then forsake her'. Owen and Sir William Stanley both spoke highly of Fawkes, who when approached by Winter seemed willing to embark on a resolution to 'doe some whatt in Ingland if the pece with Spaine healped vs nott'. Accordingly, they returned to England together and told Catesby that they had heard 'good words' from the Constable, but that they feared 'the deeds would nott answere'.

Catesby then met Percy again. Percy's first words were a frustrated call for action: 'shall wee alwais talk gentlemen and neuer doe any thing?' Catesby quietly took him aside, telling him that a plan was in hand and that they should meet again at Catesby's lodging in the Strand two or three days hence to swear an oath of secrecy and hear the full details. Gathering there as arranged they went into another room in the house to take communion from a Jesuit priest, Father

John Gerard, before Catesby told Percy the full details with Wright and Winter telling Fawkes. On 24 May 1604 Percy, employing the good offices of Dudley Carleton and John Hippesley, fellow-officers of the earl of Northumberland,[39] sub-leased a small house adjacent to the Lords' chamber from one Henry Ferrers of Baddesley Clinton,[40] who in turn held a lease on the property from John Whynniard, keeper of the Old Palace of Westminster. From there, they proposed to drive a mine through the foundations of the parliament house. Fawkes, 'becaus his face was the most vnknowen', assumed the name John Johnson and received the keys of the lodging. Catesby's house in Lambeth seemed the ideal place in which to store the powder and pit props which might then be ferried across the river at dead of night, and because they felt the need of a guard for this property they admitted Keyes – 'a trusty honest man' – to the conspiracy. When they heard that parliament had been prorogued until February 1605 due to an outbreak of plague in the city the plotters dispersed into the country, reassembling in London at the start of the Michaelmas law term.

Their plans received an immediate setback when they discovered that the Scottish commissioners negotiating the proposed union between England and Scotland had taken over Percy's lodgings for their deliberations, preventing any work on the mine until just before Christmas. They were at least able to assemble gunpowder[41] and lay in a store of baked meats 'the lesse to need sending abroad' for provisions. Work began at last, and by Christmas Eve they had tunnelled to the wall of the parliament house, but upon hearing of a further prorogation they called a halt until around early February. Then they brought over the gunpowder from Lambeth by boat and stored it in Percy's house because, as Winter pragmatically put it 'wee were willing to haue all our dainger in one place'. They spent another fortnight attacking the foundations, but progress was so slow that they decided to recruit Christopher Wright as extra labour. Robert Winter and John Grant were also admitted to the conspiracy at about the same time, and one of them at least worked in the mine.[42]

Then Providence seemed to take a hand. As they were tunnelling they heard a rushing sound overhead. Fearing that they had been discovered, Fawkes was sent out to reconnoitre, but he came back with encouraging news that the tenant of the ground-floor vault below the Lords' chamber, a coal merchant by name of Ellen Bright, was selling off her wares and vacating the premises. Percy at once set about obtaining the lease from Whynniard[43] and the plotters thankfully abandoned the mine, resolving to lay the powder in the vault.

Long hours of shared toil and concealment had given the conspirators a chance to plan how best to capitalise upon their blow. They resolved to kidnap the next heir, and working on the assumption that Prince Henry would die with his father, Percy undertook to use his position as a gentleman pensioner to abduct Prince Charles, the duke of York, declaring to any bystanders that he was taking the boy to a place of safety. No one, Percy apart, seems to have had much confidence in this project, however, for in London their friends were few, their enemies many. Princess Elizabeth would be the first target of a Catholic insurrection in the midlands, and Catesby decided to gather Catholic gentlemen of the region together on 5 November – ostensibly to hunt – at his home at Ashby St Ledgers, not far from Lord Harington's estate. Especially following the Treaty of London which had brought to an end the war between England and Spain on terms which, as the plotters had gloomily foreseen, made no effective provision for the security of Catholics in England they were disillusioned with foreign princes, feeling that none could be trusted with prior knowledge of their intentions. As for friends among the nobility, they agreed in principle to preserve as 'many . . . as were Catholick or so disposed'. Catesby assured new recruits unwilling to see patrons die that 'tricks' would be used to dissuade certain noblemen from attending the parliament, but when it came to the crunch his low opinion of the nobility in general meant that he would rather see them all blown to perdition than have the plot miscarry.[44]

Because there was little else to be done in London at that stage they again dispersed, Fawkes, having concealed the gunpowder with billets and faggots, overseas, the others into the country. Catesby, though, took with him an increasingly pressing problem. He had borne the financial burden almost alone for over a year, and his funds were virtually exhausted. Percy may have promised large sums purloined from his master's rents, but nothing had as yet materialised.[45] Accordingly, Catesby sought permission from his colleagues to admit new recruits to the plot – men with the financial resources necessary to pay for the planned rising in the midlands. He undertook to tell Percy and one other of any new admissions, but all agreed that some prospective supporters might be deterred if their participation was known to a wider circle.

Fawkes, while in Flanders, told Owen about the plot, and would have told Sir William Stanley too had he not been absent in Spain. Owen thought that Sir William, who was making some effort to obtain a pardon in England, would be none too keen to learn of treason, but nevertheless agreed to tell him and to send the experienced military commander into England following the explosion. After four months on the continent Fawkes returned at the end of August. Meanwhile, Catesby had apparently done nothing to bring new men into the conspiracy, but meeting Percy in Bath at about the same time he gained his colleague's consent to admit men on his own. Subsequently he told the secret to Ambrose Rookwood and Sir Everard Digby, a handsome, athletic and wealthy young Catholic gentleman in his mid-twenties, with wide estates in Rutland.[46] Last of all, he told Tresham. None took the news very well, although Digby and Rookwood were soon won over, consenting to take leading roles in organising the midlands 'hunting match'. Tresham, though bound by his oath of secrecy, seemed much perturbed, promising Catesby money if he would only call a halt to the treason at once. Meanwhile, Fawkes and Winter put fresh powder into the vault, fearing that the existing store might have become dank. On 3 October parliament was again prorogued for one month, and to Winter – attending the ceremony in Monteagle's entourage – the presence of Salisbury and the leading nobility must have been a comforting confirmation that as yet nothing was suspected.[47]

The plotters again left London. Around 26 October Catesby and Fawkes returned to White Webbs in Enfield Chase, home of the Catholic Vaux family and resort of several Jesuit priests, where they heard from Winter that Prince Henry would not be attending the opening ceremony. Catesby at once decided that they must change their plans and attempt his capture in place of the younger Prince Charles, but we have no further details of what he intended. On the night of 27 October, though, Winter received a visitor in his chamber – possibly a servant of Lord Monteagle[48] – who told him about the delivery of the warning message and his master's immediate reaction. Winter hurriedly sought out Catesby, convinced that the game was up and that they all must flee for their lives. But Catesby was determined to 'see further as yett' and sent a willing Fawkes to check the cellar. When he returned, reporting that nothing had been touched, their minds were somewhat eased.

Catesby and Winter immediately suspected Tresham to be the informer and lost no time in directly accusing him at Barnet on 1 November and again in Lincoln's Inn Walks the next day. On both occasions Tresham stoutly denied the charge, urging them at the same time to give the plot up as lost.[49] His arguments again convinced Winter and almost swayed Catesby, who nevertheless decided to wait for Percy's return from the north before taking a final decision. Although he had probably arrived in London a day or two earlier, Percy met his fellow conspirators again on 3 November. He remained resolute, and following a visit to Syon the next day when he dined with his master, returned full of confidence, declaring that all was well.[50] So Fawkes took up his station with watch and match beside the gunpowder,[51] and the rest is a story already told. Realising on the morning of 5 November that their plans had been discovered the plotters in London, the Wrights, Percy, Catesby, Thomas Winter, and Rookwood, took horse for Warwickshire, casting cloaks aside in their quest for speed. The Catholic gentry duly assembled in the midlands on 5 November for their hunting match, but as soon as the weary and dishevelled Catesby arrived to tell them something of what had occurred in the capital that day, the vast majority vanished as rapidly as they could into the November darkness. Tension and confusion crackled in the night air; George Prince, a servant at the 'Red Lion' at Dunchurch, later remembered hearing a man speak 'owt at a casement in the ynne' saying 'I doubt wee are all betrayde.'[52]

An impressive, dramatic story, but one which was clearly incomplete. When they took stock, the commissioners realised that they still did not have evidence strong enough to charge any nobleman with treason, and they still had little evidence to incriminate any priest. They had not obtained the extradition of any of the suspects known to be on the continent, and they could still not quite credit that plans for following up the anticipated destruction of parliament house and political nation had been quite so cavalierly thought through. If the work was not so pressing, much work remained to be done.

Notes

1   BL Additional MS 12497, fols 285–91, Sir Julius Caesar's papers
2   PRO SP 14/216/134
3   BL Additional MS 12497, fol 380
4   *ibid*, fols 378–9
5   BL Additional MS 12503, fol 368; 12497, fols 370, 372, 380
6   Essex was executed seventeen days after his rebellion, and all trials in connection with that treason were over within a month, although some of the lesser participants were fined in star chamber in May 1601 (*PRO Deputy Keeper's Fourth Report*, appendix II, pp 292–7; Jones, 'Journal of Levinus Munck', pp 241–2)
7   PRO SP 14/216/108, 111, 118, 119, 121, 123, 128, 138, 139, 140, 142, 144, 153, 157, 159, 161, 240; PRO (Transcripts) PRO 31/6/1 (transcripts from Phelips papers at Montacute House)
8   Jeayes, *Letters of Philip Gawdy*, pp 162–3. Stourton, like Mordaunt, was a friend of Catesby, and had intended to miss the opening of parliament. Huddlestone had unwittingly associated with the plotters during their flight from London on 5 November (PRO SP 14/216/103, 104; 14/17/13). While Stourton remained in the Tower, Huddlestone was soon transferred to the Marshalsea prison (SP 14/17/14; Hatfield MS P461, petitions of his wife)
9   Lane wrote from the Tower to Salisbury on 28 November that 'my lords fyrste cominge hether was full of passion, but now more reposed' (Hatfield MS 113/50)
10   For example see PRO SP 14/216/116, 124, 126, 135, 136, 146; Bodleian MS Tanner 75, fols 141v–142, 203
11   PRO SP 14/16/38, 57, 100, 101, 116. See also Coke's notes c5 November (SP 14/16/7); Hatfield MSS 113/3, 115/18
12   PRO SP 14/16/116; 14/3/16
13   See part II chapters XI–XIII below
14   Some information added colour to the lives of the conspirators (eg Hatfield MS 112/160, list of Catesby's dining companions during visits to London in 1605) while some supplied further details of their movements in recent weeks (eg PRO SP 14/16/11, 13, 15, 16)
15   Hatfield MS 191/80. For the petitions see the final two volumes of the published HMC, *Hatfield* calendar. For example Hatfield MSS P353, 464, petitions of William Hilliard; P1465, petition of William Shaw. Some of the more deserving or better-connected cases were indeed beginning to secure their rewards. Henry Bromley received £210 from the exchequer on 8 December, while Sir John Folliatt and Humphrey Salway were generously reimbursed for their expenses in conveying prisoners and assisting the county authorities (PRO E403/2725, fols 143, 147, 151; Devon, *Issues of the Exchequer*, p 28)
16   *Sir Henry Whithed's Letter-Book*, pp 42–3
17   Hatfield MS 191/69. The sheriff of Pembroke ordered prayers of thanksgiving, bonfires to be lit, and bells to be rung in Haverfordwest
18   Hatfield MS 112/174
19   Nicholls, 'Sir Charles Percy', p 245. Catesby had not lived there for

some time, leasing the house out to the earl of Northumberland's brother

20   Hatfield MS 191/78. See also PRO SP 14/216/57, 58 for the response to the alarm in Staffordshire. The council supported Walsh's action, issuing a proclamation to this effect on 19 November (Larkin and Hughes, *Stuart Royal Proclamations*, i, pp 129–31)

21   For one such anonymous attack on the sheriff of Staffordshire see PRO SP 14/16/37

22   Hatfield MSS 113/22; 191/140. See also PRO SP 14/216/72 and 94, further letters from Hastings. In what may have been another expression of local rivalries another member of his family, Sir Henry Hastings, was accused of complicity in the plot (Hatfield MS 214/54)

23   Hatfield MS 113/11, dated 15 Nov 1605

24   Hatfield MS 112/172, Sir Francis Vere to Salisbury, 12 Nov 1605

25   PRO SP 14/16/116

26   See his reaction to Sir Charles Percy's efforts to obtain the colonelcy of the regiment (Nicholls, 'Sir Charles Percy', pp 243–4)

27   Lunn, 'Chaplains to the English Regiment', pp 136–42; Willaert, 'Negociations', pp 596–8; Edwards, *Guy Fawkes*, pp 93–8

28   Nicholls, 'Sir Charles Percy', pp 244–5

29   Hatfield MS 112/91; PRO SP 14/216/124

30   See PRO SP 14/216/117 and 124 for two examples where Monteagle's name is edited out of confessions to be read at the Gunpowder trials. Garnett had purchased a pardon for all treasons plotted in Elizabeth's reign

31   Hatfield MS 112/91

32   For example PRO SP 14/216/124, 125; Bodleian MS Tanner 75, fols 141v, 142

33   PRO SP 14/16/116. Fawkes had supplied details of his mission before Winter's statement regarding the Spanish treason (Bodleian MS Tanner 75, fol 141v)

34   See PRO SP 14/216/6 and 37; 14/16/100 and 101; Hatfield MSS 107/108; 113/25 and 33. See Shirley, *Thomas Harriot*, p 334

35   PRO SP 14/16/116, it would appear that this is a reference to John rather than to Robert Winter, whose guilt by then was manifest to all; Hatfield MS 113/48

36   Hatfield MS 113/91

37   Bodleian MS Add C86, fol 3–3v

38   Much of what follows is derived from Hatfield MSS 112/91 and 113/54, and from PRO SP 14/216/49, confessions of Thomas Winter and Fawkes

39   PRO SP 14/216/39 and 115

40   PRO SP 14/216/1

41   On the collection of gunpowder see PRO SP 14/216/126, 136, examinations of Keyes and Rookwood

42   Gardiner, *What Gunpowder Plot Was*, pp 71–6; PRO SP 14/18/25, examination of John Grant, 17 Jan 1606

43   PRO SP 14/216/6, 24, 39, 49

44   PRO SP 14/216/126

45   See below, p 151

46   Edwards, *Greenway Narrative*, pp 104–7; for an interesting, if sympathetic, biography of Digby see [Thomas Longueville], *The Life of a Conspirator*, 1895

47   *Lords' Journals*, ii, p 351

48   See Durst, *Intended Treason*, pp 303–7

49   See Thomas Winter's confession (Hatfield MS 113/54) and Tresham's confessions (SP 14/16/62 and 63)

50   PRO SP 14/216/126

51   PRO SP 14/216/100

52   The story of the hunting meet can be established from several documents in Gunpowder Plot Book (PRO SP 14/216/33, 47, 55, 64, 67, 108, 109, 121, 135, 136, 138, 140, 153, 176, 233, 240)

IV

The plotters condemned

One must be wary of confusing the interpretations which later generations placed on the plot with the reaction of James's government at the time. Over the following centuries, the most vehement criticism of Catholics and Catholicism has come during periods when the critics feared, often with good reason, that the authorities were inclined to treat Catholics leniently. We see this in 1678–80 with the Popish plot, and as late as the 1850s when the final stages in Catholic emancipation were marked by a resurgence of religious xenophobia in traditional bonfire night celebrations throughout the land.[1] When writing about the plot it has become customary to assume that, even if the government was not itself instrumental in shaping the treason, it at once seized upon the fact to illustrate to domestic and external audiences the depths of iniquity to which professors of the Roman Catholic faith would stoop.

But forgetting later events and looking solely at what happened in 1605–6, it is clear that Salisbury and his colleagues were if anything rather embarrassed by the potential for anti-Catholic propaganda inherent in their discovery. For the government did not use the horror generated by the plot as a weapon with which to deal a 'crushing blow' to English Catholics.[2] When the rebels were proclaimed traitors on 7 November, their crime was described – quite deliberately – in clearly political terms, 'howsoever cloaked with zeale of Superstitious Religion'. Care was taken 'to distinguish betweene all others, calling themselves Catholickes, and these detestable Traitours'.[3] In his speech to parliament two days later, the king seemed genuinely torn between distaste for the traitors' professed religion and his sincere wish to avoid a general witch hunt directed against all Catholics:

For although it cannot bee denied, That it was the onely blind superstition of their errors in Religion, that led them to this desperate deuise; yet doeth it not follow, that all professing that *Romish* religion were guilty of the same. For as it is true, That no other sect of heretiques . . . did euer maintaine by the grounds of their Religion, That it was lawfull, or rather meritorious (as the *Romish* Catholicks call it) to murther Princes or people, for quarrell of Religion. . . . Yet it is true on the other side, That many honest men blinded peraduenture with some opinions of Popery, as if they be not sound in the questions of the *Real presence*, or in the number of the Sacraments, or some such Schoole question: yet do they either not know, or at least not beleeue all the true grounds of Popery, which is indeed, *The mysterie of iniquitie.*[4]

Especially considering the composition of his audience and the effect which so close a brush with death must have had on a timorous man the demand for restraint behind his words is as remarkable as it is evident. Salisbury too, that arch-enemy of the Jesuit faction and alleged oppressor of Catholics, showed no overpowering desire to launch into full-scale persecution. Earlier in 1605 he had told the Venetian ambassador that, so long as the Catholics remained quiet, he had no wish to see their blood spilt, and his extremely cautious and politically oriented negotiations with some of the secular clergy continued after 5 November.[5] Of course there were many who tried to hold all Catholics responsible for the treason. The anonymous author of *Feareful Newes of Thunder and Lightning*, a work published in 1606, announced that all Catholics must *ipso facto* be traitors, for

whosoeuer holdeth the Popes supremacie, is a traitor, euery Catholick holdeth the Popes supremacie: my assumption neede here no more wordes, for this very name telleth me, that he holdeth the vniversality of the church of Rome, and so the vniversall authoritie of the Pope of Rome. And this will alwayes be the keeping of the dirige, a Papist, a Catholick, a traytor, a traytor.[6]

Sir Francis Hastings, Sir George More, and other hardline protestants lost no time in echoing such simplistic views when parliament reassembled in January 1606. Pressing for the better execution of the penal statutes against papists they urged the manifest religious motivation of the plotters as a valid reason to restrict recusants' liberties still further.[7] But this argument struck no chord with the government, which through patronage was able to sway the House of Commons whither it pleased. For all the rhetoric of individual members, the penal legislation passed was hardly severe, and there was greater enthusiasm for Sir Edward Montagu's uncontentious motion that 5 November should thereafter be marked as a day of public thanksgiving. This bill passed swiftly through all its stages in both Houses, although an attempt by Sir Henry Poole to include Monteagle in the congratulations was blocked, ostensibly because his inclusion would detract from the king's role in the discovery.[8]

When examined closely, stricter anti-Catholic legislation passed in the parliament of 1606 amounted to little more than the enforcement of an Oath of Allegiance to the king. Tendered to any convicted recusant and to anyone who had declined to take the sacrament for twelve months, the oath demanded an affirmation of loyalty to James as the rightful monarch, and an explicit denial of papal powers to depose the king, order an invasion, or release the king's subjects from their oaths. It also required recusants to denounce tyrannicide as an heretical doctrine and to promise that they would reveal any plot against the king which might come to their notice. If the Catholics of England could bring themselves to take the oath, as the Archpriest George Blackwell along with many others managed to do, then central government was, by and large, appeased, even though individual counties could as ever make life more or less tolerable for their Catholic minorities according to the religious convictions of influential men in the shire.[9]

Of course, that government's belief in the political threat posed by the Society of Jesus remained undiminished, but even here there was a strange hesitancy to make capital out of links between principal plotters and eminent Jesuits. One feature of the November investigations is an absence of any concerted attempt to force from the plotters details of their Jesuit friends and contacts. While in early December James was eager to have the prisoners answer some very obvious questions about the extent of priestly involvement, it looks as if his ministers held back, for when the king ordered them to learn the names of those who had regularly confessed and absolved the traitors, reasoning that these priests must have been aware of what was afoot, Salisbury replied via James's secretary that the prisoners were wilfully denying that any priest had been told of their plans 'yea, what torture soever they be put to'.[10]

All the same, Salisbury simultaneously sent the king a statement recently made by Thomas Bate. In it, Bate admitted that he had confessed to the Jesuit Oswald Tesimond immediately after his master had admitted him to the conspiracy, and that he had then told Tesimond – who had not been 'desirous to heare' them – the details of the plot. Bate said further that Tesimond had subsequently absolved him, telling him that he ought to keep his master's secret, 'because yt was for a good cause'.[11] Pointing to this promising document, Salisbury urged the king to be patient, a few days more would surely bring the desired results. But although armed with firm evidence against Tesimond, and although recent testimony provided grounds for investigating further the activities of several other Jesuits, enquiries into these matters seem to have been promptly set aside and not resumed until well into the new year.

On 23 December, Francis Tresham died of a strangury in the Tower.[12] Shortly before his death Coke had searched Tresham's chambers at the Inner Temple, finding there two copies of a Jesuit 'Treatise of Equivocation', the doctrine that a man suspected of a crime was justified in 'answering doubtfully' under oath to the investigating authorities in order to avoid incriminating himself or others. Coke set to work listing the moral and legal pitfalls inherent in such an argument. This discovery, coupled with the suspect's death, made it easier to portray Tresham as a traitor, although one may feel that his role in the affair was indeed as he himself had described it. Certainly there were those who believed at the time that he would escape the block.[13] At any rate, Christmas at court seems to have occupied the commissioners' energies for the next few weeks. It was only on 9 January that a principal plotter was again questioned,[14] although from then on they all were, frequently and repeatedly.[15]

When examinations resumed in the new year they were often left to Popham and Coke, with the other commissioners visiting the Tower on only a couple of occasions.[16] This probably reflected the absence of any serious political danger in the situation, the legal necessities of preparing for a trial now taking precedence. There was, though, a new emphasis to these January investigations marking them out as a third phase of the enquiries into Gunpowder plot. The questions, at last, concentrated on securing information against the Jesuits. Of course, it may well be that other questions were put on a wider range of topics, and that answers went unrecorded because they told the investigators nothing new. All the same, it was only on 15 January – nearly two-and-a-half months after the discovery – that a proclamation went out for the arrest of Henry Garnett, John Gerard, and Tesimond.[17] When Stephen Littleton and Robert Winter were captured soon after[18] they were immediately confronted with questions concerning the priests.[19] One can only speculate on reasons for this apparent delay, but it is at least possible that the authorities, while looking to incriminate the Jesuits, had rather hoped that those concerned would take a hint and leave England. Propaganda victories are often less messy than more concrete successes, and the propaganda would have been just as effective had none of those named in the proclamation ever been brought to trial.

While great efforts have subsequently been made to clear the names of the three proclaimed Jesuits, it is difficult to believe that any one of them, with the possible exception of Gerard, was ignorant of the plotters' intentions. Tesimond, in confession, had heard about the plot from Catesby and had himself told Garnett of the treason under circumstances which seem to have fallen short of those required for confession.[20] During the midlands rebellion, Tesimond had shown himself to be the conspirators' ally in their extremity. He had come to the rebels on the afternoon of 6 November during their stay at Huddington, Catesby greeting him warmly as a gentleman who would 'live and die' with them.[21] Subsequently, Tesimond had ridden to Hindlip, hoping to secure the support of its owner Thomas Abington for the rebels, and failing in this had ridden off angrily, vowing to rouse the Catholics in Lancashire.[22] As for Gerard, Fawkes admitted that it was he who had administered the sacrament to the original group of conspirators, immediately after they had taken the oath of secrecy among themselves.[23] Both Tesimond and Gerard eventually made their escape to the continent[24] where they wrote – or translated – accounts of the plot in English and Italian.[25] At the end of January, however, Garnett was captured at Hindlip House, together with another Jesuit Edward Oldcorne and their two menservants Richard Chambers and Nicholas Owen.[26] Having accused him of complicity in the treason in the recent proclamation, the authorities were now in a position to see whether Garnett could answer those questions left open after the interrogation of his alleged accomplices.

Shortly before Garnett's capture, proceedings against the prisoners received a spur with the reassembling of a parliament eager to see all those guilty of the treason receive their just deserts and only too ready to pick up an injudicious suggestion by the king in his prorogation speech that the plotters should be tried in parliament.[27] There was even talk of appointing 'some more greavous death' for them, once convicted.[28] The authorities seem to have anticipated trouble from this quarter, since shortly before the first meeting of parliament they began the process of bringing the leading prisoners to trial,[29] thus nipping in the bud any such extra-legal and pre-cedent forming action.[30] A thorough indictment was drawn up, naming the three priests, Catesby, Percy, Fawkes, Thomas Winter, the Wrights, Keyes, Bate, and Tresham as the principal traitors, who had subsequently drawn Rookwood, Grant, and Robert Winter into the plot.[31] Digby had first been told of the conspiracy in Northamptonshire, and accordingly his indictment was taken at Wellingborough.[32] On 24 January special commissions of oyer and terminer were addressed to Nottingham, Suffolk, Worcester, Devonshire, Salisbury, Northampton, Popham, Sir Thomas Fleming, Sir Thomas Walmisley, and Sir Peter Warburton, requiring them to try the accused, and writs of habeas corpus went out that day ordering the gaolers to present their prisoners at Westminster.[33] Following a final round of examinations the previous day, seven prisoners – Digby, Grant, Fawkes, Keyes, Rookwood, Robert and Thomas Winter – were brought from the Tower up river to Westminster on 27 January. Bate, a mere serving man, had been lodged in the Gatehouse, but he was brought from that city prison to stand trial with the rest.[34] Other gentlemen prisoners still held in London, among them John Winter and Henry Morgan, were not yet brought to justice, the intention being to arraign them in the various midland counties, where their crimes of treason and rebellion had been committed.

After standing in star chamber for half an hour, the eight men were led into Westminster Hall. They were well-dressed, Digby in 'his tuff taffatie gowne and a sute of blacke satten', the others 'all very gallante at the kinge's Charge, they themselues desyringe to haue it so'. Of the seven prisoners facing the main indictment, all pleaded Not Guilty, denying certain points within the indictment, while confessing to the whole. It was difficult for them to do otherwise, for seldom could traitors have offended under more articles of the 1351 Treason Act.[35] Digby, tried separately at the end of the day, alone pleaded Guilty.

Although lasting all the short January day, the trial was apparently rather lacking in spectacle for the crowds of onlookers, many of whom had paid high prices to be present.[36] According to one account, 'the Kinge and Queene were bothe there in pryuate', as were most of the peerage and a majority of 'all the whole parlimente'.[37] Coke, for once, was relatively restrained, forgetting, at least in the scanty reports that survive, his instructions received from Salisbury that he should clear Monteagle from slanderous rumours accusing him of involvement in the plot.[38] The occasional choice turn of phrase, such as his description of Catesby as '*homo profundae perfidae*' was no more, perhaps rather less, than the spectators had anticipated. Aware no doubt that he was retelling a familiar story, he urged the wickedness of the conspiracy as best he could, showing the relationships between the Spanish treason and Gunpowder plot. He was at pains to reject Catholic claims that the criminals were financially ruined men 'of noe relligion, and of base Condition'. On the contrary, Percy the 'Archerebell' was of the house of Northumberland, Winter, Tresham, and Digby all of ancient and honourable birth, while Sir John Talbot – whom Coke described without much justification as 'guiltie in the higheste degree of misprision of Treason' – was heir-presumptive to the earldom of Shrewsbury. As for being men without religion, how, he asked, could that be when they were continually associating with Jesuits, and when 'theise priestes were the forwardeste men in them, Desmonde [Tesimond], Baldwin, Creswell, Hammon[d], Garnette, Jarette and Westmerlande, makinge relligion there mantell of impietie'. They had scorned the king's lenity towards papists – indeed, it had only served to nurture their schemes, so that they had aimed at the place of justice as well as the persons, 'and Justice Fauxe showlde haue bene the gunpowder Justice'.

To liven up the proceedings, Coke told an old fable concerning the cat that had slaughtered most of the 'mise and rattes' in a country, obliging survivors to keep to their holes. Perceiving this, the cat had shaved her crown and had put on a friar's habit, luring the mice into the open by promising them that, having taken orders, her character had wholly changed. Alas, the gullible rodents soon discovered that the cat 'had the same Cruell and bloodie harte still'. The story was not there simply to show that an evil man remained evil, howsoever disguised. There was more to it: for had not a friar discovered gunpowder? And here was the ideal moment to describe to an appreciative audience how God's judgement had dealt the fugitives one final, resounding blow while they were attempting to dry the powder at Holbeach.

As a concluding gesture, after the speeches of the condemned men were done, the court was told how conversation between Robert Winter and Fawkes, lodged in adjacent cells within the Tower, had been monitored by carefully positioned eavesdroppers. Winter had said that he hoped another generation – his son and Catesby's son in particular – would avenge their execution, and that, though no one had yet published a defence of their actions, they should maintain the justice of their cause to the end. 'Our deathes will be a sufficient justifficacion of it. And it is for Gods cause.' In addition, according to the eavesdroppers, he 'seemed to express some part of his sorrow that their busines being brought within one day or twoe of the execucon, it should so vnhappely be crossed'.[39] Winter also described a lurid dream in which he had seen steeples of St Paul's and other churches standing awry as if blasted by an explosion, and strange disfigured faces within the churches which, after the explosion at Holbeach, he had recognised as those of his injured colleagues. Both Fawkes and Winter had confirmed the truth of these conversations under subsequent examination.[40] This fanatical testimony, no doubt, went down very well in the court.

Most excitement was aroused during Digby's trial, when Sir Everard tried to maintain that the king had gone back on promises of toleration for Catholics and had made the penal laws more savage. In mitigation of his offence Digby said that he had been led into the plot through his love for Catesby and for the 'Catholic Cause', and that he had not been motivated by any particular or personal discontent. Northampton and Salisbury both spent much time refuting these points, Northampton's speech in particular being a masterpiece of turgid rhetoric.[41]

None of the accused men had much to say. Thomas Winter sought mercy for his brother, Bate and Robert Winter simply begged for mercy. Both Rookwood and Fawkes attempted to explain why they had entered pleas of Not Guilty, Fawkes declaring that he had been unaware of certain conferences alleged in the indictment, Rookwood explaining frankly that he would 'rather lose his life than give it', suggesting with desperate optimism that – as he had been drawn into the plot only through his love for Catesby and seeing as it had been his first offence – he might be punished 'corporaliter non mortaliter'. Digby sought clemency for his wife and children, whose livelihood would be snatched away under the penalties for treason, and asked that he might suffer death by beheading rather than undergo the rigorous form of execution reserved for traitors. He left the court with a flourish, bowing to the lords of the council and declaring that, were they to forgive him, he would go to his execution in better heart. Their lordships, no less ceremonious, or perhaps genuinely moved, replied: 'God forgiue you, and we doe.'[42]

Keyes showed the most resilience. Popham had learnt something of the man by 6 November, when he described him as being 'of spyryt, but of noe state'.[43] At his trial, he said defiantly that his fortunes had been desperate before the action, that he was as ready to die then as at any other time, 'and for this cause rather then for an other'.[44]

No place of execution was specified at the trial,[45] and some debate might have continued as to the most suitable site. On 30 January, however, four of the condemned men: Digby, Robert Winter, Grant, and Bate, were drawn on hurdles through streets lined with guards recruited from among the householders of London to St Paul's churchyard and there put to death.[46] The following day Fawkes, Thomas Winter, Ambrose Rookwood, and Robert Keyes were executed in the Old Palace Yard at Westminster. None made any significant confession at his death, although Keyes apparently exuded defiance once more. One contemporary – unsympathetic – account of the executions tells us that he

like a desperate villain, using little speech, with small or no shew of repentance, went stoutly up the ladder; where, not staying the hangman's turn, he turned himself off with such a leap, that with the swing he brake the halter; but, after his fall, was quickly drawn to the block, and there was quickly divided into four parts.[47]

A Catholic source insisted that Keyes met his death very devoutly, but conceded that, when asked if he did not then regret the plot and recognise it to have been a grave sin, 'he still refused to see any wrong in it. All he would admit was that the conspiracy had its unfortunate aspects.'[48]

The execution of the conspirators had been delayed long enough, but the continuing resolution shown at their deaths must have confirmed lingering suspicions that more information might yet have been won from them. Over the years there has been a good deal of sympathy for the plotters; they have been portrayed as men who, under extremes of torture, were forced to reveal all they knew.[49] While it would not do to suggest that the investigators were particularly humane, the course of examinations surely illustrates that such views are well wide of the mark. Fawkes was probably the only conspirator to be tortured, our only certain evidence for its use being the king's directive of 6 November, already mentioned.[50] Salisbury's letter to the king's secretary on 4 December, also cited above, is sometimes quoted to prove the use of torture on Fawkes's associates, whereas in fact it implies the exact opposite.[51]

A series of secret letters written by Sir Everard Digby to his family and smuggled out of the Tower was rediscovered among the papers of his son Sir Kenelm Digby after the latter's death in 1675.[52] These letters, a series which apparently continues right up to the eve of Digby's trial, contain no hint that he had ever faced torture, although at one point Digby fancied that it had been 'in a fashion, offered' to him.[53] From the Gatehouse, Thomas Bate specifically acknowledged that his captors were treating him well in a letter which he too managed to have smuggled out to friends and which John Gerard subsequently published. Not unnaturally suspicious, Bate expressed his fears that the authorities anticipated some return for showing him such unexpected kindness, saying that while he had admitted acquainting Tesimond with the plot he had done so only in the hope of saving his own life, and that he now regretted having been so weak.[54]

Fawkes and some of his colleagues, while admitting their own guilt, lied desperately and defiantly in order to save their associates.[55] Only one short confession made by John Grant has been preserved, and while this may simply be due to the fact that he had nothing significant to add it is possible that he refused to talk.[56] Nor was Digby at any stage completely frank with his examiners. At his first examination, he fed his questioners a diet of lies from start to finish[57] and in his letters he would boast of his deceptions. Thus on 10 January 1606 he wrote:

Yesterday I was before Mr Attorney and my Lord Chief Justice, who asked me if I had taken the Sacrament to keep secret the plot as others did. I said that I had not, because I would avoid the question of at whose hands it were.[58]

In another letter, he insisted that he could not say anything which might make the plot appear less odious to fellow Catholics 'for divers were to have been brought out of the danger, which now would rather hurt them than otherwise'. He did not think that there would have been as many as three men 'worth Saving that should have been lost', writing that some of his own friends had been in danger, 'which

I had prevented, but they shall never know it'.[59] It must be pointed out, though, that Digby had in effect lost all touch with reality. In a bizarre letter from prison he volunteered to procure any priest in England to go to Rome and secure guarantees from the pope that any 'as shall goe about to disturbe the kinges quiet and hapie raygne' would suffer excommunication. He warned Salisbury that if the authorities were resolved to deal severely with Catholics 'in breife [there] wilbe massakers, rebellions, and desperate attemptes agaynste the kinge and state, for it is a generall receued reason among Catholikes, that there is not that expectinge and sufferinge course now to be run that was in the queenes time'.[60] Both Gerard and Gardiner argued that this letter was written before Digby had been admitted to the plot, an argument which flies in the face of Digby's repeated insistence that he is ready to suffer punishment, ready to die for his faults, whether or not the privy council made use of him in this way — and which also ignores the fact that one of Digby's secret letters from the Tower records Salisbury's curt rejection of his overture.[61]

One further example of the prisoners' procrastinations is worth mentioning. Thomas Winter and Fawkes, when examined about their part in the Spanish treason, both assigned to their dead colleague Christopher Wright the role played by one Anthony Dutton in this affair. Dutton/Wright had been sent by Catesby on the queen's death to discover whether the Spanish court intended to honour its promise to invade England in support of a Catholic claimant. It is possible that Dutton was Wright's alias, but it is equally possible that, while Wright could suffer no further, Dutton still lived at liberty and might be protected by such a fabrication. Certainly the English authorities never connected the name 'Dutton' with the Spanish treason and it has taken recent research to redis-cover the part that he played in negotiations at Madrid.[62] Thus, as many have argued over the past century, the testimony of Winter and others may indeed be held somewhat suspect, but not necessarily for the reasons usually put forward. For our purposes, the point is that the council may have realised these shortcomings only too well.

Yet if the authorities felt that secrets were escaping them it may be wondered why they did not resort to torture to obtain a fuller picture. There can be no certain answer to this, but it must have been as clear to them as it is to us that torture, while it can produce a confession shaped to the requirements of the questioners, does not necessarily produce the truth. And there is no need to doubt that James and his council desperately wanted to know the truth about the involvement of the nobility in Gunpowder plot and other enduring mysteries. Progress was being made by other more orthodox and approved means, and while such progress was slow there was no great incentive to resort to what were clearly distasteful methods of interrogation which hazarded the lives of precious informants; too many plotters had already been silenced through violence. Fawkes's case apart, the only extant references to torture being used come after the plotters' deaths. Evidence in Garnett's case is inconclusive, lying open to differing interpretations, but he may at least have been shown what was in store for him if he remained silent. In February 1606 the privy council issued warrants authorising the use of torture on Chambers, Owen, and possibly others 'inferior prisoners' then in detention.[63] Whether the warrants were ever implemented is uncertain, but there is a strong tradition in Catholic circles that Owen died under torture, the rack fatally aggravating a hernia.[64]

The reader may choose to believe this, or the official version which maintained that Owen had ripped open his stomach with a knife.[65] What seems certain is that, by then, the authorities were becoming irritated by their inability to tidy up the remaining loose ends. Garnett had yet to be tried, Northumberland and the other lords also languished in the Tower, and there was no real prospect of obtaining the extradition of Owen or any other suspect on the continent. In addition, parliament was proving difficult over agreeing to the bill of attainder against the condemned traitors. While ready to applaud the mercies of God and the divinely inspired perception of the king, and while happy to mark out 5 November as a day of national salvation, both Houses showed less enthusiasm for depriving relatives of their means of livelihood. Tresham's family, especially, had influential friends and Coke was obliged to appear more than once before the Commons to argue his case for the attainders.[66] Consequently, progress was very slow.[67]

Notes

1 Swift, 'Guy Fawkes Celebrations in Exeter', pp 6–8
2 Bossy, 'English Catholic Community', p 95
3 Larkin and Hughes, *Stuart Royal Proclamations*, i, pp 124–5
4 *His Majesties Speach*, sigs C2–C2v
5 Gardiner, *What Gunpowder Plot Was*, pp 162–7. See also below pp,

130–4

6 Cited by J V Gifford, 'The Controversy over the Oath of Allegiance', Oxford MPhil thesis, 1971, pp 26–7. For men sharing such views, popery was indeed an 'anti-religion', thriving on the ignorance and weaknesses of mankind (Lake, 'Anti-popery', pp 75–7)

7 *Commons' Journals*, i, p 257

8 *ibid*, pp 258, 262; HMC, *Montagu of Beaulieu*, p 49; Willson, *Bowyer's Diary*, pp 4–5, 16

9 Fincham and Lake, 'Ecclesiastical Policy of James I', p 186; cf Ryan, 'Jacobean Oath of Allegiance', pp 171–83; La Rocca, 'James I and his Catholic Subjects', pp 251, 253–4, 258–9

10 Hatfield MS 113/77

11 PRO SP 14/216/145

12 PRO SP 14/17/56, Waad to Salisbury, 23 Dec 1605, see also Wake, 'Death of Francis Tresham', pp 31–41

13 Malloch, 'Garnet's Treatise of Equivocation', pp 390–3; PRO SP 14/17/33 and 56

14 On that day Fawkes was questioned on Sir Edmund Baynham's part in the plot (SP 14/216/163, for Baynham see below, pp 67–8) and Winter was asked about Father John Gerard's role when the original five plotters had sworn their oath of secrecy (SP 14/216/164)

15 PRO SP 14/216/165, 166, 170, 171, 175, 177, 178; 14/18/13

16 The lords commissioners appear to have visited the Tower on 17 January (PRO SP 14/216/168–70, 172; 14/18/25) to examine John Grant and the newly captured Winter and Littleton, and on 26 January (SP 14/216/180, 14/18/44) to examine Fawkes and Robert Winter on the eve of their trial. They also examined Thomas Bate, presumably in the Gatehouse prison, on 13 January (SP 14/216/166)

17 Larkin and Hughes, *Stuart Royal Proclamations*, i, pp 131–3

18 On the capture of Littleton and Winter see Harley MS 360, fols 92–108; see also Hatfield MSS P331 and P1185, petitions

19 PRO SP 14/216/168, 172, almost all the prisoners were asked about Father Hammond SJ who had heard their confessions whilst at Huddington on 7 November

20 See Gardiner, 'Two Declarations of Garnet', pp 510–17, esp pp 513–15

21 PRO SP 14/216/165, testimony of Henry Morgan

22 PRO SP 14/216/197

23 PRO SP 14/216/54

24 Morris, *Troubles of our Catholic Forefathers*, i, p 143; Caraman, *John Gerard*, pp 197–209

25 See the article by Francis Edwards SJ in the *Journal of the Society of Archivists*, iv, number 2, Oct 1970, pp 96–108

26 See Caraman, *Henry Garnet*, pp 330–41

27 In his speech of 9 November; see also *Commons' Journals*, i, p 259

28 *Commons' Journals*, i, p 259; Willson, *Bowyer's Diary*, p 7

29 *PRO Deputy Keeper's Fifth Report*, appendix II, pp 139–43, records of the 'Baga de Secretis' (PRO KB8)

30   See *Lords' Journals*, ii, p 365 – reporting for the committee set up to enquire into the matter, the archbishop of Canterbury said that, having taken advice from the lord chief justice, they had 'forborn and given over to proceed any further therein', since there was no 'convenient' reason to defer the executions

31   PRO *Deputy Keeper's Fifth Report*, appendix II, p 140–1

32   *ibid*, p 143; Hatfield MS 109/129, Coke to Salisbury, 18 Jan 1606

33   PRO *Deputy Keeper's Fifth Report*, appendix II, pp 141–2; Talbot, *Recusant Records*, p 272 (BL Additional MS 41257, fol 36)

34   PRO *Deputy Keeper's Fifth Report*, appendix II, pp 141–2, 143

35   Hawarde, *Les Reportes*, p 256. They had conspired to kill the king, the queen, the king's eldest son, and the lord chancellor in the execution of his duty, besides plotting to violate the king's eldest daughter and endeavouring to raise rebellion in England. Any one of these was a treasonable offence; see *True and Perfect Relation*, sigs D3–D4v

36   An MP complained in the Commons that he had paid 10s for standing room but that others had then been let into the same enclosure for much smaller sums, with the result that 'they of this howse stoode at greate disease, not without much danger' (Willson, *Bowyer's Diary*, p 10)

37   Hawarde, *Les Reportes*, p 257. The principal sources for the trial are Howell, *State Trials*, ii, cols 159–94; *True and Perfect Relation*, sigs A3–N3v; Hawarde, *Les Reportes*, pp 251–7; Bodleian MS Add C86

38   PRO SP 14/19/94

39   Howell, *State Trials*, cols 186–7; PRO SP 14/18/42; *True and Perfect Relation*, sigs L–Lv

40   PRO SP 14/216/180; 14/18/44; *True and Perfect Relation*, sig Lv

41   Howell, *State Trials*, ii, cols 187–94; *True and Perfect Relation*, sigs M–N3

42   Howell, *State Trials*, ii, cols 186, 194; *True and Perfect Relation*, sigs K4–L, N3–N3v

43   PRO SP 14/216/20A

44   Howell, *State Trials*, ii, col 186; *True and Perfect Relation*, sig K4v

45   PRO *Deputy Keeper's Fifth Report*, appendix II, pp 142–3

46   Guildhall, City of London Record Office, Journal of Common Council vol 27, fol 20v. On 28 January the privy council wrote to Waad 'willing him to deale by way of perswasion with Digby, Winter, and the rest of the traytors . . . [to] admitt and make choice of the clergie, bishop or other for their spirituall comfort, and to offer them conference with any of the clergie' (BL Additional MS 11402, fol 109v)

47   Oldys, *Harleian Miscellany*, iii, p 134

48   Edwards, *Greenway Narrative*, p 229

49   See, for example, Hugh Ross Williamson's *The Gunpowder Plot*

50   PRO SP 14/216/17

51   Hatfield MS 113/77 – the plotters are clearly defying the authorities to use force

52   Barlow, *Gunpowder-Treason*, pp 229–63. Admittedly the originals do not survive, and Barlow's history is hardly impartial, but the letters do not give the impression of having been modified or tampered with in any

way. Barlow, one feels, published them so that they might speak for themselves, no doubt hoping that they would serve as an awful warning against the perils of adhering blindly to a false religion. To a more-sympathetic audience, however, the letters show Digby in a better light: as an idealistic, poetic young man, devoted to his family and to his faith. The points therein which augment our knowledge of the investigations, illuminating as they are, would not have satisfied a forger who, presented with such scope for invention, could hardly have failed to carry through a more-thorough job

53   *ibid*, p 248
54   Morris, *Condition of Catholics*, p 210
55   Nicholls, 'Politics and Percies', p 276
56   PRO SP 14/18/25, dated 17 Jan 1606
57   Compare PRO SP 14/16/94 with 14/16/95
58   Barlow, *Gunpowder-Treason*, p 241; cf Digby's examination of 9 Jan 1606 (PRO SP 14/18/13)
59   *ibid*, p 251
60   PRO SP 14/17/10
61   Barlow, *Gunpowder-Treason*, p 245; See also Gerard, *What was the Gunpowder Plot?*, pp 245–9; Gardiner, *What Gunpowder Plot Was*, p 169
62   Loomie, 'Guy Fawkes in Spain', pp 45–6, 59–60. See also the extracts from Fawkes's confessions printed in Abbot's *Antilogia*, pp 167v, 168), copied by Sancroft (Bodleian MS Tanner 75, fol 141v), and cited at Garnett's trial (BL Harley MS 360, fol 115**v)
63   For Garnett see below, p 77 n14. The council first permitted the use of manacles, later allowing the rack to be employed as well (BL Additional MS 11402, fols 109v, 110)
64   Foley, *Records*, iv, pp 263–7
65   Abbot, *Antilogia*, p 114; Jardine, *Narrative of Gunpowder Plot*, pp 198–200
66   PRO SP 14/19/93; See also *Lords' Journals*, ii, pp 401, 404; *Commons' Journals*, i, pp 301–2
67   The bill did not receive its Third Reading in the Commons until 12 May, and even then there were those prepared to express disagreement with the attainder of Tresham, maintaining that it set a dangerous precedent (*Commons' Journals*, i, p 308). The bill had its Third Reading in the Lords on 17 May (*Lords' Journals*, ii, p 435)

V

Further suspects, further trials

At this stage the commissioners might have been tempted to concentrate both on exploiting the plot's propaganda potential abroad and on following through foreign leads, for the revelations concerning the Spanish treason had indeed given an international dimension to the investigations. But they had little incentive to pursue such a course. England was at peace with all western European powers and it could serve no political purpose to incriminate France – or even the old enemy Spain – in any way. Writing to Parry on 6 November Salisbury had been quick to point out that both the Spanish and Flemish ambassadors had sought permission to attend parliament on the previous day – they would have been blown up with everyone else.[1] The proclamation of 7 November specifically refuted rumours that a foreign prince had been involved, and in his speech to parliament James was only too ready to accept Fawkes's assurances – subsequently confirmed by other statements – that he and his fellows had at no time sought foreign aid.[2]

So attentions were again turned inwards, for the authorities had still to decide when and where the remaining prisoners would be tried. Since Garnett had been named as principal traitor in the indictment framed against the recently executed plotters it was logical enough to proceed against him first, delaying the trial of the suspect noblemen who, in point of law at least, faced lesser charges. The case against the Jesuit, however, was anything but fully formed, and while it had been quite possible to argue his guilt in abstract terms – as an instigator of treason if not an active participant – the evidence on which these accusations rested was rather thin. Bate had testified against Tesimond, and Gerard was implicated through his association with the initial group of plotters in 1604, but Garnett's guilt still seemed to depend upon the supposition that as head of the Jesuits in England, and as a close confidante of Catesby, he must have been aware of what was going on. Much time and effort was thus thrown into constructing a damning case against him. At his trial, Coke stressed that in the space of six weeks Garnett had been examined no less than twenty-three times,[3] and it was in truth only slowly that the investigators learned the full extent, or what had to pass as the full extent, of his involvement in the treason.

Garnett had been born in 1555 in Nottingham, the son of a schoolmaster. He was educated at Winchester and worked briefly for the law printer Richard Tottel in the 1570s before embracing the Roman Catholic faith, joining the Society of Jesus in 1575 and studying under Bellarmine in Rome. A successful academic career there was cut short when in 1586 Robert Persons proposed him for the English mission. The appointment found favour in high circles, although some felt that his mild nature was not ideally suited to the current hardships endured by his colleagues in England. Garnett was in the country no more than a couple of years when the imprisonment of the Superior of the Jesuits led to his own promotion, and he continued to serve in this role until his death.[4]

After capture, Garnett was brought up to London by Sir Henry Bromley – whom he much impressed by his modest manner and obvious erudition – arriving in the capital on 12 February. Initially he was lodged in the Gatehouse, but after two days he was transferred to the more secure confines of the Tower, prior to examination. On 13 February, facing a list of questions prepared in advance and based wholly on earlier discoveries, Garnett, when charged with involvement in Gunpowder plot, admitted only that on the previous 6 November he had received a letter from Sir Everard Digby via Bate while staying at Coughton, Thomas Throckmorton's house in Warwickshire. So much had already been disclosed by Bate in his examination of 13 January. Digby had informed him of the plotters' enterprise, had asked Garnett to pardon their rashness, and had sought his support, Garnett replying that he 'marvelled they would enter into so wicked actions, and not be ruled by the advice of frends'. He admitted that Tesimond had also been present, but denied having then told him what was afoot, and further denied having sent Sir Edmund Baynham with a message to the pope, or of having any knowledge of either Fawkes's or Wright's missions to Spain in 1603. He rejected any suggestion that he had encouraged Catholics to pray for the success of the 'Catholic Cause' when parliament met, conceding only one further significant point: that he had taken part in the 'pilgrimage' made by a number of Catholics, suspects in the plot and their families among them, to St Winifred's Well in Flintshire during the previous September. In all, this told the authorities virtually nothing new.[5]

On 20 February, according to a testimony surviving only as extracts in Abbot's *Antilogia*, Garnett confessed that he had supplied Fawkes with letters of recommendation on his mission to the continent,[6] but that apart, subsequent interrogations seem to have made little progress. Realising this, the investigators employed a trick already used with Fawkes and Winter. They made it possible for Garnett and Oldcorne to converse together in apparent secrecy in the Tower while two strategically placed officials recorded what was said. Good plans do not always work out perfectly and the eavesdroppers were unable to hear the ensuing conversations very well. But their conscientious and truthful efforts did at least reveal that Garnett was anxious he should not be pressed to state why he had been at Coughton in November, which he obviously felt to be the most damaging circumstance telling against him.[7] In one of these so-called 'interlocutions' Garnett also admitted that he had indeed prayed for the success of the 'Catholic Cause' on the previous 1 November.[8] He further expressed every confidence that 'Little John' – Nicholas Owen, one of the lay brothers captured with them at Hindlip – would give nothing away.[9] He clearly knew his man well, for as we have seen Owen did not disappoint him.

Garnett, during these conversations, conceded that the council had so far treated him with respect and consideration, even if they had occasionally lapsed into crude and unnecessary jokes at his expense. He even turned a critical eye on the efforts of his interrogators, feeling that the questions asked had often been too general and inconsequential to serve any purpose: 'they prest me with so many trifles and circumstances, that I was troubled to make answer, and I told them if they would demand anything concerning myself I was ready to deal plainly, but to accuse any other that were innocent, might be some matter of conscience to me'. He admitted that Coke in particular adopted classic interrogation techniques, treating him by turns kindly and aggressively so as to weaken his resistance.[10]

Armed with this testimony from the eavesdroppers, the lords commissioners questioned Garnett and Oldcorne on 5 and 6 March 1606. Each initially denied having spoken to the other while in the Tower, Garnett maintaining stoutly that, while others were free to slander him, he would never accuse himself falsely.[11] When confronted with the listeners' statements, though, Oldcorne was persuaded to confess that the conversations had indeed occurred, and when re-examined on 6 March he freely admitted all that had passed between himself and Garnett.[12]

This was more promising, and Garnett was at once confronted with his colleague's testimony. He too was soon obliged to drop his pretence, admitting in examination on 6 March that he had met Fawkes the previous Easter, subsequently writing to Father William Baldwin on Fawkes's behalf when the latter went over to Flanders, and also, later, to recommend Sir Edmund Baynham as a soldier 'as often he had done before'. He also admitted having spoken to Catesby in private during the spring and early summer of 1605.[13] Now the investigators scented a breakthrough, and Garnett's resistance began to crumble. On 9 March, after either being tortured or at least being threatened with torture, he wrote out a declaration admitting that he had 'dealt very reservedly with your Lordships in the case of the late powder action', believing that his course would best be served by maintaining silence. Now, though, he had resolved to speak plainly. He conceded that Catesby had asked him in June whether it might ever be God's will that innocent people should die in a just cause. Thinking it an idle, hypothetical question he had remarked that all arguments for a theory of 'just war' would be untenable were one to insist otherwise. Pondering on these exchanges later, Garnett admitted that he had wondered whether there might be something dangerous afoot, subsequently warning Catesby against making any rash moves.

He proceded to admit that the patience of many among his lay friends had been wearing very thin by 1605, recalling that he had discussed the possibility of armed insurrection by the Catholics with Francis Tresham and Lord Monteagle. The latter, so he claimed, had seemed to favour such a move, arguing that if ever there was a chance of success it was now, the king being 'so odious to all sorts'. No one had expected any assistance from foreign powers, although Garnett insisted that he had used this argument to back his own firmly expressed counsels of continued patience. Such advice had been lost on his unreceptive audience. Catesby, 'seldome long from us', was soon admitting that he had some plan afoot but would not at first give Garnett any details, so sure was he that the pope would unhesitatingly sanction what he had in mind. Doubting this, Garnett had urged him to send a 'lay gentleman' to the pontiff to inform him of the state of affairs in England, proposing Sir Edmund Baynham for this 'embassy'. Once Catesby had received clearance from his comrades and was ready to tell him about the plot, Garnett insisted that he had in turn refused Catesby a hearing, not wishing to become embroiled in treasonous schemes.

Soon afterwards, however, events had overtaken him. Tesimond, having heard details of the plot 'out of confession', had passed the information on to Garnett 'by way of confession', not kneeling as was customary, for it had been a long story. Garnett then proceeded to set down what he had heard from his colleague – essentially the familiar story of the plot. He recalled that Catesby and his associates had planned to capture either the duke of York or the Princess Elizabeth – although 'of any protectour, it seemeth they thought not, untill the noble men came togither which should be left alive'. Garnett, who had clearly been left in no doubt of the importance which the commissioners attached to this point, was ready to elaborate. Although Catesby had hopes of saving some noblemen whom he respected, he 'was of mind that rather then in any sort the secret should be discovered, he would not spare his owne sonne if he were there'. The full horror of the enterprise, Garnett insisted, only now began to dawn upon him, and the dawn had heralded a day filled with the darkest clouds of foreboding. From that moment on he had enjoyed no rest, writing continually to Rome to obtain a general prohibition 'of all attempts'. None came, and from snippets of overheard conversation he had realised that the plotters intended to go ahead with their enterprise. He had also learnt with dismay that Sir Everard Digby had entered the plot, and his subsequent journey to Coughton had been made with great reluctance, Garnett fearing 'an intention in him to draw us to that country for their owne projects, which I could well imagin but was not in particuler acquainted withall'. Hence his earlier anxieties on this subject.

On this he stood, the next day settling down again to give additional information on points where the king – who had wasted no time in reading his statement – considered his information rather 'drye'. Among other matters he admitted that Catesby had been unhappy at the thought of the earl of Rutland meeting his death in parliament house 'but it seemed then he was contented to lett him go'. The plotters had also considered 'wounding or disabling' the earl of Arundel so that he could not attend parliament, and Catesby had been unable to visit 'Lady Darby or the Lady Straunge at their houses, though he loved them above all others, because it pitied him to think that they must also dye'.[14]

Seeing the accusations made against Lord Monteagle, the king at once placed a ban on Garnett's testimony being used in evidence at any future trial, and so a more structured examination on set points proved necessary. This was taken on 12 March before Popham, Coke, Waad, and one of Waad's officials. Garnett then confirmed that, while he had had no knowledge of the conspiracy before Easter 1605, Tesimond had informed him of Catesby's project shortly before St James's Day (25 July), and that Catesby himself had subsequently spoken to him about it at St Bartholomewtide (24 August), promising that he would not take the matter further until Garnett had sought papal advice on the matter. Catesby had then agreed to Garnett's proposal that Baynham should be sent to Rome for this purpose, although he expressed his personal belief that the pope would 'not hynder' such a scheme.[15]

Baynham, who had apparently been planning to travel on the continent for at least the past two years, would have been an obvious choice. He was, as the plotters knew from long personal experience, a reckless and unpredictable man, but his loyalty to their cause could not be faulted and he had, above all, the great advantage of being a layman. There would consequently be no risk of their message being 'watered down' by compassionate or fearful priests. 'Soone after midsomer', therefore, Baynham came to see Garnett for a 'very short' conference. He was then briefed on evidence of persecution, and recommended 'to take his instruction of gentlemen of experience, which he or Mr Catesby should know'.[16] Garnett insisted that he knew nothing of Catesby's instructions to the envoy, although he supposed that something would have been said of general enterprises for the Catholic cause.

This evidence confirmed Fawkes's testimony that Catesby had told him Baynham was to make known to the new pope, Paul V, the hardships endured by English Catholics. Both Fawkes and Winter confessed that Baynham's role was to have been that of a 'sleeper': that as soon as news of the plot's success reached Rome he was to have explained the conspirators' actions to the pontiff.[17] In itself, this does not add further to assumptions of Garnett's complicity. He seems to have made no effort to speed Baynham's journey, but this too can be interpreted in different ways. As it was, Sir Edmund did not leave until early September, and only passed through Florence around 20 October. He was never to return to England, and much of his later life remains a mystery. Soon after the plot, however, he sent his servant Nicholas Burte back to England on some personal business. Burte, no doubt concerned for his own safety and clearly in no mood to suffer for his master's indiscretions, showed the letters he carried to the new English envoy Sir George Carew upon his arrival in France. When this news reached the English court there was great excitement. Arriving in London Burte was at once interrogated by Popham on 26 February, at eleven o'clock at night, and was subsequently committed to the King's Bench prison. It transpired, however, that the servant had not shared his master's more intimate secrets. He could add nothing to the story beyond adding to suspicions that Baynham had spent some time in Owen's company while in Brussels the previous September, throwing in also the picaresque detail that his master had been well feasted by Father Persons during his stay in Rome.[18]

In this revealing deposition of 12 March, Garnett further admitted having written a testimonial to Father Baldwin for Catesby when the latter had sought a command in Flanders, and confirmed that he had written more than once to the pope since the Herefordshire disturbances asking for a prohibition of 'all generall stirres'. At no time, though, had he been more specific. Nor, he conceded, had he answered a letter from Persons requesting him to outline any current plots which the Catholics had in hand. In addition, he recalled only too clearly that his friend and follower Anne Vaux[19] had spoken to him during the autumn of her fears that 'some troble or disorder was towards [them], for that some of the gentlewomen had demaunded of her where they should bestowe themselves vntill the bruit was past in the beginning of the parliament', although she had refused to disclose the source of her information, 'for she was charged with secrecye'. Vaux was duly brought in for questioning.[20]

On the following two days, still perhaps hoping to avoid a charge of treason, Garnett confessed further details which he thought might be of interest to the authorities but which he judged could not harm him further. He admitted that Catesby and Winter had hinted at a project in hand which would 'sure preuaile', and that he had advised them against any wild enterprises. Also on 13 March, he admitted that he had received two papal letters or *breves* the year before Elizabeth died, one directed to lay Catholics, the other to the clergy, which insisted that no Catholic should support or tolerate a successor to the English throne who did not 'with all his might sett forward the Catholicke religion, and according to the custome of other Catholicke princes submitt himself to the Sea Apostolicall'. These had come accompanied by the copy of a letter from the pope to his nuncio in Flanders directing him to pass on these instructions to all English Catholics on the queen's death. Garnett said that, with the country disinclined to dispute James's accession, he had burnt the *breves*, but he admitted that both Winter and Catesby had seen them and 'so they made vse of them'. When Catesby had asked him why they were now submitting to one who had shown no sympathy to their cause, he had been able to reply only that the pope had since 'geven other order'. He also admitted that he had heard of plans laid by the pope and the kings of France and Spain to place a Catholic claimant on the English throne at Elizabeth's death, plans which had been incomplete in 1603.[21]

The next day, examined by Popham and Coke in the presence of Waad and his colleague John Corbett, Garnett admitted that Percy had been shown the *breves* at White Webbs immediately before one of his journeys into Scotland, and that it had been Catesby who had brought him first news of the queen's death and of the subsequent 'proclamation [of James] and applause of the people'. It was then that he had burnt the papal letters, 'fyndinge the state setled'. Elaborating on a still more important matter, he confirmed that either Catesby and Winter or Catesby alone had visited him in midsummer 1604 and had told him that 'there was a plott in hand for the Catholique cause against the kinge and the state which would worke good effect', justifying it by the words of the *breves*. Again Garnett insisted that he had urged the pope's ban on all 'stirs' and that Catesby had 'promised to surceasse'. He also repeated that Tesimond had been 'bounde to secrecie' when he had told Garnett of the intended treason.[22]

The time had clearly come to take stock, and on 15 March Popham drew up a list of proofs against Garnett – it was a long and, as portrayed, damning catalogue, running to three pages. Garnett had allegedly known of Catholic efforts to solicit support from Spain both before and after 1603, he had assured Catesby that his proceedings were lawful in the sight of God, he had done everything in his power to smooth the journeys of Winter and Fawkes to and from the continent, and he had known of Catesby's plot for many months but had said not a word to the authorities, rather choosing to dwell in places frequented by the plotters. Nor, when Tesimond had expressed a determination to support the rebels, had he lifted a finger to stop him. This list, subsequently seen and annotated by Salisbury, was probably used at Garnett's trial.[23]

Garnett also faced questioning on several loose ends which required tidying; he was asked for example to outline all recent contacts with Francis Tresham, an exercise designed to prove that Tresham – who had died insisting that he had not seen Garnett in the past sixteen years – had perished with a soul burdened by falsehood and deceit.[24]

Perhaps as another token of appreciation of the help afforded by the citizens of London during the Gunpowder investigations,[25] Garnett was tried in Guildhall by special commission on 28 March 1606,[26] much to the chagrin of the lieutenant of the Tower who had a longstanding dispute with the lord mayor over privileges and who insisted to Salisbury that the prisoner should remain in his charge until the court decided otherwise. The trial was another showpiece, with another crowded court and with James again said to have attended incognito.[27] Garnett was brought to the bar at around nine o'clock, the court assembling about thirty minutes later. Although he had been cited first among the plotters in the original indictment drawn against the executed conspirators, the new evidence discovered from recent examinations had led to the construction of a fresh bill which stated that Garnett had first entered the Gunpowder treason on 9 June, the date of his speculative conversation with Catesby.[28]

Initially speaking quietly, Coke described Garnett's background. Here clearly was a traitor of long standing, a man experienced in villany. He dwelt long on the treasons of 1602 and 1603, devoting much time to the iniquities which he ascribed to Catholics in general, to those particularly foul crimes attributable to Jesuits in particular, and to the doctrine of equivocation which Garnett had used to cover his colleagues and to avoid incriminating himself. Garnett's defence rested on his insistence that, while he knew of the treason by mid-1605, he had been bound by the seal of the confessional not to reveal what he knew, and that, labouring under this moral handicap, he had nevertheless done what he could to defuse the conspiracy. Coke was, however, ready to demonstrate that everything Garnett might argue in his favour could quite easily be turned against him. For example, while the prisoner insisted that he had written to the pope urging him to forbid all stirs, Fawkes had confessed very early on that the suppression of all minor plots in favour of the grand design had been one of the conspirators' established aims.[29]

The proceedings were rounded off by both Salisbury and Northampton propounding theological questions to Garnett, and with Salisbury returning to the subject of equivocation. Much was made of Garnett's economy with the truth in his examinations – to the judges and to the less-than-impartial audience his insistence that a man was justified in telling falsehoods to save his own skin sounded like another devious Jesuitical argument to make black appear white. The authorities also played on his theological 'approval' of Catesby's scheme, even though the approval had been given to a theoretical and generally dissimilar hypothesis. Garnett, however, stood by his opinion that lesser evils might be condoned provided that they led directly to or were the result of establishing a greater good.[30] Referring to Tresham's final statement, Garnett was asked what the dying man had meant by so clear an untruth at such an hour of peril for his soul. So far as he could, Garnett charitably put this down to equivocation also, an opinion again seized on by the court. Nottingham finally summed up the authorities' thoughts on equivocation by saying 'Garnet thou hast don more goode in that pulpit this day (for he stoode in a pew by himself) then in all the pulpits thou ever camest in in thy life.'[31]

Ever mindful of 'image', Salisbury pointed out to Garnett that he had been tried in an impartial court, sufficient for the noblest prince of the church. No one, he maintained, however prejudiced, could possibly deny either Garnett's guilt or the clemency of a king who had allowed him so fair and open a hearing.[32] The jury took very little time to find the prisoner guilty, at which he said nothing besides 'God save the king', placing his life wholly in the king's hands. Sentence of death was duly passed.

The verdict, both from a legal and a political point of view, was hardly surprising. Since English law took no account of the inviolability of confession, even as Garnett's story stood he was guilty of misprision of treason, the bare knowledge and concealment of a treasonable act. But indeed it becomes difficult to believe that Garnett, had he wished to reveal the secret, could not have done so in some way that would have satisfied his conscience. Equally, it is difficult to credit that one who has known about the existence of so violent a scheme for so long has not taken some action which can be construed as giving support to the enterprise. Thus we may understand Garnett's apprehension on the point of his trip to Coughton. Here is an already marked man, knowing that a blow is intended against parliament, knowing too that parliament is shortly to meet, declaring that he came to Coughton to see Catesby and dissuade him again from any violence, yet surely knowing that Catesby would not come to the area again until the blow had been struck and the time had come to employ the assembled Catholic gentry in his bloody cause. It is perhaps no slur on Garnett to suggest that he knew full well what was coming, but believed that the deed, however bloody and savage, might indeed lead by catharsis to a spiritually cleaner England. He had been living for twenty years in a climate of intrigue, pitted against those who sought the extirpation of himself and his order. It may be that, while he felt that he had done what he could to stop a violent act, he felt also that there were limits to the steps which he could justifiably take in this case.

Not that condemnation marked the end of his interrogations. In writing of the trial on 2 April Chamberlain told Dudley Carleton that it was 'thought he shall not die yet, yf at all, for they hope to win much out of him'.[33] For a full month after, Garnett faced lengthy examinations by members of the council. There were still many points which required illumination, and sentence was not carried out until 3 May, by which time the investigators had come to the conclusion that he would say no more. Immediately after the trial, on the prompting of Waad, Garnett wrote out for Salisbury his further thoughts on equivocation, which still appeared to the protestant mind as nothing more nor less than a justification of deceit.[34] The interest on this point continued to within days of his death, but it is a remarkable fact that the authorities, despite some very clear clues, apparently never realised that Garnett himself had been the author of the treatise found in Tresham's study.[35]

Further questions set out to clarify his notions of just and unjust laws, the authorities obviously believing that statements from a Jesuit on the subject might be turned to some good propaganda purpose in the future.[36] Garnett was told – falsely – that Tesimond had been captured, and the information did indeed seem to have the desired effect of making him fear a difference in their testimony. This is shown best in one of his final confessions, made on 25 April 1606. When asked to state honestly whether he had believed Tesimond's relation of the intended plot had been made in confession, he answered cautiously that it had been 'not in confession but by way of confession, which may be done in conference of greate poyntes or neede of studye, or wante of tyme, though it be a good whyle after'.[37]

Again he was asked to name the man whom the plotters had designated as protector, and again he replied that the issue had, so far as he knew, never been decided. Tesimond, he insisted, had told him that a settlement of this matter had been postponed until it became clear who had survived the explosion and who had not. There had, he added, been no agreement between himself and Tesimond 'not to discover any noble men since the plott was revealed'.[38] The investigators' persistence here is instructive, for much the same question had been asked over and over for two months. During the 'interlocutions', Garnett and Oldcorne had mentioned the 'great', ensuing words having been inaudible.[39] It was apparently thought that this was a reference to 'great men', but on 12 March Garnett explained that he had been discussing a great house in Essex where he had spoken to Catesby and others.[40] Earlier still, on 25 February, the eavesdroppers reported that they had heard Garnett mention 'my lord of Northumberland, my lord of Rutland, and one more (whom we heard not well), but to what effect they were named we could not hear, by occasion of a cock crowing under the window of the room, and the cackling of hens at the very same instant'.[41] Such small pieces of tantalising information would have only made the investigators hunger for more substantial results.

Like him, others went to their deaths elsewhere without saying anything new. We know little about the trials in Worcestershire, Warwickshire, and Staffordshire over the following few months. Henry Morgan and Stephen Littleton were executed at Stafford, Humphrey Littleton, who had sheltered his fugitive brother and Robert Winter, after a desperate bid to save his life by helping the authorities locate Garnett, died with John Winter at Worcester. On a happier note Thomas Abington, host to Garnett in the weeks before his capture, escaped the gallows and made a virtue out of being confined to Worcestershire for the rest of his days by embarking on an historical survey of his native county.[42] While the executions no doubt served as further warning to the Catholic and discontented folk of the west midlands, they also served to an extent as an admittance of defeat: the authorities were letting justice take its course knowing that there were still issues – and important ones at that – extant and unresolved.

With Garnett's case decided, the king at last resolved to see justice done in the cases of the suspect peers. Lord Montagu, who had given least cause for suspicion, was able thanks in part to the help of influential friends to secure his release later in 1606 without facing trial.[43] Mordaunt and Stourton, however, were less fortunate. With Fawkes having admitted that Catesby had known neither man would be present at the opening of parliament, and after examinations conducted by the most active commissioners – Nottingham, Suffolk, Devonshire, Northampton, Salisbury, Popham, and Coke – early in February, which as we have seen might well have been intended to be followed shortly after by a court appearance, the evidence was thought sufficient to arraign them in star chamber where they were fined and imprisoned on 3 June 1606.[44]

Neither man could offer a convincing excuse for his actions. Stourton, a friend of Catesby, had not even begun his journey to London from Wiltshire before 6 November, explaining that he had been deterred by a pressing debt owing to the dowager Lady Stourton, his wife's sickness, and the reported spread of the plague in London.[45] Mordaunt, brother-in-law of both Francis Tresham and Lord Monteagle, had also consorted with several of the plotters in the previous summer and autumn, and Keyes's wife taught his children. His household was, moreover, known to be full of Catholics. Endeavouring to allay suspicion, he insisted that he had sought permission to be absent from the opening of parliament even if he had not received such permission by 5 November, and said that he had been prevented from attending by a search for 'evidences concerning his assart lands'.[46]

The few surviving accounts of their trial provide us with frustratingly brief details of the *ore tenus* proceedings. This summary form of justice could only be adopted if the accused admitted guilt, and consequently the two lords, standing 'within a barre made of purpose for them', were shown their examinations by Coke so that they could confirm the contents. It was then Coke's task to describe the manifest errors which they had committed. He made no effort to portray their offences as anything other than misprision, a crime that carried penalties extending to life imprisonment and confiscation of property. In this case, however, the king was insisting on treating them merely as contempts: the lords were being punished only for ignoring their summons to attend the opening of parliament. Coke could not quite hide his own doubts at this decision but set about making the best of his brief, enlarging upon the responsibilities required of those summoned to parliament in their own right, and reflecting that *dignitas personae auget culpam* – 'yf a litle corrupte bloode come to the harte, yt is either deadlye or daungerous; and this offence is farre greater in theise great lordes, for it is an offence againste there creation'.

Not, Coke added, that one could have expected anything else from those who harboured priests on their estates – it was, he announced, in Lord Mordaunt's house that the Gunpowder plotters had resolved to preserve the lives of the two noblemen. At this point, the attorney went off at a not-unexpected tangent, condemning Catholic priests as 'serpentes, vipers'. Worse still, the missionary clergy were often young men. 'An olde preiste maye easilye be founde oute, but theise younge preistes, in fethers and fashions, they doe infecte and affecte too, and ouerthrowe all with whome they conuerse'. But serpents, as was well known, have their natural enemies. 'A greate prince is resembled to an elephante, *et elephantem propter iustas causas serpente percusso terra non patitur.*' With this off his chest, Coke turned to the excuses offered by the accused. These, he declared, only served to condemn them further. Stourton's catalogue of difficulties which had allegedly prevented him coming to London on the Tuesday had not stopped him arriving in town on the following Friday, while Mordaunt's argument that he had gone down to the country on 18 October to investigate his claim on some lands was hardly convincing, seeing that he had had all summer to accomplish the task. In any case, he had 'kepte Contynuall Companie with all the greate Traytors'. That was quite enough.

Coke then embarked upon a long list of precedents, showing that since the time of Edward I, lords disobeying the summons to a parliament had either suffered forfeiture of goods, or had been 'greeuouselye fyned'. Not for the first time, he felt moved to comment both on the justice of God and on the amazing clemency of the king:

Blessed be god, those are preserued that showlde have bene destroied, and all those that showlde haue beene preserued (but that the kinge extendes greate mercye) showlde haue bene destroyed. He is a blessed man therefore whome a traitor dothe not affecte: thoughe they Curse, wee will blesse.

It only remained for him to read from various confessions of the Winters, Keyes, Digby, Fawkes, and Garnett. The extracts themselves are not recorded, but it must be presumed that they included all references to the two lords, together perhaps with material designed to remind those who scarcely needed reminding of the horrors intended by the conspirators.

Few further excuses seem to have been offered by the accused. The nineteen privy councillors and judges present appear to have agreed unanimously in fining Mordaunt the sum of ten thousand marks (£6,666), Stourton six thousand marks (£4,000), and imprisoning them both 'in the tower from whence they Came duringe the kinge's pleasure'. The discrepancy is probably best explained by the fact that Mordaunt was the wealthier man and that his contacts with the dead conspirators were the more blatant and frequent of the two. As each judge, beginning with Justice Williams, the most junior in rank then present, explained his sentence, they differed only in their emphasis: Williams rather irrelevantly outlining precedents for depriving of their goods men who left the realm without leave, Popham noting that contempts of absence could be serious or trivial, but that 'the absence in progres, in warre, or embasie, ys a greate Contempte'.

Salisbury's comments express the unexceptional but no less heartfelt relief of those whose destruction had been intended: 'This Damnable plotte', he said, 'had broughte desperate Calamitie, and a masse of confusyon.' He too complimented James on his clemency. 'The greater the offences are, the more hydden they lye: but the kinge of his grace hath bowed the Cedar so lowe as to stoope to the iudgemente of this Courte.' As usual, Northampton was more long-winded on the same theme, drawing on Persian history and classical diagnostical treatises to explain that in the state as in the body there were three remedies for diseases: 'diete' and 'medecine', besides 'bloud lettinge'. Bancroft made up for lost time, explaining that since all agreed with the 'atturnie's inuention' 'he woulde be shorte'. Finally, Egerton, while observing that 'theise exorbitante offences are not subiecte to an ordinarye Course of lawe', agreed with both the fines and imprisonment.

In practice, both Mordaunt and Stourton were treated with con-siderable lenity. Although initially lodged in the Tower, they were both transferred to the Fleet prison in August 1606 and Stourton was released in 1608. Mordaunt died the following year and their full fines were never enforced.[47]

Notes

1 PRO SP 78/52, fol 340v
2 *His Majesties Speach*, sigs C2v–C3
3 Foley, *Records*, iv, p 166
4 Garnett's career is best explored in Caraman's biography. His prior knowledge of the conspiracy has been discussed at great length (particularly by Jardine, *Criminal Trials*, ii, pp 190–403; Foley, *Records*, iv, pp 145–93; Caraman, *Henry Garnet*, pp 348–429), and what follows is intended only as a summary showing how evidence was amassed
5 PRO SP 14/18/86 and 87; 14/216/166
6 For the examination of 20 February see Abbot, *Antilogia*, pp 139v–40, 144v, 145, 163v–4, 165v, 167, 172v
7 Bodleian MS Tanner 75, fol 189v, interlocution of 25 Feb 1606
8 PRO SP 14/18/111, interlocution of 23 Feb 1606; 14/18/122, interlocution of 27 Feb 1606
9 PRO SP 14/19/7. Owen had indeed been examined by Waad and two of his men on 1 March. He confessed only that he had served Garnett for about four years, that they had been at Coughton in November 1605, that Garnett had celebrated mass there, that they had stayed in the Vaux household at White Webbs several times, and that they had been at Hindlip for six weeks prior to their capture, Garnett dining and supping with the master of the house (SP 14/216/194)
10 Bodleian MS Tanner 75, fol 189v; PRO SP 14/18/111
11 PRO SP 14/19/15; 14/216/196
12 PRO SP 14/216/197 and 198
13 PRO SP 14/19/16
14 Gardiner, 'Two Declarations of Garnet', pp 510–19. Garnett's testimony with regard to Monteagle has been uncritically accepted by most authorities, although if we may assume that Garnett sought some revenge against this 'renegade' who had betrayed his erstwhile friends, what better available means was there than to accuse him of fomenting sedition? Caraman accepts the testimony of the fugitive priest John Gerard that Garnett was tortured, although he admits that his torment cannot have been prolonged (*Henry Garnet*, pp 371–5). There is no firmer proof that Garnett was physically ill-treated, apart from his own subsequent admission that he had feared going to the torture for a second time (Hatfield MS 115/13)
15 PRO SP 14/19/40
16 Sprott, 'Sir Edmund Baynham', p 102
17 PRO SP 14/216/163, 170
18 Sprott, 'Sir Edmund Baynham', pp 103–4; Hatfield MS 110/17
19 For Anne Vaux, see Anstruther, *Vaux of Harrowden*, passim
20 *ibid*, p 279; PRO SP 14/19/40

21   PRO SP 14/19/41 and 42

22   PRO SP 14/19/44

23   Hatfield MS 115/19

24   PRO SP 14/216/205–212; Wake, 'Death of Francis Tresham', pp 40–1

25   The first was the execution of four of the plotters in St Paul's churchyard (see above, p 55)

26   For the trial see Howell, *State Trials*, ii, cols 217–355; *True and Perfect Relation*, sigs N4–Eee4v; Jardine, *Criminal Trials*, ii, pp 235–314; Foley, *Records*, iv, pp 164–90; BL Harley MS 360, fols 109–25v; BL Additional MS 21203; Morris, *Condition of Catholics*; McClure, *Letters of Chamberlain*, i, pp 219–22. There is some evidence to suggest that the authorities had considered condemning Garnett without trial (Caraman, *Henry Garnet*, pp 358, 397, who derives the story from the Narrative of John Gerard)

27   McClure, *Letters of Chamberlain*, i, p 220

28   *PRO Deputy Keeper's Fifth Report*, appendix II, pp 140–1, 144

29   PRO SP 14/216/37

30   Cf Rookwood's confession PRO SP 14/216/136

31   McClure, *Letters of Chamberlain*, i, pp 221–2

32   Foley, *Records*, iv, p 189

33   McClure, *Letters of Chamberlain*, i, p 222

34   PRO SP 14/216/217, 217A

35   PRO SP 14/216/218; Malloch, 'Garnet's Treatise of Equivocation', pp 390–2

36   PRO SP 14/20/2

37   PRO SP 14/20/44, examination before the lords commissioners. Garnett wrote to Tesimond apologising for having accused him (Hatfield MS 115/154)

38   PRO SP 14/20/44

39   Bodleian MS Tanner 75, fol 189v

40   PRO SP 14/19/40

41   Bodleian MS Tanner 75, fol 189v

42   Oxford, Corpus Christi College MS 297, fol 38v; Hatfield MS 109/149, Sir Richard Lewkenor to the privy council, 27 Jan 1606; 109/147, Humphrey Littleton's information; PRO E403/2725, fol 171v; Devon, *Issues of Exchequer*, pp 31, 32, 297–8; Jardine, *Narrative of Gunpowder Plot*, p 212; PRO SP 14/16/96; Humphreys, 'Habingtons of Hindlip', pp 62–5; Humphreys, 'Wyntours of Huddington', p 72; Nash, 'Littleton's Death-Warrant', p 130 (plate 8)

43   PRO SP 14/23/10, Carleton to Chamberlain, 20 Aug 1606; BL Additional MS 11402, fol 115, privy council order of 16 Aug 1606

44   PRO SP 14/216/175, examination of Fawkes, 20 Jan 1606. For the trial see Hawarde, *Les Reportes*, pp 287–92; BL Harley MS 1330, fols 9v–10v, cf *The English Reports*, Edinburgh, 1900–32, LXXII, pp 901–2, from Francis Moore's Reports. Hawarde gives the most detail and the following account of the trial is derived principally from this source

45   PRO SP 14/216/181

46   PRO SP 14/216/182. For further corroborative evidence against Mordaunt see Hatfield MSS 115/22 and 34, 119/154, 191/61

47   BL Additional MS 11402, fols 115, 138v, privy council orders of 22 Aug 1606 and 28 Apr 1608. Mordaunt's son was pardoned his father's fine in 1620 (Cokayne, *Complete Peerage*, ix, p 197; see also R Halstead, *Succinct Genealogies*, London, 1685, pp 641–3). Stourton paid £1,000 in April 1614 (PRO IND 6745)

Part II

The traitor? The earl of Northumberland and Gunpowder plot

I am afraid of this Gunpowder Percy

I Henry IV, V iv

More than one hundred and fifty years ago, David Jardine, in his introduction to the second volume of *Criminal Trials*, expressed regret that the work as then published fell a long way short of his original plan. It had been his intention, he explained, to investigate the supposed complicity of Northumberland, Montagu, Mordaunt, and Stourton in the treason, for as a lawyer he regarded these to have been the most interesting cases arising from the discovery of Gunpowder plot. Unfortunately, the *Library of Entertaining Knowledge* series in which *Criminal Trials* appeared was aimed at the interested general reader rather than the subject specialist, and Jardine well knew that in producing one of the early nineteenth-century's finest historical monographs he had already imposed somewhat on the tolerance of his publishers. While having to admit that a lack of available material on the trials of these noblemen had contributed to their exclusion from his volume, he observed pointedly that the sources at his disposal would at least allow some development of the facts respecting all four suspects, and in particular Northumberland, 'one of the most extraordinary men of the age in which he lived'.[1]

In the intervening century and a half, however, no one has taken up the challenge implicit in his words. Despite the success of *Criminal Trials*, which was constantly reprinted until the stereotype plates wore out, even Jardine himself, when returning to the subject twenty years later in his *Narrative of the Gunpowder Plot* confined himself to retelling an already very old story. This neglect has produced some persistent misconceptions. Although Northumberland was arraigned in star chamber, fined an enormous sum, and imprisoned for over fifteen years, almost every writer on the subject has seen his case as no more than an awkward appendix to a tale that

ought properly to end with the execution of Garnett. He has, however, won the sympathy of those who believe that Cecil fashioned or
manipulated the conspiracy to serve his own devious ends. In their
view Northumberland was the unwitting victim of a crafty and
unscrupulous man bent on removing a possible rival for power and
influence under James I. It is fair to say, though, that those who
favour this attractive but rather simplistic interpretation have never
troubled to look closely at the political career of the 'victim', or at the
way in which a case was assembled against him.

Since Jardine's day, many relevant additional sources have
become widely accessible, notably the collections of Salisbury-Cecil
papers at Hatfield and the archives of the duke of Northumberland
at Alnwick Castle and Syon House. An examination of the case
against Northumberland is consequently long overdue. It is in itself
an intriguing example of proceedings on the grounds of 'pregnant
suspicion' without the comfort of firm evidence. Through it we can
more readily appreciate the religious background to the conspiracy,
and we learn much that is new about that obscure but important
conspirator Thomas Percy. Most significant of all, however, it
affords a well-documented and specific example of how the lords
commissioners looked into and were ultimately frustrated by a
particular case arising out of Gunpowder plot. But the tale is
involved and often confusing, dealing as much with men's reputations as with their deeds. Northumberland's fall cannot be seen
simply in terms of events in and after November 1605, for it is in his
relationships with King James, with Salisbury, and with his fellow
privy councillors that the heart of this story lies. In the nature of these
indefinite things we may never lay that heart bare, yet by looking first
at the earl's career in court life and politics before the plot was
discovered we shall be in a far better position to judge proceedings
thereafter.

VI

A family's burden

Henry, eldest son of Sir Henry Percy and nephew of Thomas, seventh earl of Northumberland, was born at Tynemouth in 1564. Although Thomas was executed at York in 1572 following the northern rebellion, Sir Henry, who had remained conspicuously loyal during the rising, was allowed to inherit the title. Unfortunately, the eighth earl did not learn from his brother's misfortune, becoming involved in plots to liberate Mary Stuart. In 1584, suspected of complicity in the Throckmorton conspiracy, he was committed to the Tower, and it was there, on 21 June 1585, that he shot himself through the heart with a dag. Under these unhappy circumstances his son became ninth earl of Northumberland.

The younger Henry at least avoided the fate that had overtaken his immediate predecessors. He outlived the queen, and at the beginning of James I's reign he held, briefly, a position of political importance rivalling those enjoyed by some of his mediaeval ancestors. Contemporaries both English and foreign then accorded him a prominence not always appreciated today, and the historian James Spedding once went so far as to suggest that Northumberland's power in 1603 ranked second only to that of Secretary Cecil.[2]

But this importance was to some extent illusory and was certainly short-lived; the earl was by nature ill-suited to the difficult task of capitalising on abnormal opportunities offered by the queen's death. An intelligent, well-educated man, proud and quick-tempered, he was also shy and retiring, conscious of an impediment in hearing that seems to have afflicted him from his youth. One well-disposed contemporary emphasised the two sides to his nature: while the earl was said to keep a good table and to enjoy good company, he was also a 'civill, modest, and quyett' man, characteristically 'inward and reserved', very deliberate and considered in his speech.[3] Northumberland was unquestionably studious, well-read, deeply interested in geographical, scientific, philosophical, and military matters. A sometimes laboured style does not obscure either an originality in his writings or a sharp, enquiring mind. At the same time, though, he was rather too easily led by more dominant personalities, a prey to flattery, and incapable of keeping a secret.

Naturally his enemies saw these defects in his character all too clearly. Henry Howard, who sought to destroy the earl's credibility as a statesmen in the eyes of their future king, described him in 1602 as an isolated, incompetent, gullible figure, clay in the hands of more experienced men.[4] Northumberland was by no means so contemptible, but in attempting to assume a role for which he was unsuited he inevitably appears – at times – in a somewhat poor light.[5]

A wealthy young man living in London was then as now susceptible to various temptations, and in later life the earl confessed that his youth had been profligate. During the difficult days of 1585 his mother the Countess Katherine wrote that her husband was distressed to see 'how vnproffitablye his twoo eldest sonnes doth bestowe their tymes here, yea in that sorte that rather he wissheth them to carye a hargebuse vpon their neckes to sarue a worthie prince then to live as they do'.[6] Relations between mother and son were often strained, though such loose living might charitably be ascribed to a reaction against the anxiety both Henry and his brother Thomas must have felt for their father at that time. Also, the eighth earl's suicide might help explain his son's lavish and wasteful expenditure, and his wilder excesses, over the next couple of years. The household accounts from 1585 to 1587 show levels of spending on luxuries and losses through gambling unmatched in any later period.[7]

A rumour that the eighth earl had been murdered in the Tower – which was strong enough to warrant publication of the inquest's findings[8] – must have left its impression on the heir and may initially have bred in him a dangerous 'discontent'.[9] Not surprisingly, those concerned in the Babington plot were confident of his support, although it seems that he was never actually approached by any conspirator and so was spared the temptation to dabble in what must have proved a fatal enterprise.[10]

Such amateur psychology is, however, dangerous.

Northumberland himself said little about his father's death; even in his *Advice to his Son*, written years later, he merely reflected that:

if ever father loved a son, he did me (and whether his death was such as vulgarly it was bruited, is not for this place), only this I must say and conclude, that his care was to leave me well to maintain the honour of his house behind him.[11]

In any case the earl soon mended his ways. 'Within a little time,' he wrote later, 'these errors having unmasked themselves to me, I began to take up, and to look to mine own affairs, partly constrained by an imperfection that God laid upon me to call me back, partly out of necessity, so as in time I redeemed myself out of the disquiet of disquieted thoughts.'[12] The 'imperfection' was almost certainly a reference to deafness. In addition, the earl found cause for sober reflection in the death of his brother and companion Thomas at the age of twenty.[13] Court life soon absorbed him. Early in 1589, William Herbert described Northumberland as 'a fine gentleman and a wise, and of good courage and begins to be a good courtier'. He added pointedly that the earl was 'like to live' and that his correspondent – the earl of Shrewsbury – might 'conjecture the rest'.[14] The story that Northumberland served as a volunteer against the Armada was almost certainly one invented by Camden,[15] but he did visit the Netherlands in 1588, an experience which doubtless helped stimulate his lifelong interest in siege tactics and other military matters.[16]

Over the next few years Northumberland basked in the favour of a queen who, although she had no reason to feel affection for the Percy family, often displayed a weakness to indulge the young men at her court. She greatly reduced a fine imposed on his father in star chamber two decades earlier,[17] restored him to the eighth earl's governorship of Tynemouth Castle in 1591,[18] and made him a knight of the garter in 1593.[19] The latter honour gave him particular satisfaction, even to the extent of rewarding the poet George Peele with three pounds for a congratulatory ode which was inescapably worth far less.[20]

Northumberland was a highly eligible bachelor, and there were rumours abroad in the early 1590s that he might prove a suitable candidate for the hand of Arabella Stuart, potentially a successor to Elizabeth. However, he eventually made a far less ambitious – and a far less risky – choice, marrying Dorothy Perrott, sister of the favourite Robert Devereux, earl of Essex, and widow of Sir Thomas Perrott, son of the late lord deputy of Ireland.[21] There is little doubt that he was genuinely attracted to Dorothy, although the match-makers would have, of course, taken care to weigh all financial, dynastic and political implications of the union. It has been suggested that the earl of Huntingdon and Lord Burghley encouraged the match, hoping in this way to tie Northumberland firmly to the world of London and the court, thus ensuring that there would be no Percy earl residing in his distant northern estates and so providing a focus for religious or regional discontent.[22] In fact it must be said that the earl never showed the slightest inclination to live in the north. When offered the wardenship of the Middle Marches between England and Scotland in 1597, he immediately wrote to influential friends expressing his desire to avoid this 'honour', stating that he had no wish to see his 'purse picked' on the border.[23] Either through choice or compulsion, he spent almost his entire life in the south of England.

This aversion to public employment was not simply brought about by the unpleasant and unwelcome prospect of a difficult command. When appointed special envoy to France in July 1596 he hurriedly wrote to Cecil pleading both deafness and poverty:

The imperfection of my hearing, what absurdites of nessessite it must begette, as trouble to the king, euell performance of my part of her majestys affaiers, and disgrace to my selfe, I hope she will rightely vnderstand when her highness shall remember, how by the first I shall force a king to speake with often repeticions, and to strain his voice abouue ordenary, boeth whiche my secret conceite must needs hold as indecorum in course of good mannors.[24]

Although Northumberland avoided public duties when they threatened to inconvenience him, he was quite prepared to accept more congenial employment. He supervised the ceremonial reception of French envoys on missions to Elizabeth's court – perhaps in this way establishing important contacts in France – and during the shortlived invasion scare of August 1599, when rumour had it that a Spanish fleet was under sail for England, he was general of the horse in London, a post which combined his equestrian and military interests. Granted that public employment under Elizabeth inevitably entailed financial sacrifice, it still seems that an otherwise alert mind was less than taken with the chores and tedious complexities of diplomacy. Here, apparently, was an essentially half-hearted statesman, happiest when carrying out simple though conspicuous tasks.[25]

Dorothy Perrott brought with her the leasehold of Syon House, a crown property on the Thames, and a disputed title to some former Perrott lands in Wales – the fact that Sir John Perrott her late father-in-law had been attainted of treason shortly before his death gave the crown an interest in those lands, although a conveyance of the properties apparently made before he had entered into any treasonous act seemed to protect the rights of his heirs.[26] She also brought a daughter from her first marriage, Penelope, and an intangible but very important alliance with Essex. The marriage, however, proved constantly tempestuous, while the Devereux association weakened with the decline of Essex's fortunes at court and Northumberland's continuing affection for Essex's old enemy, Sir Walter Ralegh. It was with feeling that the earl in later years advised his son against hasty marriages.[27] He confessed ruefully that even though he himself had chosen his bride with great care their marriage had proved far from ideal.[28]

Although deeply interested in military science, circumstances conspired to frustrate the earl's ambition to experience conflict at first hand. In 1587 the queen would not allow him to sail with Drake's expedition,[29] while a decade later the death of his young son prompted him to withdraw from Essex's Islands Voyage.[30] Only in June 1600 did he obtain permission to visit the Low Countries once again. He was accompanied by the earl of Rutland on the outward journey,[31] and rumours – officially denied – sprang up at court that they had been charged with some secret mission.[32] Earlier in the year Northumberland had been first proposed and then passed over as a commissioner for the abortive peace negotiations with Spain, and it is possible that this ostensible pleasure trip had some connection with those talks.[33] Whatever the reason, he found life in Holland quite to his taste and had not yet returned when in the following February Essex staked – and lost – everything on an attempt to take the Tower and overthrow his rivals by force.

The size and scope of Northumberland's library bears witness to the wide range of his interests.[34] Early in life he fell under the spell of Ralegh, and their mutual circle came to include some notable and notorious scholars, including John Dee, Thomas Harriot, Walter Warner and, later, Robert Hues.[35] Yet while he advocated the pursuit of academic study, while his concept of a 'well-fashioned mind' was of one 'free from perturbations and unseemly affections', his own mind hardly answered to this cool and unemotional ideal.[36] Household accounts provide ample evidence to show that he lived court life to the full, participating in ceremonial and enthusiastically indulging a taste for gambling.[37] In 1587 he and his boon companion John Wotton were committed by the privy council to the Fleet and Marshalsea prisons for causing a disturbance in the home of the earl's mother,[38] and in 1597 he came close to fighting a duel with the earl of Southampton.[39] Two years later, his longstanding marital problems came to a head when Dorothy left him, the couple temporarily living apart.[40] This breach alienated the queen, who took a dim view of courtiers incapable of keeping such discord discreetly hidden.

Since this is not intended as a study of Percy finances it will be sufficient here to note that the earl enjoyed a competent income from widespread estates, an income which was to grow steadily from the 1590s onwards. The most important Percy lands lay in Northumberland and, especially, in Yorkshire, but there were also substantial holdings in Sussex, Somerset, Dorset, and South Wales, with further estates scattered through southern and central England. The latter were in part a legacy from the earl's mother, a co-heiress of John Nevill, Lord Latimer, after her death in 1596. In addition, further Welsh lands came through the marriage to Dorothy.

Increasing returns were largely the result of capable estate management.[41] Outgrowing the youthful extravagance which had plunged him into debt, the earl began to show real interest in the care of his lands. As a result, while the income inherited from his father had not been 'enough for a young man's fancy', by the 1600s an older, wiser Northumberland had initiated those improvements which transformed him 'from a relatively poor nobleman with a net income of £3,000 a year into the possessor of a secure income from land of more than double that amount'.[42] Deliveries of rents and revenues in the 'North Parts' averaged £2,050 a year between 1592 and 1596. Between 1598 and 1604, however, the annual average had risen sharply to stand at £4,150. Furthermore, these improvements were made on every part of his estates since similar increases were recorded for Sussex lands.

Consolidation of holdings, increased rents on fallen leases, and enclosure all played their part in this process, yet arguably the most important factor was the earl's personal and meticulous supervision of his estates. He naturally had more time to spare for such attention during his years in the Tower after 1605, and annual returns rose accordingly, but the process had begun earlier. Nothumberland's involvement in political life during the early seventeenth century was thus based upon sound financial foundations. As early as November 1594 one of his creditors, Sir Thomas Tresham, considered him to be a 'very good payer' of his debts.[43]

With the dawn of a new century the earl was absent from his native land, showing no great inclination to return. Intrigues at court apparently held no great attraction for him. While in the great faction struggle between Robert Cecil and the earl of Essex, then approaching a bloody climax, one would have to include Northumberland among the Secretary's supporters, his commitment to that party was hardly wholehearted, owing more to his friendship with Ralegh and his marital problems than to an excess of affection for Cecil. It is against this background, then, that we must see his actions and the manoeuvrings of others in the changed circumstances which prevailed after Essex's death on the scaffold in February 1601.

Notes

1 Jardine, *Criminal Trials*, ii, p xv

2 Spedding, *Letters and Life of Sir Francis Bacon*, iii, p 56

3 BL Hargrave MS 226, fols 241–3

4 Hailes, *Secret Correspondence*, p 107

5 It was doubtless principally for this reason that sympathetic family historians devoted less space than they might have done to this particular period in his career. The most comprehensive family histories of the Percies are those by Thomas Percy (in the 1779 edition of Collins' *Peerage*), De Fonblanque, and Brenan. The first two had access to archives at Alnwick and Syon and are, generally speaking, more reliable than Brenan. There is an excellent summary of the ninth earl's career in G B Harrison's introduction to his edition of Northumberland's *Advice to his Son*. Mention should also be made of Gordon Batho's detailed investigations into many aspects of the ninth earl's life

6 Harrison, *Advice*, pp 80–1; BL Egerton MS 2074, fol 95, dated 9 Apr 1585, Katherine to the tutor of her younger sons in Paris

7 Batho, *Household Papers*, pp 19–21, 45–80

8 *A True and Summarie Reporte*, pp 13–20; Stow, *Annales*, p 707

9 PRO SP 12/241/112; 12/243/11

10 Murdin, *A Collection of State Papers*, pp 521, 533–4; BL Egerton MS 2124, fol 60; Camden, *History*, for the year 1586 (a year included in W T McCaffrey's abridged edition, University of Chicago, 1970, pp 214–77,

esp p 250)

11   Harrison, *Advice*, p 79

12   *ibid*, pp 83–4

13   See Syon MSS U I 1y, Thomas Wycliffe, declaration, 14 Feb 1587–14 Feb 1588; X II 12 Box 5a, Thomas Wycliffe's book of payments

14   HMC, *Bath*, v, p 99, 22 Feb 1589

15   Camden, *History*, p 414. See Laughton, *Armada State Papers*, i, pp lxxvi–lxxvii. Stow (*Annales*, p 711) says that the earl went to the Low Countries in 1585, but this is not supported by Camden, *History*, p 326

16   HMC, *Ancaster*, pp 213–14; PRO SP 46/18, fol 154

17   *Calendar SP Domestic 1591–4*, p 568, PRO docquet dated 10 Dec 1594

18   De Fonblanque, *Annals*, ii, p 194

19   *ibid*; BL Additional MS 5756, fol 242, warrant for his garter robes

20   Harrison, *Advice*, p 11; De Fonblanque, *Annals*, ii, p 195

21   PRO SP 12/235/19; De Thou, *Histoire*, v, p 1056. The earl did not marry until he was thirty; among others spoken of as possible partners were Lady Susan Vere and Lady Bridget Manners (HMC, *Rutland*, i, p 300)

22   Cross, *The Puritan Earl*, pp 167–8. See also Hatfield MS 168/70 in which Northumberland seems to hint at a suggested marriage alliance with the Cecils in an obscure letter to Burghley

23   Hatfield MS 53/73; 170/40, Northumberland to Cecil and to the privy council; Lambeth MS 3203, fol 415; Lodge, *Illustrations*, ii, p 505, Robert Cecil to the earl of Shrewsbury; Watts, *From Border to Middle Shire*, pp 120–1

24   Hatfield MS 71/59. He hurried to court from Petworth to put his own case, and the queen changed her mind. The earl even showed some reluctance to travel to the Low Countries in 1600 (Hatfield MS 180/99, Northumberland to Cecil, 27 May 1600)

25   See PRO SP 12/259/98, Lord Burgh to Cecil, 14 Aug 1596; Hatfield MS 42/87, Cobham to Cecil, 25 July 1596; Syon MS V X 1, commission from the earl of Nottingham to the earl of Northumberland to be general of the horse, Aug 1599; Foley, *Records*, i, p 24, letter from Anthony Rivers, 17 Mar 1602. See also Rymer, *Foedera*, vii part 1, pp 224–31, special commission to exercise ecclesiastical jurisdiction in the province of York, 1599

26   There are many papers at Alnwick concerning legal proceedings over the Perrott lands, notably in Syon MS Y III 1. See also Syon MS X II 1 Box 2 bundle c. For the rest of Elizabeth's life Dorothy enjoyed a pension from the queen rather than the lands themselves. See below, p 190. See also Hatfield MS 169/18

27   Harrison, *Advice*, pp 54–5

28   *ibid*, p 94

29   Hatfield MS 165/139

30   Collins, *Letters and Memorials*, ii, p 54, two letters from Rowland Whyte to Sir Robert Sidney, 27 May and 2 June 1597

31   *ibid*, ii, p 205, Whyte to Sidney, 5 July 1600; McClure, *Letters of Chamberlain*, i, p 100

32   Sawyer, *Winwood Memorials*, i, p 215

33   Collins, *Letters and Memorials*, ii, pp 177–9, 181, Whyte to Sidney, 1 and 22 Mar 1600; Hatfield MS 78/26(2), Cecil to Nicholson, 1 Apr 1600; *Calendar SP Venetian 1592–1603*, p 410

34   Syon MS W II 1; Batho, *Household Papers*, pp 7–8. See Batho, 'Library of the Wizard Earl', pp 246–61

35   Shirley, *Thomas Harriot, passim*, esp pp 358–79; Wood, *Athenæ Oxonienses*, i, p 492; French, *John Dee*, pp 171–2; G R Batho, *Thomas Harriot and the Northumberland Household*, London, 1983

36   Harrison, *Advice*, p 71; See also PRO SP 14/11/9, Northumberland's 'Discourse on Love'

37   He was present at the Gray's Inn Revels of 1595 (Harrison, *Second Elizabethan Journal*, p 1

38   PRO SP 12/206/9; Stoye, 'An Early Letter of John Chamberlain', pp 529–30; Syon MS X II 12 Box 6b, Thomas Power's book, 1587. For Wotton see Tighe, 'Gentlemen Pensioners', pp 476–7; *Archaeologia*, xxxviii, pp 400–1

39   Birch, *Memoirs*, ii, p 274

40   Collins, *Letters and Memorials*, ii, p 133, Rowland Whyte to Sir Robert Sidney, 16 Oct 1599; HMC, *De L'Isle*, ii, p 421; Hatfield MS 179/157(2), Essex to countess of Northumberland

41   Batho, *Household Papers*, pp xlvii–lvi

42   *ibid*, pp xlviii, l

43   HMC, *Various Collections*, iii, p 86, Sir Thomas Tresham to Lady Tresham, 23 Nov 1594

VII

An uncertain future

Pondering increasingly upon the misfortunes of ageing monarchs, Queen Elizabeth once remarked that loyalty was ever bound up with personal expectations, and that human nature being what it was, more people pinned their future hopes upon possible alterations made by her successor after her death, upon the rising rather than the setting sun.[1] Her mind dwelt uneasily on the threat of deposition, and in worsening fits of melancholy she would draw parallels between the current state of affairs and the political strife of the 1390s, gloomily sensing that she might share the fate of her forebear Richard II.[2] Faction at court, the turmoil of Essex's rebellion, and widespread unease over the succession, all contributed to the sense of impending calamity that more and more ruled her mind, and gave rise to speculation over the future of the realm among high and low alike.

Late on the evening of 8 Febuary 1601, forces beseiging the earl of Essex in his mansion received 'store of powther, shott and ordinance brought thether from the Tower to batter the house'. Even his most resolute followers appreciated at this point that further resistance would serve no purpose, and after a short consultation the doors of Essex House were thrown open, Essex and his friend the earl of Southampton 'upon their knees' surrendering 'their swordes into the Lord Admirals [the earl of Nottingham's] hands'.[3] So ended 'suche a hurrle burlye in London and at the courte',[4] the like of which had not been seen in almost half a century. At the close of that eventful day, Essex stood condemned by his own actions. Ever since he had abandoned his command in Ireland more than a year earlier his fortunes had been on the wane. Now, with a suddenness that had taken the shrewdest observers by surprise, his fate was sealed.

Within seventeen days he had been tried, convicted of treason along with Southampton, and executed in the Tower.[5]

Essex's death did not simply decide a lengthy and increasingly bitter struggle for supremacy among the queen's courtiers,[6] it also posed new problems for the future. The most important of these arose from Elizabeth's continuing reluctance to name her successor. Essex had vigorously championed the claims of James VI of Scotland, and at the time of his insurrection two Scottish envoys were preparing for a journey to London with secret instructions to meet him and plot ways in which James might frustrate moves by possible rivals.[7] On hearing of Essex's abortive coup the king might have been forgiven for reflecting that the fates had been less than kind. He remained – as he had been for some years – the queen's most likely heir; his was certainly the strongest claim, both by blood and experience. But he was well aware that his parentage and nationality cast more than just a shadow of doubt over his chances. There was no shortage of adverse comment on the prospect of a Scotsman – and a Scotsman who was Mary Stuart's son at that – ascending the throne of England. Elizabeth was periodically warned, tactfully, that 'a king born in Scotland, and so a Scottes man' would not be welcomed as her successor.[8] While none of his potential rivals had so good a title as James, there was always the possibility that another's cause might be adopted by factions unwilling to stomach the thought of being ruled by a Scottish king.

But while rumour mongers and tavern pundits might have gained fleeting currency for their prognostications of impending trouble, any threat posed by James's 'rivals' was always more apparent than real. An assiduous investigator into the competing claims enjoyed the challenge of a genealogical game but succeeded only in convincing himself that there was no viable alternative to the Stuart king.[9] James's cousin Arabella[10] was hardly the stuff of which queens were made, while the claim of Edward Seymour, Lord Beauchamp was technically as well as practically inferior.[11] Those who counted in the political realm of England had already resolved that James was by far the most palatable prospect for the future. Although less than enthusiastic at the idea, they were prepared to face rule by a Scotsman rather than endure the anarchy that could result otherwise.

The consequences of Essex's fall were thus – in reality – minimal. Those connected to him by ties of kinship or loyalty were quick to distance themselves from the fallen star. Northumberland returned home from the Low Countries just too late to attend the trials of Essex and Southampton, although he was at least able to intercede for his brothers Sir Charles and Sir Josceline Percy, by then indicted for treason after their participation in the revolt, securing their release from the Fleet prison.[12] Though he and Essex had once been close,[13] Northumberland had in recent years drawn apart from one whose fortunes were visibly waning. Consequently, he was able to join in the condemnation of Essex's actions while avoiding any suspicion of complicity in the rebellion.

Writing to Dudley Carleton in April 1601, Northumberland lost no time in expressing the accepted view that Essex had simply lost touch with reality; his had been the actions of a madman. When told by Carleton of widespread sympathy in the Low Countries for the fallen earl he replied resignedly that, concerning such 'oppinions of my Lord of Essex marterdom, they will know it better one day, or if they will not then must wee of this state giue them leaue to thinke as they list'.[14] Court factions realigned, Northumberland telling Carleton with some distaste that outward displays of friendship and affection there were but a facade, concealing 'inward' factions and rivalries 'according to the old faschion'.[15] He was doubtless relieved to return to Holland on 1 June,[16] and his long, informative, and animated letters to Cecil over the next few months show his spirits rising as he participated in the summer campaigns.[17]

Robert Cecil was unquestionably the rising star of English political life during the 1590s. The younger but more-capable son of Elizabeth's great statesman William Cecil, Lord Burghley, he had been groomed for high office by his father and had been since 1596 the queen's principal Secretary. Physically small and slightly deformed, Cecil had little of the presence of his father, but matched Burghley's assiduous attention to work and his unrelenting ambition to rise in the service of the crown.[18] Inevitably, he was at the centre of these renewed 'inward' intrigues. After the fall of Essex – which when all was said and done owed more to the earl's own shortcomings than to the manoeuvrings of his rivals – relations between Cecil on the one side and Sir Walter Ralegh and Henry Brooke, Lord Cobham on the other – a triumvirate formerly united in opposition to the earl – became increasingly cool.[19] Cecil wasted no time in opening negotiations with James's emissaries to London, the earl of Mar and Edward Bruce, who arrived in London shortly after the February upheavals. Through them, he and his associate

Henry Howard – younger brother of the late fourth duke of Norfolk – began a secret correspondence with the Scottish king.[20] Subsequently Ralegh, who like Cecil had hitherto been thought of as lukewarm towards the Scottish claimant, held tentative and obscure discussions with the duke of Lennox.[21] Others with political ambitions followed suit, the earl of Northumberland among them after his return to England via Ostend at the end of September 1601.[22]

It is still not wholly clear why the earl took such an initiative, the move marking a departure from his efforts to avoid involvement in politics during the 1590s. Viewed in another way, however, the change is not so startling. All that had been on offer under Elizabeth was the occasional embassy or the supervision of the remote Middle March – and with the fate of several former Percy earls never far from his mind he clearly had no wish to re-establish the family's fateful, hereditary, political influence in those parts. It is probable that, were the chance of public employment to present itself, the earl would have far preferred a role in central rather than peripheral politics. Besides, any public service under the parsimonious queen generally proved a thankless labour. How different things might be if one were instead the trusted confidante of a new king keen to express in all possible ways his gratitude for services rendered.

By the end of Elizabeth's reign there were, moreover, new considerations to be taken into account. Perhaps Northumberland felt that as the mature representative of a great house it was his duty to play a greater part in the government of his country – possibly one greater than any the queen would allow to a Percy. There was a broad hint to this effect in his first letter to James, where he claimed that some of the nobility, although they would never back a premature attempt on the crown by a Scottish king, were nevertheless discontented due to Elizabeth's reluctance to allow them responsibilities in the state. Perhaps he also wished to circumvent any misconstruction of his friendship for Ralegh. It is also possible – it would have been quite in character – that the earl initiated the correspondence out of a genuine concern to see the just cause prevail – and he was no doubt sincere in wishing to avoid the bloodshed which he and others feared might result from any attempt by James to assert a claim 'before its time'.

There are at least two further matters which he must have taken into account. It made obvious financial sense for him to back the

Scottish succession; anything that might lessen the endemic border strife that had so wasted his Northumbrian lands in years past could only serve to increase returns from these estates. Not that we should accord this consideration too much importance. It is true that in 1596 Northumberland had used the Scots' depredations as one reason why he would be unable to meet the costs of ambassadorial employment to France,[23] but on that occasion he had deliberately exaggerated the effect of such raiding on his revenues. Since he was by no means simply a border landlord – much of his income being derived from more-southerly estates – his future prosperity was at no time dependent on a cessation of the reivers' activities.[24]

The second consideration, while more important, is also far more difficult to analyse. There is undoubtedly some truth to allegations made in the aftermath of Gunpowder plot which accused the earl of seeking to secure some measure of toleration for English Catholics. But what were his motives? They could have been patriotic and selfless; he may have seen in such concessions the surest way to smooth James's path to the crown. Alternatively, he could have hoped to establish a personal clientage among grateful Catholics sufficiently powerful to make his services indispensable to the king. Complicating our assessment is the fact that Thomas Percy carried Northumberland's letters to Edinburgh. In his examination on 23 November 1605 the earl confessed that it had been Percy who had first suggested an overture to James,[25] and Percy at least hoped in this way to secure better times for his co-religionists after the death of the queen. We know that far more on the subject of toleration passed verbally through Thomas Percy than ever appeared in the written correspondence between king and earl, and it is equally certain that the king's sentiments as related by Percy or as understood by the earl were not those which the king thought he had expressed. Here were the seeds of much future trouble.

For Northumberland these were all possible motives, but behind everything lay a less-tangible but very important consideration. Given the family history under the Tudors, it would hardly have been surprising if the earl had done everything in his power to secure a 'clean sheet' from the new dynasty, a dynasty which might well have been disposed to look kindly on the Percy family. Had not the earl's father and uncle suffered in the cause of the king of Scots' mother? Northumberland, surely, was one man entitled to have his eyes fixed optimistically on the new dawn of the Stuart monarchy.

The secret correspondence, particularly that drafted by Henry Howard, makes unedifying reading. Employing minimal discretion, Howard finds targets in overt and potential rivals alike.[26] Thus his tirade against a 'diabolical triplicity' comprising not only Ralegh and Cobham, but Northumberland as well, whom he repeatedly branded as a man 'beloved of none, followed by none, trusted by no one nobleman or gentleman of quality within the land beside his faction'.[27] Worst of all, perhaps, Howard's Northumberland was out of favour with a queen irritated past endurance by his refusal to patch things up with Dorothy. Howard wrote of Elizabeth's 'deep hatred and daily invectives' against the earl, 'a mortal wound to a mind that is ambitious'.[28] Moreover, the earl was said to be incapable of discretion 'for such a leaking sieve did never water the wild gardens of Hesperides'.[29] Howard was clearly aiming principally at Ralegh and Cobham – the 'triplicity' soon becomes a 'duality' – and his florid 'ample, Asiatic and endless' style completely obscures his meaning at times,[30] yet there is no doubt that by portraying Northumberland as the stupid dupe of cleverer men he sowed some seeds of doubt in James's mind as to the capacity of his noble correspondent.

But Howard's vituperation cannot necessarily be taken to represent the views of Cecil. The Secretary's mind in these murky matters as in other more open affairs is a constant puzzle – as with statesmen of every age there is a tendency to attribute personal malice to actions which might more profitably be seen in other lights. The secret correspondence unquestionably provides strong arguments to support a view that Cecil was the earl's covert enemy. Through his colleague Howard he was denigrating one who was his declared friend and who clearly trusted him implicitly. Even Howard admitted that Northumberland was showing his correspondence with the king to Cecil, although he managed to place a sinister construction on the action.[31] Outwardly, though, Cecil returned the earl's respect and affection. On 13 October 1601 he solicited a colonel's appointment in Ireland for Northumberland's brother Sir Richard Percy. 'You know', he wrote to the lord president of Munster, Sir George Carew, 'how much I loue and honor the noble erle, who, notwithstanding his obligation in former tymes to those who esteemed us as Iewes, dyd euer loue us for the trueths sake.'[32]

There is a danger here in special pleading, yet the apparent duplicity does not have to indicate personal antipathy. It is probable that

Cecil did not so much dislike Ralegh, Cobham, and Northumberland as fear them for potential rivals. Put crudely, Cecil was a worrier. As Howard once told Edward Bruce, referring to a letter in the secret correspondence that had gone astray:

if Cecil had seen [the letter that conveyed Bruce's fears on the subject], I protest to God all the course of convey and intelligence had been ruined for ever . . . upon the multiplicity of doubts his mind would never have been at rest, nor he would have eaten or slept quietly; for nothing makes him confident, but experience of secret trust, and security of intelligence.[33]

Moreover, in too-readily ascribing the views expressed in Howard's correspondence to his ally Cecil, we perhaps do both men an injustice. Although less the master of his feelings than his father had been, Cecil never employs such immoderate language, in keeping with the able statesman that he was.[34] Howard's attacks are at least some way understood when one takes account of the thirty years he had spent in the political wilderness under Elizabeth, following his brother's execution for treason. Although this cannot be proved – there is little other evidence on which to assess their relationship – one suspects that his dislike of Northumberland in particular was something essentially his own, that he wished to discredit one whom he saw as a rival for the position which he himself wished to occupy under James – that of the most trusted associate among the higher nobility. Henry Howard was, after all, no mere lackey of Cecil's. His survival instincts sharpened by the long years of adversity, he had his own long-nourished hopes of the future king that had probably led him to serve Essex in much the same way that he now served the Secretary. It was James – not Cecil – who had chosen him as their contact.[35]

The Ralegh-Cobham-Northumberland 'triplicity' is essentially Howard's creation. Although there is no doubt that the three men were on close terms, Northumberland's links with Cobham in particular were of quite recent origin, and his description of his old friend Ralegh in one of his letters to James is balanced, perceptive, but by no means wholly favourable. While insisting that there were still 'excellent good parts of natur in hem', the earl admitted that Sir Walter was 'insolent, extreamly heated, a man that desirs to seeme to be able to swaye all mens fancies . . . a man that owt of himselfe, when your time sall come, will neuer be able to do yow muche good nor hearme'.[36]

If both Cecil and Howard feared the earl as a possible rival, it is fair to say that Lord Henry's fears were the better founded. While it is possible that Northumberland sought the type of influence Howard was later to enjoy under James, it is most improbable that he ever thought of supplanting Cecil. Despite all his doubts and anxieties the Secretary probably realised this – for him, the threat posed by Ralegh was more immediate. Yet even Ralegh was unlikely to prove another Essex. In many respects Cecil was fortunate in his enemies; Essex had lacked the resources of money, patronage, and political sagacity necessary to halt the Secretary's rise to power, and once established in that power it would have taken more than a man like Ralegh, who despite his personal gifts had far less influence than Essex, to bring him down.[37] Moreover, and most importantly, James was not inclined to overlook talent in his subordinates.

Given the difficulty of foreseeing just what would happen when Elizabeth died, it is not surprising that Cecil encouraged Howard's attempts to destroy the credit of potential rivals. In writing to the king Cecil was not merely attempting to develop an already-settled intimacy with James, rather he was trying to establish such a happy state of affairs against what he might have suspected to be a field full of rivals. Furthermore, for obvious reasons, it was imperative to keep the whole correspondence secret from the queen, notoriously touchy and suspicious on the subject of her successor. This was, indeed, a most difficult and uncertain time.[38]

It is, though, this very uncertainty which helps explain why it was that men with ambition were prepared to use what influence they had – and stake their all – to gain favour. Northumberland's correspondence with the Scottish king is in many ways unremarkable – as events were to prove, the earl was a man of no pronounced political acumen, and his letters, while expressing good sense, make no special impact upon the reader.[39] That said, James was no doubt glad to receive these overtures from the representative of an ancient border house who could, simply through open acceptance of his claim, make the king's succession so much easier, and he would have particularly taken to heart the earl's opinion that – while it could and would be overcome by the examples set by their betters – anti-Scots xenophobia would be a real problem for red-blooded Englishmen faced with the prospect of a Scottish succession. 'The name of scotts', wrote Northumberland, 'is harche in the earres of the wulgar.'[40] Himself a red-blooded Englishman, the earl could not resist pointing out, somewhat inaccurately, that as one who was 'half englishe',

James had in fact precious little reason 'to be so far enamored wyth the fayth of there subiects that willingly thay will repose a greater truist in them then in the englishe'.[41]

The real significance of Northumberland's correspondence for the later events which concern us here is his readiness to speak on behalf of the English Catholics. In the very first surviving letter in the secret correspondence he wrote:

For the papists, it is treue there faction is strong, there encrease is dayly, and there diffidence in your maiestie is not desperat. Somme of the purer sort of them, who hathe swaloued the doctrine of putting doune princes for religion, may perhapps be whoter then there ware reason, wishing the enfanta [of Spain, sister to Philip III and wife of Archduke Albert of Flanders] a better scare [share] in the kingdome then your selfe. But since your maiestie vndirstandeth better whow to leede this cause then I can giue instruction, I will dare to say no more, bot it weare pittie to losse so good a kingdome for the not tollerating a messe in a cornere (if wppon that it resteth) so long as they sall not be too busy disturbers of the guuernement of the state, nor seeke to make vs contributers to a peter prist.[42]

In the earl's first two letters to the king, this was his only reference to Catholics, but it is a clear enough recommendation of toleration in some form. Northumberland probably believed that his words would not prove unpleasant to James, but there can be no doubt that in venturing to speak on behalf of an embattled minority in this way he was laying up potential difficulties for himself in the future. Here again we are confronted with the problem of guessing, in the absence of any evidence, what verbal messages were conveyed – and how accurately they were conveyed – by Thomas Percy.[43]

This choice of a messenger, although ultimately disastrous, was logical enough. An adventurous man, distantly related to the earl and the constable of his principal seat in Northumberland, Alnwick Castle, Percy must have seemed an obvious choice. The earl was later to describe him as 'a tall gent and one whom he trusted' – inasmuch as trust was placed in any estate official.[44] Certainly in 1602 the determined and brave Percy was very much a 'coming man' in Northumberland's entourage. Descended from a younger son of the fourth earl of Northumberland, very little is known of his early life. He matriculated at Peterhouse, Cambridge, in 1579 and may possibly have sailed with George Clifford, earl of Cumberland, on his Azores voyage of 1589.[45] An estate officer since 1595, he had travelled with his master to the Low Countries in 1601 and had been rewarded with two hundred pounds shortly afterwards.[46]

Although he did not join in Essex's rebellion he was on cordial terms with some who did, notably Robert Catesby, John and Christopher Wright, whose sister he had married,[47] and Lord Monteagle, who as we have seen had undertaken to pay Percy's wife an annuity of five hundred pounds.[48] In contrast to his friends, however, the 1600s began successfully and profitably for Percy. In 1603 he became receiver of the earl's rents in Cumberland and Northumberland, replacing weaker men who – in a lawless area – had fallen considerably in arrears on their payments. It was a hard job, requiring a ruthless energy that gave rise to some complaints about his conduct, not least from one of the officers he replaced.[49] The darker side of his character is also illustrated by his enthusiastic participation in a plot engineered by Essex to entrap the Scottish warden of the Western March in the late 1590s.[50] This escapade having given Percy a taste of cloak and dagger operations, the chance seemed now at hand for Northumberland to use him in an altogether bigger game.

Unfortunately, this reasoning proved faulty. Percy, in common with many on the English side of the border, harboured a virulent antipathy towards Scotsmen and all things Scottish.[51] There is even some evidence to show that he killed a Scot in the 1590s, presumably during some border affray.[52] Beyond that, and in common with many of his closest friends, Percy was a fervent adherent to the Roman Catholic faith.[53] A man of divided and conflicting loyalties was about to embark on the greatest adventure of his life.

The beleaguered church to which he belonged, although viewed as a monolithic and inimical whole by many who held to the faith of the Thirty-Nine Articles, was in fact itself riven by disputes, divisions, and that most bitter form of fratricidal conflict found in small and persecuted minorities. The most fundamental split of all was that between those Catholics who wished to come to some agreement with the authorities and those who were reluctant to contemplate compromising their beliefs in return for what might well prove to be but transient or illusory benefits. At the end of Elizabeth's life, this split found expression in the so-called Archpriest controversy, an argument over the most appropriate form of church government for the English Catholics. On one side stood the 'secular' priests who sought the appointment of a bishop and ecclesiastical hierarchy in England, while against them were arrayed those, including most English Jesuits, who felt that – in a country where the church had to contend with open persecution – a form of government more suited to a protracted campaign of resistance was called for.[54]

Some of the most virulent language used against the Jesuits came, not from protestant sources, but from the pens of the 'Appellant' secular clergy, opposed to government by the Archpriest George Blackwell. 'Their platforme', wrote the argumentative William Watson, 'is heathenish, tyrannicall, Sathanicall, and able to set *Aretine, Lucian, Machiauell*, yea and *Don Lucifer* in a sort to schoole, as impossible for him by all the art he hath to besot men as they do.'[55] These divisions were hardly conducive to efficient propagation of the faith, and while both sides angled for support from the Catholic nobility and gentry, missionary activity among the humbler folk was inevitably neglected. The services of a priest were seldom to hand in many country areas, and as has been convincingly argued, there was in consequence a 'high risk of leakage from the Catholic community'.[56]

Of course, the same applied to the other side. English protestantism ran at best only skin deep in many adherents, and cries of outrage at the poor provision of the gospel to the mass of the English people set up by the 'puritans' at the end of the sixteenth and early in the seventeenth centuries was by no means unwarranted. Hungry sheep were going unfed.[57] What all this bred, on both sides of the religious divide, was a sense of deep uncertainty and unease, feelings sharpened by a genuine vagueness over the king of Scots' own religious persuasions. James himself took a practical attitude towards those with deeper religious convictions. The Calvinist faith in which he had been reared appealed to him in its way, but far more attractive was a church in which Calvinist doctrines were wedded to an episcopal hierarchy with the king, naturally enough, at its head.[58] He was, moreover, the son of a Catholic 'martyr' – though he never liked to be reminded of that fact – and his queen was a Catholic. While Anglicans could fear that the weak flower of their faith might be plucked by a king who saw an advantage in favouring the Catholic community for his own purposes, the Catholics equally saw James's accession as a chance to put behind them over forty years of growing restrictions on their freedom.[59]

These, then, were the troubled religious waters into which

Northumberland dipped in the spring of 1602. He did not, however, have the chance to wade deeper. At the end of his second letter to the king, which had contained a long denunciation of Essex and an assessment of leading figures at court, he made clear his intention to write again and describe the dispositions of other prominent Englishmen.[60] James, however, deciding that enough was enough, repeated more forcefully advice given in his first reply. Now that the earl had made so frank a display of his 'wpryght sinseritie' and affection, he cautioned, it would be prudent to suspend correspondence until 'some great and wrgent occation' necessitated a resumption. Although in accordance with Cecil's advice as relayed by Howard, the pause need not be ascribed to their insinuations: both king and earl may have favoured a self-imposed reticence at this point. Neither would want to run the risk of their letters falling into the queen's hands, and neither quite trusted the discretion of the messengers involved.[61] So, by mutual consent, the exchange of letters ceased, only to be resumed in March 1603 when Northumberland wrote again on the 'great and wrgent occation' presented by the mortal sickness of his queen.

Before leaving the secret correspondence it is interesting to reflect that Howard, although successfully planting seeds of doubt as to Northumberland's abilities in James's mind, may have harmed his case through overstatement. Some of the earl's failings were only too obvious. His inability to keep secrets was to be illustrated in later years, and there is little doubt that he was out of favour with the queen, especially after a scandal involving an abortive duel with Sir Francis Vere in 1602, which had shown him in no very favourable light.[62] Although a temporary reconcilement to Dorothy led to a relaxation in Elizabeth's wrath,[63] and to the birth of a son and heir – Algernon, the future tenth earl – in 1602,[64] the diarist John Manningham had heard rumours of another separation as early as December 1602. Manningham, with some degree of sober satisfaction as to the mutability of human emotions, depicted the earl wallowing in melancholy, only happy when he was with the child.[65]

So much was true, but the king remained ignorant of other important defects. The Vere incident had shown a childish, petulant side to the earl's character. Moreover, Northumberland could himself dissimulate when he chose. In his second letter to the king he blamed Essex for blocking his appointment to any northern office,[66] conveniently omitting to point out that he had himself been reluctant to take on such positions. It was to be the earl's inexperience rather than either his incompetence or his naivety that would eventually tell against him.

Northumberland's accounts permit us glimpses of his life during the last year of Elizabeth's reign. Any regrets for his new marital troubles did not keep him away from court for very long, since one finds him there in Christmas 1602. His brother Sir Richard Percy, over on leave from his regiment in Ireland, hired a fool for the new year festivities at court, and on 1 January the fool provided entertainment for the earl who gave him sixpence as a 'philipe'.[67] When a Frenchman brought 'babions to daunce before your lordship' he was rewarded with ten shillings.[68] On 2 January 1603, Northumberland managed to lose fifty pounds in gambling to the earl of Worcester – a man of Catholic sympathies, an ally of Cecil and himself a privy councillor – and to the French ambassador. These accounts show how, with an eye to the future, the same French ambassador – Christophe Harlay, comte de Beaumont – was doing all he could to win the earl's friendship. He gave Northumberland a horse, and a further present of some wine. On 15 March, shortly before Elizabeth died, a French cook was rewarded for helping to dress a dinner at Syon when the ambassador was there.[69] Beaumont's foresight was soon to pay dividends.

The earl had good reason to live quietly after his return from the Low Countries. His travels overseas had led him to spend over £4,000 in the space of thirty-three weeks on living and travelling expenses alone, besides a further £1,212 spent on horses.[70] In December 1601 Carleton had remarked that the earl was then living away from court at Syon, hoping in this way to offset some of the financial costs of his travels and perhaps even to make possible another trip abroad in 1602.[71] Whatever its cause, a period of quiet living would have allowed him time to enjoy his extensive library. Early in 1603, Sir Henry Saville wrote to Carleton, then in Paris, informing him that a Mr Dalrimple was travelling to the French capital with 'bookish matters' in hand both for Saville himself and for Northumberland.[72] Over the following few months, however, the earl could have had little time to spare for these 'bookish matters'.

Notes

1   Black, *Reign of Elizabeth*, p 71

2   Smith, *Treason in Tudor England*, pp 268–9

3   HMC, *Bath*, v, pp 280–1. See also Smith, *Treason in Tudor England*, pp 239–68

4   Wall, 'An Account of the Essex Revolt', p 132

5   For the trials of Essex and Southampton see Howell, *State Trials*, i, cols 1333–60; of Sir Christopher Blount and others involved in the Essex revolt see *ibid*, cols 1403–52

6   Illustrated in the contents of Anthony Bacon's papers and in Birch's *Memoirs*

7   Stafford, *James VI of Scotland and the Throne of England*, pp 214–16

8   Bain, *Calendar of Border Papers*, i, pp 530–1, quoted by Wormald, 'Two Kings or One?', p 209

9   See Fisher, 'The State of England by Thomas Wilson' for an examination of the various claims

10   Arabella Stuart was first cousin to James. She was the daughter of Charles Stuart, earl of Lennox, himself a great-grandson of Henry VII

11   Edward Seymour, earl of Hertford, son of the Edward Seymour, duke of Somerset who had been Protector in Edward VI's reign, secretly married Lady Catherine Grey, sister of Lady Jane Grey and great-niece of Henry VIII. Lord Beauchamp was his eldest son

12   Nicholls, 'Sir Charles Percy', pp 239–40

13   There is a series of friendly letters 1596–9 among the Aylesford MSS at Warwick CRO. These are calendared in HMC National Register of Archives 10782. Copies by Thomas Birch can be found in BL Additional MS 4124

14   PRO SP 12/279/59, from London, 6 Apr 1601

15   *ibid*

16   Batho, *Household Papers*, p 137n. The earl's route from London is traceable in Syon MS U I 50a(2), Rocke Church's book of payments

17   He describes the siege of Rheinberg particularly vividly (Hatfield MS 182/81–2). See also Hatfield MSS 86/153–4; 182/104; 183/1 and 118

18   The definitive biography of Robert Cecil remains to be written. Alan Haynes's *Robert Cecil* is a readable if brief introduction. For Cecil's later career, the best source is arguably still Thomas M Coakley's doctoral thesis 'The Political Position and Domestic Policy of Robert Cecil 1603–12', and Coakley's article 'Robert Cecil in Power: Elizabethan Politics in Two Reigns' is worth reading. For a brief but significant study see Hurstfield's 'Robert Cecil, Earl of Salisbury: Minister of Elizabeth and James I', while a rather less flattering view is offered in Francis Edwards's 'Robin Goodfellow or Robin the Devil? The Enigma of the First Earl of Salisbury', *The Month*, NS XXX, 1963, pp 12–21

19   Nicholls, 'Politics and Percies', pp 20–35

20   Stafford, *James VI of Scotland and the Throne of England*, pp 254–9. The so-called 'secret correspondence' between James and his ministers on the one hand, and various leading figures at the English court on

the other, can be found in Hailes, *Secret Correspondence*, and Bruce, *Correspondence*. In addition, there are letters apparently connected with the correspondence in BL Cotton MS Titus C VI, fols 64–5, 382–92, and see also Stafford, *James VI of Scotland and the Throne of England*, p 255n. For a recent reflection on the correspondence see Akrigg, *Letters of James VI and I*, pp 178–207

21   Stafford, *James VI of Scotland and the Throne of England*, p 259

22   The earl had hankered to witness the siege of Ostend (HMC, *Rutland*, i, p 379, Thomas Screven to the earl of Rutland, 16 Sep 1601) but the attractions of a beseiged town soon waned. Ostend, he wrote to Cecil, 'is soe foule at this present with this euell wether as the soldiers or any that sterrs out in any place wades deepe in myer and water' (BL Cotton MS Galba D XII, fol 321, dated 18 Sep 1601)

23   Hatfield MS 71/59

24   For the northern revenues see Batho, *Household Papers*, pp xlvii–lvi; James, *Northumberland Estate Accounts*, pp xxxv–lv; Watts, *From Border to Middle Shire*, pp 160–74

25   PRO SP 14/216/113

26   Howard's letters are printed in Hailes, *Secret Correspondence*

27   Hailes, *Secret Correspondence*, pp 107, Howard to Edward Bruce, 1 May 1602

28   *ibid*, p 109. There is a further letter, extracts from which are printed in Edwards, *Life and Letters of Ralegh*, ii, pp 436–44 (BL Cotton MS Titus C VI, fols 386–92) which refers to Northumberland's anger at having been passed over for martial employment in the Low Countries. Howard pointed out more than once his comparative military inexperience

29   *ibid*, pp 29–33

30   Hailes, *Secret Correspondence*, p 116; Akrigg, *Letters of James VI and I*, p 190

31   Hailes, *Secret Correspondence*, pp 29–33, 66

32   Lambeth MS 604, p 110; Maclean, *Letters from Sir Robert Cecil to Sir George Carew*, p 99. In a letter of 11 October 1601 (Folger Shakespeare Library MS X d 480) Cecil wrote similarly to Mountjoy. He professed great respect for the earl, though he 'wold not be bound to all his affections'

33   Hailes, *Secret Correspondence*, pp 202–3

34   In Cecil's surviving correspondence with James and his ministers he makes no reference to Northumberland, and only once ventures to criticise Ralegh (Bruce, *Correspondence*, pp 17–20). Like Howard's most vituperative letter of 4 December 1601, this followed Ralegh's and Cobham's attempts to make contact with Lennox. Cecil's position was never that easy, since as an opponent of Essex he could be seen as opposing Essex's plans for a Stuart succession. Hicks has argued ('Sir Robert Cecil, Father Persons and the Succession', *Archivum Historicum Societatis Iesu*, XXIV, 1955, pp 95–139) that Cecil had seriously considered backing the Infanta Isabella's claim to the throne. Hurstfield in 'The Succession Struggle', pp 369–89, disagrees. It is worth noting that

Isabella had no wish to advance her claims (Wormald, 'Gunpowder, Treason, and Scots', p 155)

35 Peck, *Northampton*, pp 13–19

36 Bruce, *Correspondence*, pp 66–7

37 Hurstfield, 'The Succession Struggle', p 394

38 *ibid*, pp 391–4

39 Handover thought that they displayed political acumen, although in her view their effect was lessened through Northumberland's inability to present his advice 'in a tactful and agreeable form' (*The Second Cecil*, p 284). Shirley in his recent study of Thomas Harriot, which looks quite closely at the correspondence, concluded that, while not particularly astute, the earl's letters and his support for James were at least motivated by patriotism and not by hopes of personal gain (*Thomas Harriot*, pp 296–301). Such views are – through their simplicity – rather condescending. The earl's views on the problems that James might encounter, if obvious in hindsight, are at least realistic, and James justly described the first despatch that he received from Northumberland as a 'most wyse plaine and honest letter' (Bruce, *Correspondence*, p 61)

40 Bruce, *Correspondence*, p 56

41 *ibid*. James himself admitted to Cecil (*ibid*, p 31) that his Scottish subjects were 'farre more barbarouse and stiffe nekkit' than the English

42 *ibid*. It is worth noticing that Cecil too had assured the king that most Catholics were backing his claim (*ibid*, p 35)

43 We have copies of the letters carried by Percy on two visits to Scotland in 1602 made by the Scots for Howard and Cecil (Hatfield MSS 135/90, 92a, 95, 97, 99, 100 – printed in Bruce, *Correspondence*, pp 53–76). A marginal note on the examination of Northumberland taken on 23 November 1605, however, recorded that Percy had been to Scotland three times, carrying no letters with him on the first occasion. Nothing further is known of the alleged preliminary approach (PRO SP 14/216/113; Bruce, *Correspondence*, p 53)

44 PRO SP 14/216/113; see part II chapter X note 58

45 Venn, *Alumni Cantabrigienses*, part 1, iii, p 346; Williamson, *Third Earl of Cumberland*, p 44, but the latter may be a reference to another Thomas Percy

46 PRO SP 14/216/113

47 It has been suggested that Percy was a bigamist. All that can be said for certain is that he had two wives (Hatfield MS 113/91; *The Athenaeum*, 3646, 11 Sep 1897). It *looks* as if both were alive in November 1605, one living in London, the other in the midlands, but in the absence of certain proof one should be wary of certain conclusions. It is difficult to believe, although not impossible, that the Wrights would have remained friendly with a man who treated their sister in such a fashion

48 For details of the debt see PRO E134/7 James I Easter/39; E134/Miscellaneous James I/24. To be precise, Monteagle owed Percy's wife Martha and daughter an annuity of £50

49 De Fonblanque, *Annals*, ii, pp 589–98 (see also *History of Northumberland*, ii, pp 374–5, 402). De Fonblanque uses this material to

show that the earl had early proof that Percy was defrauding him, and took no action. However, he is quoting from Syon MS Q I 12, and papers in this collection which he does not cite, notably letters of Percy himself and of his predecessor Anthony Felton, show clearly that Felton's was the position under threat. William Wycliffe laid several accusations against Percy in 1602 which Percy repudiated and further answered with charges of his own against Wycliffe, claiming that he was being blamed for the 'idell vanites' of his youth, even though he had now 'put on a firme resolution of better cources'. This seems to have convinced the earl, and Wycliffe later worked happily enough with Percy (Syon MSS P II 2l; Q XI 2). It is worth noting that the former receivers for Cumberland and Northumberland, Thomas Dikes and Felton, still owed large sums in 1608 and 1609 (Syon MSS Q I 30 and 33, letters from Thomas Fotherley to Northumberland, 21 Sep and 18 Aug 1608). In 1607 Felton, while acknowledging his debt, still owed £518 (Syon MS C IV 3, Robert Delaval's receiver's account, 5 James I). On the indebtedness of receivers, common enough on the Northumberland estates, see James, *Northumberland Estate Accounts*, pp xxxv–xxxviii

50   Hatfield MSS 98/164; 176/48, letters of Thomas Percy, Jan 1599. There are several other letters among the Hatfield papers concerning the conspiracy to capture Sir Robert Ker of Cessford, using as bait the Scottish hostages for the truce between England and Scotland, then held at York

51   Note the low opinion of Scots expressed in his letters (Syon MSS Q I 20; Q III 1a)

52   Alnwick MS Letters and Papers vol 5, fol 99, letter from Essex on behalf of Percy, who was being held prisoner in London in 1596

53   Tesimond wrote that, on his conversion to Catholicism, Percy had forgone his old violent ways, subsequently 'giving much satisfaction to the Catholics and considerable cause for wonder to those who had known him previously' (Edwards, *Greenway Narrative*, p 58)

54   For the Archpriest controversy see Bossy, 'English Catholic Community', pp 96–8

55   Watson, *A Decacordon*, p 62

56   Haigh, 'Church, Catholics and the People', pp 200–5

57   *ibid*, pp 196–200, 205–19; Collinson, 'Elizabethan Church and the New Religion'

58   Wormald, 'Two Kings or One?', p 203; Willson, *James VI and I*, pp 219–20; Fincham and Lake, 'Ecclesiastical Policy of James I', pp 169–70 *et seq*; Lee, *Great Britain's Solomon*, pp 164–95

59   La Rocca, 'Who Can't Pray With Me, Can't Love Me', pp 22–30; Fincham and Lake, 'Ecclesiastical Policy of James I', pp 182–5

60   Bruce, *Correspondence*, p 69

61   In his second dispatch, Northumberland had warned James that there appeared to be some 'vntrustie serwants' at his court, since the king's every move was known and discussed in England (Bruce, *Correspondence*, p 69)

62   Northumberland's altercation with Vere was the sensation of its day, with both his challenge and Vere's reply being published and surviving in many contemporary collections (for example, see McClure, *Letters of*

Chamberlain, i, pp 150–1 and PRO SP 12/284/37 i and ii; Queen's College Oxford MS 144, fols 30v–31v; Braunmuller, *A Seventeenth-Century Letter-Book*, pp 122–9, 422–3). The clash seems to have grown through the mutual antagonism between the amateur soldier and the career officer (see McClure, *Letters of Chamberlain*, i, p 127; Hatfield MS 182/93; SP 12/281/19; Markham, *The Fighting Veres*, p 317n; BL Cotton MS Julius C III, fol 134; Nicholls, 'Politics and Percies', pp 48–50). Northumberland, as challenger and aggressor, did not come out of the affair well, especially since he had accused his opponent of cowardice *after* a duel had been expressly prohibited by the queen

63   At the end of 1601 Chamberlain reported speculation that Northumberland might be sent to France to attend the dauphin's christening (McClure, *Letters of Chamberlain*, i, p 178. See also PRO SP 12/283A/6. Brenan even suggested that the earl opened his correspondence with James as a direct result of this period of improved relations with Dorothy (*History*, ii, p 78)

64   The queen agreed to be godmother to the child (Lambeth MS 3201, fol 58v; Lodge, *Illustrations*, ii, pp 583–4; Maclean, *Letters from Sir Robert Cecil to Sir George Carew*, p 136; McClure, *Letters of Chamberlain*, i, p 167

65   Sorlien, *Diary of John Manningham*, p 120

66   Bruce, *Correspondence*, pp 65–6

67   Syon MS U I 50(3), Sapcoates Harrington's book of rewards

68   Syon MS U I 3q, Robert Delaval, declaration, 27 Mar 1602–29 Mar 1603

69   *ibid*; Syon MS U I 50(3)

70   Alnwick MS Letters and Papers vol 7, fol 29, a brief account of Low Countries expenses in 1600 and 1601

71   PRO SP 12/282/48

72   PRO SP 12/287/38, from court, 26 Feb 1603

VIII

The Stuart succession

When considering the crises which periodically confronted govern-
ments then as now, a distinction should be drawn between those
which burst suddenly on the scene, with little or no warning, and
those which could be anticipated and countered in advance. Gunpowder plot, we have argued, falls into the first category, while the
Essex rebellion, thanks to the earl's increasingly unpredictable
behaviour, must be placed somewhere between the two extremes of
the scale. The death of Elizabeth, however, was obviously going to
pose problems for the ministers who outlived her, and her passing,
when it came, cannot by any stretch of the imagination be described
as unforeseen.

For some months before her death, the queen's health had been
visibly declining. Writing to Cobham in August 1602 while accom-
panying the court on its annual summer progress, Northumberland
had confided to his friend that 'vppon Weddinsday night the queen
was not well, but she will not be knoen of it, for the next day shee did
walke abroad in the parke lest any should take notisse of it'.[1] Soon
there was no concealing that something was wrong. At the end of
February 1603 Elizabeth fell sick, and it rapidly became apparent to
her council that she was unlikely to recover. The nature of her illness
remains uncertain – it was put down by most observers to a
'melancholy sickness', to an increasing weariness of life. Rumours,
however, were soon to spread that dark mischief had been at work –
that the queen had fallen victim to a curse placed on a piece of Welsh
gold 'of the bigness of an angel, full of characters', that the Queen of
Hearts had been found nailed through the forehead to the underside
of her chair, and that her *doppelgänger* had been seen stalking the
corridors of the palace, even in broad daylight.[2]

While the slow progress of the disease did allow the council time in which to prepare for the end, the calm efficiency with which they proceeded to take all necessary precautionary measures is impressive. Obviously, the first requirement was to preserve order and prevent unrest in the countryside. To that end, any recusant likely to cause trouble was placed under restraint,[3] seminary priests were banished,[4] unlawful assemblies were prohibited,[5] vagabonds were rounded up,[6] and extra guards were set round prisons and important buildings in London.[7] Significantly, the council also ordered the closer confinement of Arabella Stuart, whose recent, troublesome behaviour was thought by some to have contributed to the onset of Elizabeth's decline.[8]

The council, by now in almost constant session, took the greatest pains to repudiate rumours that the queen was dying. Writing to the lord deputy in Ireland, Lord Mountjoy, on 13 March, they insisted that the royal physicians and, indeed, the evidence of their own eyes had convinced them that there was 'no doubte of her safe and perfect recouery'.[9] But the success of these measures was limited. A secret of such far-reaching importance could hardly be concealed, and rumours of all kinds were rife. Sir John Carey, commander of the exposed frontier garrison at Berwick, wrote in near-hysterical terms of a threatened Scottish invasion,[10] while in London Giovanni Scaramelli the Venetian envoy in England expressed fears that the country might soon be engulfed in religious civil war, with the factions of the Scottish king, Arabella Stuart, and the earl of Hertford all striving for the crown. So far as he could see, Catholic peers had shown no sign of obeying a direction from the council for their repair to court, and many of the religious ministers were hated by the people. It was, he summed up, enough 'to make most men blench'.[11]

To those with a better grasp of the situation, however, there was only one possible successor. Camden, perhaps the greatest propagandist of the Elizabethan regime, wrote scathingly of the great speed and determination shown by 'Puritans, Papists, Ambitious persons and Flatterers of all kinds, and other sorts of men, all of them prompted by their particular Hopes' riding or sending messengers northwards, their sole object being 'to adore the rising King, and get into his Favour'.[12] Channels of communication were indeed reopened now that the time seemed right. Whether or not he should be included in any of Camden's less-than-complimentary categories, Northumberland evidently felt that he should once again send Percy north. On 17 March he wrote, almost certainly with Cecil's knowledge and quite possibly with his encouragement,[13] that the queen's health had been deteriorating steadily over the past month, and that the end could not now be far off. 'This accident', he told James, 'hathe made all the wholle nation looke about them. Men talkes freely of your Maiesties right, and all in generall gevis you a great allowance.'

As for the 'counsell of the staite' he reported with satisfaction that he was now in a position to impart inside knowledge. Realising that their authority would be terminated by the queen's death,[14] the privy councillors had invited noblemen from outside the council to join their deliberations. As it happened, only Northumberland, Lord Thomas Howard, and Lord Cobham had been at court to answer the summons, but plans were in hand to co-opt a more formidable array of peers, plans delayed only by a last lingering hope that Elizabeth might yet recover.

Should the worst happen, the earl was at pains to stress that everything necessary was being done to ensure that the king's accession would be untroubled, a none-too-difficult task given the widespread support for James's cause. At this point, assessing any potential opposition, Northumberland again ventured to express his opinion on the Catholic problem. He maintained, accurately as it transpired, that no trouble should be expected from the Catholics, unless it came from the small minority of 'puritane papistes that thrist after a spanish tytle'. But to his mind even this threat seemed minimal. Only that notorious firebrand Sir Edmund Baynham, captain of the appropriately named 'Damned Crew' had voiced opposition to James, but before he had been able to foment any real trouble he had been arrested and imprisoned. It was at this point that the earl descended to details which were – probably – re-emphasised by Thomas Percy, explaining that he knew some Catholics personally, and that there were others among his household 'famylie' who kept him in close touch with the feelings of co-religionists. Even with such a tight finger on the pulse of Catholic opinion, however, he had been unable to detect anyone opposed to the 'fruiton of your right'. It seemed as though the Catholics had resolved

that if suplications might procure them tollerations of there contienses, they should hold them selves happy; if not they must, by the lawes of god and right, endure it with patience; to which hoapes I ever geve comfort that it wold be obteaned; your Maiesty may doe in this case as your wysest judgement shal derect you

One part of a long letter, these words can obviously be seen in differing lights depending upon the reader's point of view. It is quite legitimate to interpret them as a largely unwarranted assumption of authority to speak for 'the English Catholics', and – if the previous letter in the correspondence is taken into account – even as an attempt to try to suggest terms on which Catholics would support the Stuart claim. This construction would indeed be placed upon them in later years when the earl fell under suspicion of complicity in Gunpowder plot. To a more-charitable or more-practical mind, however, the same phrases can appear simply as a move – possibly encouraged by the council – on the part of a great nobleman to assure the king that all was being managed competently in England and that there was no call for him to consider asserting his rights by force before events ran their natural course.

I have laboured in your vynyard with all the industrie my poore vnderstanding would give me leave. If it shal happen, or pleas god to take from ws oure mistres, you shal have instantly woord, and I think newes of her departure will be sooner with your Maiesty then woord of your being proclaimed amongst ws will ouertake it. I speak it confidently, and therfore I hoope your Maiesty will pardon my ryche thoghts, which are deuoted to your Maiestys service and my cuntries good.[15]

Indeed, this letter perhaps illustrates most clearly, not the political ineptitude of the earl, nor his ambition, but the sagacity of Cecil and the council. At so critical a time, the co-operation of men like Northumberland was essential and Cecil would probably have been the first to advance a suggestion that, even while the queen still lived, the council ought to enter into full consultation with such important figures. And Northumberland was naturally quite prepared to play his part. While it would perhaps be unfair to suggest that he wrote to James purely to ingratiate himself with the king-to-be, there can be no doubt that he, in common with other noblemen in England, harboured hopes of better times under the new dynasty, hopes which would now extend to his son and heir.

But the other side of the argument was no less apparent to contemporaries, and to the earl himself. The Percy family was ancient in name and rich both in lands and dependants. Elizabeth's parsimony with titles had given rise to a situation where in 1603 there were just seventeen peers above the rank of viscount, and apart from the three privy councillors Charles Howard, Earl of Nottingham, Gilbert Talbot, Earl of Shrewsbury, and Edward Somerset, Earl of Worcester, none could match both Northumberland's evident ambition and his credentials of birth and experience at court.[16] The clash with Vere, in which his actions had been widely censured, lay almost a year in the past, long superseded by other scandals. On all sides, those in authority were desperate for the support of anyone wielding actual, potential, or even symbolic power in the country. The attraction of Northumberland was that he offered all three. What Cecil realised, though – and it is something which the earl perhaps never quite saw until it was too late – was that prominence arising at such a moment from these elements alone was bound to be transitory; if Northumberland sought a permanent role in English politics once the new monarch was settled on the throne, he would be called upon to display real political gifts in areas of day-to-day administration. For all his birth and breeding, the earl was a novice in such matters.

These considerations, however, lay in the future. James received the earl's letter about five days after it was written, and replied on 24 March, praising Northumberland's loyalty and good sense. In common with his other replies to the earl – both in contrast to his correspondence with Cecil and against his usual inclinations – James kept his letter brief. He dismissed any idea of staging an invasion of England to establish his title and said very little on the subject of the Catholics:

I will nather persecutt any that wilbe quyet, and give but ane wtward obedience to the law, nather will I spare to aduance any of them that will by good service woorthelly deserve it; and if this cours wil not serve to win every particular honest man, my prevy dealing with any of them can availl but lytle.[17]

Such a reply, of course, left every option open, and in this verbal fencing prior to the event Northumberland can have expected nothing else. At first sight, what the king said here, as in a similar, more-extensive passage during his correspondence with Cecil,[18] seems to provide grounds for Catholic optimism, but the natural condition of 'outward obedience to the law' – a law designed to impose rather than ease burdens on Catholics – makes it plain enough that James was promising nothing. The one point to note from this exchange, indeed, is that the king probably meant exactly what he said. His religious views were tolerant; with hindsight showing us how policy unfolded through his reign, it can be said with some justification that he stood opposed to extreme persecution and undue toleration of Catholics alike. So long as they showed no sign of militancy and so long as their numbers did not begin to rise dramatically, he was genuinely prepared to allow them at least a tacit liberty of conscience, for he held sincerely to the view that the Catholic church, however 'clogged' with impurities and imperfections that made it intolerable to good Christians, remained the mother church and deserved respect as such.[19]

No promise was therefore ever given to the Catholics that their burdens would be lifted, but the hope of such a sea-change in attitudes remained. Just what action the earl took upon receiving James's letter remains a mystery. Immediately after Elizabeth's death Thomas Percy, perhaps acting on his own initiative, was giving out 'very comfortable newes' from the king 'concerninge the Catholique cause, and for toleration of Catholique religion'.[20] Putting his own interpretation on the king's words, Northumberland too gave some assurance at James's accession that Catholics might expect more lenient treatment in future. It is safe to assert that much, but it is impossible, given the amount of exaggerated accusation and denial at the time of Gunpowder plot, to go further and attempt to gauge the extent of such assurances, to guess at the names of the people to whom he gave them, or to try to fathom his motives in so doing. Unfortunately, hard evidence is simply lacking.

With no direct, comprehensive source for the council's actions in March 1603, one is led to rely on its extant decrees, and accounts of its deliberations written by not always well-informed men. The reports of the French ambassador, Beaumont, are among the most informative, if not always the most reliable, sources on an obscure period. Seeing his contact's star in the ascendant Beaumont took to writing colourful accounts of meetings of the augmented privy council. At one of these Northumberland was proposed, in the first instance by Cecil, as protector of the realm and 'général des gens de guerre qu'il doit rallier de tous costez pour tenir la campagne'. For Beaumont, elated by his success, such high honour was no less than the man's due; ever since he had arrived in England he had judged that with such spirit, courage, and ambition, Northumberland would prove to be 'le plus emploié et recherché lors que le changement arrivera'. Still unable to claim Northumberland for the

Catholic church, Beaumont nevertheless remained convinced that
the earl was 'Catholique en son ame'.

This shortly before 18 March.[21] From an independent source we
learn that Northumberland brought fifty cavalry horses to Essex
House at about the same time, perhaps as a show of strength,
perhaps to have them ready against some unforeseen emergency.[22]
Four days later, Beaumont had virtually given up hope of the queen's
recovery. The council, he wrote, was assembling all important men
in town – although there was a rumour that the earl of Hertford had
refused to come. It had by this time decided against appointing
Northumberland as protector: 'il semble qu'a cause des jalousies des
grands ils déliberant au lieu du comte de Nortumberland seul . . .
deslire [d'élire] quatre seigneurs par les provinces'.[23]

One must allow that the obvious source of Beaumont's information was Northumberland himself, and consequently one must also
concede that the information is prone to exaggeration and
embellishment at two stages: when passing from the earl to
Beaumont and also from Beaumont to Henri IV and his ministers.
Nevertheless, the despatches do show clearly the importance of
leading noblemen at such a time. Of course, they show something
more, they bear out Howard's charge that the earl was an
untrustworthy man who could not keep a secret. It is difficult to find
excuses for Northumberland's actions. He may have felt that no real
harm could be done by disclosing this information to one whom he
clearly considered to be his true friend; all ports were closed and the
French would be unable to profit from their ambassador's
knowledge until it was too late. It is even possible that he acted with
the full consent of the council. England and France were, after all, at
peace, and as the next few years would show it was not then uncommon for councillors to pass information to and receive pensions from
friendly powers.[24] All the same, such revelations came at a singularly
inappropriate time, and were made by one who was himself no
councillor, simply someone called in on trust by the council to give
advice and assistance in the extremity of his sovereign. It hardly
made for an auspicious start to Northumberland's career as a leading
political figure.

Despite the possible alternatives outlined by Beaumont, power
was indeed kept firmly in the council's hands. As tension grew it
maintained its grip, instructing the justices of Middlesex on 23
March to comply with former directions and see to it that appointed

watches were well manned.[25] By this time, the queen was *in extremis*, and she died in the early hours of the following morning. The news was soon out. Reporting her death, Scaramelli wrote in melodramatic terms of a capital gripped by fear of Catholic revolt, sending his despatch out of the country by several different routes in the hope that, whatever happened, one copy at least would get through.[26] Not for the first time, though, the Venetian showed himself out of touch with events. A proclamation declaring the succession of James had already been drawn up, signed by an imposing array of former privy councillors and other spiritual and temporal lords then in the capital.[27] By mid-morning, the assembled councillors and peers had travelled together from the deathbed at Richmond to Whitehall, proclaiming England's first Stuart king at the court gates.

At about eleven o'clock Cecil read the proclamation to a crowd of curious, excited Londoners at Cheapside. Their reaction was muted at first, 'silent joye . . . for the succession of soe worthy a king' being concealed for the time being, perhaps out of respect for the dead queen. In what was clearly a pre-planned move to ensure the support of the city authorities, the lords then rode through London to the sheriff's house from where, after short consultation, they sent three heralds and a trumpeter to proclaim the alteration in the Tower of London and upon Tower Hill. As one might expect, the news was welcomed by many Tower prisoners, and especially by the former earl of Southampton who, his title forfeited, had been held there since the Essex rebellion. Knowing that James felt kindly disposed towards him, he now realised that his hour of release was near. Walking on the leads when he heard the proclamation he tossed his hat three times into the air, on the third occasion throwing it clear over the walls of the fortress 'that all vppon the tower hill might behold yt'.

And that was just about that. The occupation of London and the acquiescence of the city on behalf of a claimant supported by the great majority of the peerage of England would have been enough to forestall the most determined of opponents. By the afternoon, street gossip was discussing, not the imminent perils of a contested throne, but rather the possible 'advancement of the nobility'. By nightfall, bonfires blazed across the city, and bells rang in the churches. There was, to the relief of observers, 'noe tumult, noe contradicion, noe disorder in the city', and although a diligent round-the-clock watch had been set at every gate and street 'to prevent garboiles', such problems had already proved to be 'more feared then perceived'.[28]

While control of the capital was vital, no early-modern government could afford to take the acquiescence of the localities for granted. Over the next couple of days, messages were sent into the country describing events in London and enclosing copies of the proclamation to be read in shire towns.[29] Nor did the council waste a moment in sending word to James. While Sir Robert Carey had taken horse for Edinburgh the moment Elizabeth died, the official message was drawn up and despatched early on the morning of 25 March, carried by Sir Charles Percy, Northumberland's brother, and Thomas Somerset, son of the earl of Worcester.[30] Subsequently, Sir Thomas Lake, clerk of the signet, followed them, with orders to instruct the king in the immediate needs of the English administration.[31] This was essentially a courtesy. There would be scope enough in days to come for James to make any alterations he desired, but in the mean time his new kingdom awaited his coming in order and quiet.

Notes

1   PRO SP 12/284/97, dated 6 Aug 1602

2   Tierney, *Dodd's Church History*, iii, pp 70–4, from 'The Relation of the Lady Southwell of the late Q death, primo Aprilis 1607', a manuscript in the collection of Stonyhurst College

3   *APC 1601–4*, p 491, privy council order, 12 Mar 1603. For further examples of measures taken by the council see Munden, 'Politics of Accession', pp 80–2

4   *APC 1601–4*, p 491, privy council order, 15 Mar 1603

5   BL Lansdowne MS 157, fol 244; Egerton MS 2644, fol 124; HMC, *Rutland*, i, p 388; *Sir Henry Whithed's Letter-Book*, pp 9–10, copy of the draft letter to the county officials, 15 Mar 1603, and copies of the letters to the officials in Essex, Derbyshire, and Hampshire dated the following day

6   BL Lansdowne MS 160, fol 234; Harley MS 703, fol 132v; Additional MS 48591, fol 147–7v; *Sir Henry Whithed's Letter-Book*, pp 11–12. The excuse given was that these men were to be sent to serve in the Low Countries. The original order applied to a 10-mile radius round London, and was sent to four home counties on 14 March (*APC 1601–4*, pp 491–2). It was extended to eighteen further counties on 17 March (*ibid*, p 492)

7   *APC 1601–4*, p 492; PRO E407/56, fol 196, guards were set on the receipt at Westminster on 18 March and at the Gatehouse prison from 21 March

8   HMC, *Rutland*, i, p 388; *Calendar SP Venetian 1592–1603*, pp 554–7; Bruce, *Correspondence*, p 72

9   Bodleian MS Tanner 76, fol 175

10   Hatfield MS 92/42

11   *Calendar SP Venetian 1592–1603*, p 558

12   Camden, *History*, p 660

13   From what he himself says in the letter, Northumberland seems to have been working in close accord with the Secretary

14   The privy councillor swore a personal oath to serve the sovereign (Jensen, 'Staff of the Jacobean Privy Council', pp 41–4; *APC 1613–14*, pp 4–5)

15   Bruce, *Correspondence*, pp 72–5. The letter reached the king on 22 March according to Edward Bruce, who told Henry Howard (*ibid*, p 47) 'It is wery discretly and temperatly wreattin, and in all points wery nere the trewthe. He says not that he is a catholike him selfe, but that sondrie of hes retenow and dependance hath ores in there bot, and that thay ar not able to resolwe in any cours wyth the whiche he sall not be mad acquented.' Northumberland had several Catholic servants in his household (Batho, *Household Papers*, p xx). For Baynham, see also *Camdeni epistolae*, pp 347–8; Sprott, 'Sir Edmund Baynham', p 101; see also BL Sloane MS 414, fol 58v

16   See appendix 2 for a list of the higher nobility in 1603

17   Bruce, *Correspondence*, pp 75–6; Akrigg, *Letters of James VI and I*, pp 206–7

18   Bruce, *Correspondence*, pp 36–7; Akrigg, *Letters of James VI and I*, pp 204–5

19   Wormald, 'Two Kings or One?', pp 197–8, 203–4; Willson, *James VI and I*, pp 217–42; La Rocca, 'Who Can't Pray With Me, Can't Love Me', pp 22–31; Fincham and Lake, 'Ecclesiastical Policy of James I', pp 182–6. See also La Rocca's thesis 'English Catholics and the Recusancy Laws', particularly pp 181–293

20   PRO SP 14/19/40; Foley, *Records*, iv, p 156, Henry Garnett's examination of 12 Mar 1606

21   BL King's MS 123, fols 11–12, 13v–14. Other copies of Beaumont's reports 1603–5 are in PRO (Transcripts) PRO 31/3/35–41 and BL Additional MSS 30638–41. Copies all correspond in passages quoted

22   HMC, *Buccleuch*, i, p 236. The original letter (letters vol 3, p 143) gives no clue to the exact date on which Northumberland made this move

23   BL King's MS 123, fols 16–19; *APC 1601–4*, p 492 records that other lords then near London were summoned to court on 20 March. One wonders, and doubts, whether the notion of appointing a protector ever really found the degree of support Beaumont initially suggested, or even whether it was seriously considered at any stage. If such ideas were discussed, the natural reluctance to place too much power in too few hands ensured that no protector was ever named

24   Loomie, 'Toleration and Diplomacy', pp 54–5. See also A J Loomie, 'Sir Robert Cecil and the Spanish Embassy', *Bulletin of the Institute of Historical Research*, XLII, 1969, pp 30–57, esp pp 54–7; Peck, 'Corruption', p 85

25   BL Additional MS 12507, fol 69

26   *Calendar SP Venetian 1592–1603*, pp 562–3

27   PRO SP 14/1/1; Strype, *Annals of the Reformation*, iv, pp 516–19. The signatories vary in the subsequent printed versions (Munden, 'Politics of Accession', p 84n)

28   BL Stowe MS 150, fol 180, Thomas Ferrers to Humphrey Ferrers, 25 Mar 1603; Stow, *Annales*, p 817; Sorlien, *Diary of John Manningham*, pp 208–9; Scott, 'Wilbraham's Journal', p 54

29   For example see BL Stowe MS 150, fol 182; Additional MS 48591, fol 150; Folger Shakespeare Library MS V b 142, fol 65; HMC, *7th Report*, appendix, p 667; BL Harley MS 703, fols 131v–2, the lords and former councillors at Whitehall to the county officials in Derbyshire, Norfolk, Suffolk, Surrey, and Sussex, 25 Mar 1603

30   For Carey's ride see Mares, *Memoirs of Robert Carey*, pp 60–4. For the official embassy see Stow, *Annales*, p 817; Nicholls, 'Sir Charles Percy', pp 241–2

31   Stow, *Annales*, p 817

IX

A power in the land

It is easy to belittle the council's achievement in 1603 – it had warning of Elizabeth's impending demise, it had really little choice in her successor, and it followed a course of action which while logical was hardly profound. Yet for all that, its handling of events was remarkably smooth and efficient. It announced a *fait accompli* in unambiguous terms, and it announced this promptly to a country where the last death of a sovereign was forty-five years in the past and where antipathy to a Scottish succession ran high.[1] Rumour of some kind was as inevitable as it was without foundation – for a time there was talk that the earl of Hertford had risen in revolt on behalf of his son. But this was soon proved quite false by the Seymour family's wholehearted support for James,[2] and the great council of noblemen continued to administer a peaceful country, concerning itself with routine tasks until the king was ready to organise his own council with the men he wanted.[3]

Moreover, it did so with apparent amity and good grace. Gardiner, it is true, described one meeting of the great council soon after the queen's death where discord rather than harmony was the order of the day, with Northumberland the focus of dissent. Following his summons to assist the council, Gardiner maintained, an excited, determined Northumberland had appeared at the head of more than one hundred men, saying openly that it had become imperative to declare James as the successor, and threatening to slay any alternative candidate. With Elizabeth now dead, the earl

stepped forward in defence of the privileges of the old nobility. He had heard that the Privy Councillors had met at the Earl of Nottingham's, in order to take measures for removing the Queen's body to London. He thought this a good opportunity to remind them that, in consequence of the death of the Queen, they had ceased to occupy any official position, until they were confirmed in their places by the new King. He told them that the peerage had too long been treated with contempt, and that they were determined to submit to it no longer. Sir Thomas Egerton, the Lord Keeper, with admirable self-control, at once admitted that his authority ceased with the death of the Queen, and proposed that he, and all the Councillors who were not members of the Upper House, should resign to the Lords their seats at the head of the table. The Peers who were present would not hear of this proposal, and everything went on as usual.[4]

Because it bears so directly on any study of Northumberland's attitude towards the king's accession it is worth examining Gardiner's account in some detail. As its author admitted, this passage was based on four imperfect and at times contradictory sources. The suggestion that Northumberland had staged a preliminary show of strength in support of James – perhaps after bringing the fifty chargers to London – is found in a despatch composed by Beaumont's successor, newly arrived in London and writing three years after the event, on the eve of the earl's trial. Somewhat similar, no better authenticated stories remained in circulation for many years.[5]

Reviewing the evidence it appears that Gardiner confused two quite separate meetings, one on the morning of Elizabeth's death, the other on 25 March. Of his remaining authorities, two are anonymous accounts of events surrounding Elizabeth's death. Only one of these, apparently written by someone acquainted with the court, contains any hint of tension between council and other members of the nobility.[6] It suggests that some peers, well aware that much then depended on their goodwill, were only too ready to take offence at the actions of the queen's councillors. The insensitive meeting at Nottingham's house had presented them with an opportunity to express their doubts over the nature of privy council authority. But at this point in his story the author abruptly changes subject, and in any case he mentions no name. The second anonymous source, which seems to be some form of widely circulated 'official' version of events, contains not the slightest hint of such discord.[7] Referring to the council meeting which took place on the morning of 24 March, it has Egerton politely volunteering to surrender his place at the head of the council table, and the lords, equally politely, unanimously declining his offer.

It is only in the last of Gardiner's sources, another of Beaumont's despatches, that one finds any reference to Northumberland. According to the ambassador, when the great council assembled at Whitehall on 25 March the former privy councillors expressed a wish to continue holding independent meetings as if the queen were still alive. Those noblemen not of the council greeted this suggestion with dismay, and Northumberland, speaking for all the 'born councillors of the realm' is reported to have said

que la noblesse d'Angleterre avoit été trop longuement méprise et deprimée. Et qu'aujourd'huy elle n'étoit plus resolu de le souffrir et que ce seroit en donner au roy vne tres mauvaise opinion et un pernicieux example s'ils enduroient d'être ainsy traittez avec d'autres termes semblables digne de son courage et de son entendement qui firent que ces messieurs leur vserent de grandes excuses.[8]

In Beaumont's account, it was only then that Egerton made his offer promising, in order to avoid 'vn grand schisme', that the council would not be assembled without the assistance of the lords. The truth or otherwise of the story thus rests on the trustworthiness of Beaumont alone, and if one chooses to accept his version the former privy council appear to carry some share of the blame for precipitating an unnecessary conflict. By prefacing Beaumont's report with the rumour-mongering of his successor, Gardiner perhaps exaggerates the element of conflict in the exchange. In any case, harmony – universally seen as essential at such a time – was soon restored, and there is no evidence of further exchanges along these lines.

So it proved quite unnecessary for James to hurry south. Reassured by the evident tranquility in England, he did not cross the border until 7 April. On his slow journey towards London, however, the king gave much thought to the composition of his council. As an immediate, interim measure he had adopted Elizabeth's entire privy council, instructing them to continue in consultation with any nobleman they thought necessary. He intended to decide on additions to their number only after reaching London. At Berwick, however, he expressed concern that when some of his councillors came north to meet him, there would be insufficient of their number left in London to attend to all necessary affairs of state. He therefore ordered that four noblemen 'of whose maturitie of yeares, sufficiency of iudgment, and experience in employmentes vnder the queene defunct we haue very good information' be at once added to the council. Those so favoured were the earls of Northumberland and Cumberland, and Lords Mountjoy and Howard de Walden. Ostensibly, this made it possible for fitter and younger councillors to come and greet him, while 'the elder sort not so meet for painfull travaile' might await his arrival in the capital.[9]

But this bland explanation appears to have concealed a more pressing reason to appoint new councillors. As a Scottish king James had much experience of factious noblemen, and he seems to have already had in mind the early dissolution of the emergency 'great council'. In such matters, though, he would also have been aware of the advisability of treading delicately. These creations were possibly designed to draw the teeth of potential opposition to the termination of interim arrangements. Writing three days later, from Newcastle, the king repeated his commands, but gave another reason for the new appointments which pointed both to the imminent end of his great council and perhaps also to a further expansion of his privy council. Implicitly criticising his predecessor's practice he expressed fears that, 'when the rest of our peeres, with whome you are joyned, shalbe seuered from you hereafter' the council – although no smaller than in Elizabeth's last years – would be too small to carry out their duties most effectively.[10]

These appointments would have confirmed a commonly held opinion that the king would be by nature conservative in his choice of councillors. Francis Bacon, who had travelled north at an early stage, wrote to Northumberland observing that the king 'affecteth popularitie by graceing such as he hath heard to be populare, and not by any fashions of his owne' – James seemed to be a man set on his pet scheme to unite the kingdoms of England and Scotland, apparently 'somewhat generall in his favours', and preferring to look to 'tyme past' for his 'councell', rather than to 'tyme to come'.[11] Even though Bacon added a warning that it was as yet too early to form any fixed conclusions about the king's intentions his letter must have made cheering reading. When a prisoner in the Tower three years later Northumberland wrote sadly to the king that he had expected more reasons to look for 'comfort' under James than had ever in fact materialised.[12]

In 1603, many others shared his optimism. Scaramelli, writin on 21 April, passed on the latest gossip, much of it pretty crude and inaccurate, but reflecting a general belief that the king would continue to support those houses and persons who were oppressed by the late Queen. In pursuance of that policy . . . he has named the Earl of Northumberland of the Privy Council. The Earl had been as it were banished from Court because his estates on the borders of Scotland, near the North Sea, were so great, and because the Queen had some suspicion of those secret intelligences with the King of Scotland, which are now apparent.[13]

It is interesting to note that the secret correspondence was by then common knowledge. With Northumberland's fortunes beginning to 'florishe',[14] those who looked upon him as their patron also began to anticipate better days. Dudley Carleton, then employed somewhat unhappily in Paris, received letters from friends in England urging him to capitalise on his good relationship with the earl, although his cautious brother George warned him not to raise his hopes too high, fearing that Northumberland might not receive all the favours he had promised himself under a 'mean' king.[15] Thomas Edmondes, then at court, had few such doubts. He told Carleton that he had put in many good words with the earl on his friend's behalf, Northumberland having recently assured him that

for the love he beareth to you he hath reserved himself to the choice of you to use in the place of chiefest trust and neareness about him; at such tyme as he should receive better meanes of fortune and advancement in the state which for that he doth nowe promise himself in this our newe world, and thereby to be able . . . to doe you good, he desireth that you will nowe come speedelie to him, because he shall have present use of your service.[16]

Carleton was not to be disappointed. Later in the year he was employed by the earl as comptroller of his household and also as a personal secretary.

Word of Northumberland's new importance in English affairs spread fast, more than one continental observer concluding that the Percies would come into their own in James's 'newe world'. When the magistrates of Geneva sent an envoy to congratulate the king on his succession – and to solicit material assistance – they thought it worth their while to send letters to Northumberland and Cecil at the same time.[17] The earl was naturally keen to let nothing detract from his new-found status. Probably some time in May 1603, confined to Syon by illness, he wrote to Cecil remarking that he had heard of a commission to the privy council to examine 'and allow of sutche sutes as shall be thought fitt to haue waye, in which there are certain of the coram [quorum]'. 'I trust,' he continued, 'of yowr ancient loue and profession that yow hold me worthy to be one of them, if I shall not, the disgrace would wound me very nieghe, and the dishonor would appeare palpable to the whole worlde; the eies of many lookes vpon me and soe mutche the more I am sensible in this point.' Gently, he reminded Cecil that his ambitions were 'within limitts', and that these were 'not great matters'.[18]

Meanwhile, all sides waited to see what religious policy the king would follow. For some Catholics, relaxation of the Elizabethan persecutions was a sign of success in itself, but others already felt let down that more was not being done, and began to murmur against the new regime. At least there was the option of seeking redress from the new monarch, and the chance to do so through the mediation of powerful friends. When the king reached Theobalds, Cecil's Hertfordshire mansion, early in May, he met Northumberland for the first time, receiving him with signs of favour and affection.[19] One of the earl's first actions was to present just such a petition on behalf of Catholics. The petition was carefully designed to strike a favourable chord, for it dwelt at some length on the loyalty of Catholics to James's mother, working on an interpretation of James's *Basilikon Doron*. It pointed out, moreover, that Catholics alone could be made to obey the king by religious stricture.[20]

Unfortunately, the petition seems to have missed its mark, for by awakening memories of Mary Stuart, it also inevitably led to thoughts on the plots that had surrounded the queen of Scots during her captivity, and no monarch liked to contemplate treason, however well-intended. While Northumberland was subsequently to argue that he had simply been acting out of charity towards humble supplicants – he had himself refused to sign the petition, of course – James might have seen the move as one more attempt by the earl to speak with authority for the English Catholics. And this was worrying – for while James had by then tamed and lived on good terms with his once-turbulent Scots nobility,[21] his timid nature kept him fully aware of the potential such men held for ill as well as for good. Until he knew more, much more, about Northumberland and other powerful English noblemen, the king would have trodden very warily.

James reached London soon after, to a rapturous reception which pleased him immensely.[22] Almost at once he established his formal bodyguard, taking Elizabeth's band of gentlemen pensioners into his own service. The ailing Lord Hunsdon, who had recently relinquished his post of lord chamberlain to the earl of Suffolk,[23] also stood down from his captaincy of the band and the king, perhaps at the earl's request, chose Northumberland as his successor. On 18 May 1603, he wrote to his new captain requiring him to ensure that every man under his command was acquainted with certain cardinal rules governing admission and conduct.[24] In the first place, Northumberland was to see that every man joining the band took the oath of supremacy, recognising James as head of the church – Catholics were not wanted this close to the royal person. He was also told to 'take particular information whether they are of meanes and ability to maintaine themselfs in that sort as the place requires', and to make it clear that pensioners were forbidden to sell or otherwise bargain away their positions. The earl subsequently so disregarded these clear instructions that he made Thomas Percy a pensioner and failed to ensure that Percy took the necessary oath.[25] But the catastrophic miscalculation was obvious only in hindsight, for surely James could rely on the 'ancient Mercury'[26] who had risked so much to carry messages to and fro between himself and the earl – a man whom he had trusted with his replies, and who was highly respected and favoured by Northumberland?

No formal response appears to have been made to any Catholic petition, and the more turbulent spirits began to voice doubts that the king meant to help them. On the 'secular' side, William Watson decided to take drastic action, and began to hatch a scheme to kidnap the king and to hold him prisoner in the Tower of London, demanding in return for his release a pardon, full toleration of the Catholic religion, foreign Catholic guarantors of the new status quo, and the removal from office of Cecil and others seen as representatives of the Elizabethan persecution.

Through his relative George Brooke, Lord Cobham – now fully alienated from Cecil – became at least aware of this enterprise, which was to be put into effect on midsummer night while the king lay at Hanworth. Cobham, almost certainly with the full knowledge and prompting of Sir Walter Ralegh, was himself in communication with the envoy from Spanish Flanders, Aremberg, and their lengthy political discussions included clearly treasonous talk which, at some point, dwelt on means of ridding England altogether of James and his family, colourfully termed the 'king and his cubs'. Some adherents of Watson's plot did not scruple to seek help from discontented extremists on the protestant side, including a small, shady group round Lord Grey de Wilton, also considering an attempt to 'remove' the king. Coke later likened these plots to Sampson's foxes: joined at the tails, though the heads were severed – an apt comparison.[27]

It is impossible here to investigate the Bye, Main, and Grey plots in any great depth, but it is at least fair to say that attempts to demonstrate the innocence of any of these conspirators fail to convince. The obvious bitterness felt by both Ralegh and Cobham at their reception by James led both men to commit certain indiscretions which could all too easily be shaped to fit a charge of treason. Ralegh had apparently been expecting trouble, he had felt keenly his dismissal from the post of captain of the guard – he was replaced by a Scot – and the loss of Durham House, which he had been ordered to return to the bishop of Durham in June.[28] The personal attractions of Ralegh,[29] his dignified bearing during his eventual trial for treason in November 1603,[30] where he won a great deal of public sympathy, and the obscurity of the case against him – the affair was aptly described by Rushworth as 'a dark kind of treason'[31] – should not blind us to his political ineptitude. Betrayed by their opponents among the English Catholics, both as a means of demonstrating loyalty to the new king and as a token that many still expected some good from the change in dynasty, Watson and Clarke were unquestionably guilty, and the only sympathy they deserve is that accorded to the wholly incompetent. Like Ralegh, Grey's upright conduct at his trial won him a good deal of favourable comment, but he never tried to deny his crime.[32]

In fact, these treasons of 1603 demonstrate above all else the vigour of the privy council in dealing swiftly with the threat of trouble, and the king's tolerance. From the first whiff of treason, the council had stepped up its watch on known malcontents, had widened its enquiries as new information came to light, and had at no point over-reacted to the problem, moving in on Ralegh only when it had sufficient information.[33] James in turn demonstrated a clemency unusual to those brought up under his predecessor's regime, pardoning all but Watson, Clarke, and George Brooke, although decreeing that Ralegh, Cobham, Grey, and a Catholic gentleman involved in the conspiracy, Sir Griffin Markham, should appear on the scaffold in Winchester before being told that they were to live.[34]

Such treatment was in accord with what we know of James's aversion to excessive bloodshed, but it was also a calculated bid to show that the king and his administration were still prepared to start with a clean sheet. The English Catholics – divided as ever – now by and large tended to adopt an attitude of 'wait-and-see'. Understanding the wishes of his royal master, Cecil did nothing to persuade them that they were mistaken in at least tacitly accepting the Stuart monarch – throughout 1603 the recusancy laws went virtually unenforced.[35]

The divisions among the Catholics indeed probably worked in their favour, for although the cruder forms of protestant propaganda would never recognise the fact, those in power realised that the political threat posed by a small and divided community would never be that great. James and his ministers were at all times bargaining from a position of strength; tolerance not toleration was all that was on offer.[36] While the treasons in 1603 inevitably gave further ammunition to those who believed that no trust could be placed in a Catholic, the fact that they had been revealed by Catholics helped the authorities hold to their stated reluctance to persecute for religion. With Richard Bancroft, who succeeded John Whitgift as archbishop of Canterbury in February 1604, Cecil tried to work on such tensions, to persuade the 'seculars' that their dreams of toleration were by no means groundless, that they 'could expect more from their own countrymen than from foreign Jesuits'.[37] Doubtless the majority of those appealed to, stout Englishmen that they were, would hope for nothing less. Cecil's religious convictions were, like so many aspects of his character, enigmatic, but he never quite matched his father's antipathy to Catholicism, nor, perhaps, did he share William Cecil's fervency of faith.[38] He spoke in earnest when declaring his opposition to open toleration, but were the Catholics to disavow the pope's claim to hold a power of deposition over princes, and were they also to live quietly, he was prepared to turn a blind eye to what Northumberland called 'a messe in a cornere'.[39] Thus it was that, although king and Secretary found it expedient to banish all priests from the realm in 1604, those who had caused no political disturbances, which meant the vast majority, went largely unmolested about their business.[40]

During the secret correspondence, Cecil had told James that, while he condemned the Catholic priesthood, he nevertheless had no wish 'to see them dy by dosens when (at the last gasp) they come so neare loyalty'. For the subversive Jesuits, however, 'who make no more ordinary merchandise of any thing then of the blood and crownes of Princes', he had no such compassion. They were nothing but a 'generation of vypars' and in their case James would have to order him to 'abstaine [rather] then prosecute'.[41] This was partly an expression of belief calculated to reassure the Scottish king, but it was also the statement of a politically astute man.

James had agreed, although he had advised Cecil that those who 'seame to professe loyaltie' might yet pose a threat, since

lyke maried uemen or minors, quhose uowes are euer subiect to the controlment of thaire husbandis and tutoris, thaire consciences must euer be comandit and ouerreulid by thaire romishe god as it pleasis him to allowe or reuoke thaire conclusions.[42]

Yet even against the Jesuits, James inclined to a moderate course. Inasmuch as he had a clear policy in the matter, the king saw it as a problem to be solved by expulsion rather than execution. America rather than Tyburn was to benefit, colonies far from the shores of England being seen as ideal places for men of a corrupt religion to 'glutte thaime selfis upon thaire imaginated goddis'.[43] James at all times showed an ability to detach himself from the narrow confines of bigotry – even politically expedient bigotry. The years 1603–5 show him actually pursuing the remarkably ambitious goal of Christian unity, and even as they survive in his writings the range of his professions on religious matters – from a denouncement of the pope as Antichrist to an insistence that only the papacy's claim to have the power of deposing secular princes stood between Europe's rival churches and true unity – allowed him the scope to make men of all persuasions suspect that he had their interests at heart. To any observer, a court which tolerated crypto-Catholics such as Northampton, Worcester, and Lord Wotton in its highest reaches also clearly held out the promise of a toleration for all who outwardly conformed.[44] Yet the outward display was vital. On Easter Day 1603, the Catholic gentlemen of the new court failed to attend divine service. On learning of their absence, James declared trenchantly that he 'who can't pray with me, can't love me'.[45]

Early restraint shown in collecting recusancy fines did not survive pressure brought to bear from interested financial parties and growing evidence that Catholic numbers were rapidly increasing in the prevalent atmosphere of toleration.[46] The latter was understandable and was hardly due to successful evangelical activity, as men who had previously concealed their beliefs through fear were now again prepared to risk public profession, but to the leading protestant gentlemen of the counties there was no question that leniency at the top was being overdone. James was ready, when addressing the parliament of 1604, to highlight the problem in more-aggressive terms, but beneath the rhetoric he did not alter his relaxed stance. Indeed in his speech of 19 March he said openly that he wished to see a general Christian union, stressing that he would meet the Catholics half way in a search for this utopia while at the same time warning them that they should not feel thereby empowered to daily increase their numbers and strength in the kingdom.[47] Though the recusancy laws were reimposed, they were enforced in such a way that estates were often placed in the hands of the recusants themselves, or of friends who could be relied upon to act in their interests.[48] The burden, so far as central government was concerned, remained essentially financial.

Outbursts of persecution in the shires prompted the council to confirm this approach. During September 1604 the king convened a well-attended council meeting to discuss a petition which complained that some local justices had lately imprisoned Catholics, even though they had paid their fines for recusancy. Possibly informed of the details by Henry Howard, by now earl of Northampton and an active privy councillor, the Spanish ambassador included an account of the deliberations in one of his despatches. According to this report, the majority of the council, Northumberland included, had argued for a continuance of the 'soft' line towards recusants, advocated by Cecil but strongly opposed by Lords Burghley, Kinloss, and Ellesmere, and Sir John Popham. In the end there had been agreement that tolerance – dependent on Catholic docility – should not be withdrawn, 'for they intend nothing against the state of our country'.[49]

It is obviously difficult to gauge the extent to which the hopes of Catholics had been raised at James's succession and dashed thereafter, but it is probably fair to say that, with few exceptions, decades of persecution had bred in the majority of Catholics, wealthy and poor alike, a cynical attitude which would have welcomed any practical improvement in their lot rather than an ill-judged expectation that James would change their state overnight.

For the missionary Jesuits and their supporters, however, it had very soon become apparent that James's offers would never allow them the degree of toleration they sought. Indeed, some among them had probably given up hope of James before his succession, convinced that half-way houses were anathema and well realising that he could never give them their hearts' desire, a Catholic England. For men of this persuasion, it would have become ever more obvious that an effective easing of the penal laws would only encourage Catholics to compromise with the authorities, laying fresh temptations in the paths of right-thinking men hitherto united by persecution. While many Catholics could shrug their shoulders and see the new regime – with all its imperfections – as being preferable to the old, there were others who saw nothing but 'a fresh persecution more bitter and grievous than the last'.[50] These zealots, as Northumberland had warned James in 1602, had long pinned their hopes, not upon change from within, but upon an alteration imposed upon England from without. Yet with France now on friendly terms with England, and with negotiations underway to end the protracted war with Spain, prospects of such an alteration were receding fast. Articles of peace finally concluded by the Treaty of London in August 1604 made no mention of the English Catholics, Philip III resting content with verbal guarantees from James that they would escape persecution for their faith. For some, his decision signified an end to hopes of help from the Catholic continent; Englishmen would henceforth have to endure, or act, on their own.[51] This is a consideration of the first importance in understanding the genesis of Gunpowder plot.

The king and council could never be accused of exaggerating the Catholic problem. They saw it for what it was, a potentially serious political threat if harnessed by the wrong forces, but in itself incapable of sustaining a challenge to established authority – political or religious – in England. Naturally, they appreciated the dangers of complacency, and fears that the Catholics were increasing in numbers, especially when set against the failure of attempts by the state church to advance its own faith among the populace, produced growing pressure to reimpose restrictions. Any unrest, such as the 'stirs' in Herefordshire during May 1605 which arose from the refusal of a parish priest to bury the body of an excommunicate Catholic, led to adverse reactions from a king and council anxious to preserve order and peace in the extremities of the land.[52] On 9 June the king ordered the circuit judges to 'enquire of all recusants in their circuits', expressing his willingness to see the Herefordshire rioters severely punished.[53] But again, harsh words did not precede harsh actions.

For when viewing the religious situation in England, James and his ministers saw not only the potential Catholic threat but also, as Lord Grey's treason had strikingly demonstrated, a danger from quite another quarter. Here too the government, although naturally concerned, never lost its head, always realising that an 'extremist' minority of whatever persuasion could ultimately be thwarted without great difficulty. The 'purer' protestants – loosely called 'puritans' – never comprised an organised party, and contained a range of diverse views. They were, and remained throughout James's reign, an expression of dissatisfaction, of opposition to what they saw as a reformation but half carried through, and their own divisions contributed to the overwhelming endorsement of the episcopal status quo and rejection of further innovation which emerged from the Hampton Court conference of 1604.[54]

The council wisely chose to minimise puritan beliefs, and to work upon divisions between the moderates who sought a purer form of worship and the 'turbulent humours' of those who demanded an end to episcopal jurisdiction within the church.[55] James's bishops, not all unsympathetic to some forms of puritanism, exercised the same cautious approach which helped divert the main thrust of presbyterian reform in England.[56] Humour too played a part in ridiculing the excesses of the 'stricter sort', Northumberland, here apparently sharing common goals with his king, illustrating this popular stance: in what appears to have been the draft of a letter to James he gave a colourful description of an elaborate feast held to celebrate the peace with Spain, making in passing a reference to more-radical elements within the English church. 'Great intertainement wee haue had,' he wrote, 'and soe many ceremonyes, as if the puritans of the parlement had bene present, they would giue ouer making of acts against the crosse in bapty[s]me, against serplesses, and faule to composing new bills against theas new trickes.'[57] Here, perhaps, is the opinion of one who wore his religion lightly.

Notes

1 See Wormald, 'Gunpowder, Treason, and Scots', pp 158–9

2 *Sir Henry Whithed's Letter-Book*, pp 15–16; Haynes, *Robert Cecil*, p 94

3 HMC, *13th Report*, appendix IV, p 126; Hatfield MS 102/153; BL Royal MS appendix 89, fols 134–6. A rebellion in Munster that April can hardly be said to have troubled the council, since it was effectively dealt with

by local authorities before action was required in London (A J Sheehan, 'The Recusancy Revolt of 1603, a Reinterpretation', *Archivium Hibernicum*, XXXVIII, 1983, pp 3–13)

4   Gardiner, *History of England*, i, pp 85–6

5   Boderie, *Ambassade*, i, p 181, Boderie to Villeroi, 6 July 1606 ns. Goodman's account (*The Court of James I*, i, pp 24–7) reads as follows: 'and at the very instant time when it was debated in Council, I have heard it, by credible persons, that Sir John Fortescue, chancellor of the exchequer, did then very moderately and mildly ask, whether any conditions should be proposed to the king? Which the Earl of Northumberland, then present, hearing made a protestation, that if any man should offer to make any proposition to the King, he would instantly raise an army against him.' It is interesting that Osborn (*Traditional Memoyres*, p 6) would have it that James was helped to the throne by the 'ranting protestations of the Earle of Northumberland (that in all places vapoured he would bring him in by the sword)'. Yet another mid-seventeenth-century reminiscence can be found in Bodleian MS Carte 80, fol 618 (439), a memoir of Lord Grey. This maintains that in the council's deliberations at the queen's death, Grey was the first to propose that conditions should be made before the king were accepted. Fortescue seconded him but Northumberland opposed them and carried the day

6   BL Sloane MS 718, fols 34v–5. From internal evidence the author seems to have lived in Lord Burghley's household and to have held some office under Elizabeth. The piece was written before November 1603

7   BL Sloane MS 1786, fol 5v; Inner Temple Petyt MS 538/36, fols 199–202v; PRO SP 14/86/150; BL Cotton MS Titus C VII, fol 57. Although admitting that there was 'some speach of divers competitors' this account tells us that it ended once Nottingham, Egerton, and Cecil had all affirmed that the queen's last act had been to signify her wish that James should succeed

8   BL King's MS 123, fols 30v–1; PRO (Transcripts) PRO 31/3/35, fol 22

9   Bodleian MS Ashmole 1729, fol 64

10   *ibid*, fols 70–1. See Munden, 'Politics of Accession', pp 91–8. The letter of 10 April also appoints Thomas Howard lord chamberlain in place of Lord Hunsdon

11   BL Additional MS 5503, fol 24. Bacon was probably looking after Northumberland's interests at James's court. Soon after the accession he had sent a letter to the earl suggesting that a 'gratious declaration' might be made before the king's entry, and mentioning that he had just such a declaration ready prepared (*ibid*, fol 23). It seems as if many other English courtiers sent men north as their representatives (Scott, 'Wilbraham's Journal', p 55)

12   Alnwick MS 101, fol 30

13   *Calendar SP Venetian 1603–7*, p 17

14   See Bodleian MS Tanner 75, fol 81, Simon Theloal to Doctor Dun, 26 Mar 1603

15   PRO SP 14/1/14

16   PRO SP 14/1/20

17 PRO SP 96/1, fols 104, 106, 110

18 PRO SP 14/1/108. The commission was probably that set up to examine and allow suits of law (De Fonblanque, *Annals*, ii, p 247; *APC 1601–4*, p 499)

19 Cecil rode north in mid-April to meet his king at York, but Northumberland in common with most councillors did not stray far from London at this time. The earl was first received by James at Royston on 2 May (Syon MS U I 3aa, Delaval's account, recording disbursements when the earl rode post to Royston). For their meeting see Nichols, *Progresses of James I*, i, pp 138–9

20 La Rocca, 'Who Can't Pray With Me, Can't Love Me', pp 27–8

21 See Wormald, 'Two Kings or One?', p 196 and articles cited in the footnote

22 Stow, *Annales*, p 824

23 See above, note 10. George Carey, second Baron Hunsdon, was terminally ill – he died on 6 September 1603; these moves were not, apparently, intended to punish Carey in any way (Haynes, *Robert Cecil*, pp 93–5)

24 PRO SP 14/1/86

25 As we shall see, Northumberland long insisted that he had thought his brother Sir Allan Percy, his lieutenant of the pensioners, had supervised the swearing-in of Thomas Percy, but it transpired that, if he had done so, no witness had been present (PRO SP 14/216/220; Cheshire CRO De Tabley MS DLT/B 8, p 172, see also below, p 177)

26 PRO SP 14/4/85

27 For these conspiracies see Gardiner, *History of England*, i, pp 108–40; Edwards, *Life and Letters of Ralegh*, i, pp 361–82; Stebbing, *Sir Walter Ralegh*, pp 180–206; Tierney, *Dodd's Church History*, iv, appendix 1

28 Stebbing, *Sir Walter Ralegh*, pp 181–3; Shirley, *Thomas Harriot*, pp 303–4; Harrison, *Jacobean Journal*, pp 35–6

29 Shirley's, *Thomas Harriot*, offers a scholarly portrait of Ralegh, and Edwards's work remains a valuable source of information

30 While sources are plentiful for Ralegh's trial (Jardine, *Criminal Trials*, i, pp 389–520; Edwards, *Life and Letters of Ralegh*, i, pp 383–439; Howell, *State Trials*, ii, cols 1–31; BL Harley MS 39, fols 275–322v; PRO SP 12/278/102; 14/4/83; 14/6/37; Inner Temple Library MS Petyt 538/36, fols 273–313) and the Bye plotters (*State Trials*, ii, cols 61–5) they are more scanty for the arraignments of Cobham and Grey (Lodge, *Illustrations*, iii, pp 76–8; SP 14/6/37; Howell, *State Trials*, ii, pp 48–50). For the indictment of the Bye, Main, and Grey conspirators taken from PRO KB8 see *PRO Deputy Keeper's 5th Report*, appendix II, pp 135–7

31 Rushworth, *Historical Collections*, i, p 4

32 Lodge, *Illustrations*, iii, pp 77–8

33 See Jones, 'Journal of Levinus Munck', pp 244–8. The original journal kept by Munck survives at Hatfield (Hatfield MS 278) but it differs in only very slight details from the copy in the Bodleian Library published by Jones

34   See Howell, *State Trials*, ii, cols 65–70
35   Exchequer receipts for recusancy fall dramatically in 1604 and 1605 (Dietz, *Receipts of Jacobean Exchequer*, pp 136–7; Gardiner, *What Gunpowder Plot Was*, p 149)
36   Fincham and Lake, 'Ecclesiastical Policy of James I', pp 184–5
37   Usher, *Reconstruction of the English Church*, ii, pp 89–95; Bossy, 'Henri IV, the Appellants and the Jesuits', pp 94–5; see also Lake, 'Anti-popery', p 79 on the portrayal of Roman Catholicism as a 'foreign' religion
38   Haynes, *Robert Cecil*, pp 14, 16; Hurstfield, 'Robert Cecil', p 286
39   Lodge, *Illustrations*, iii, p 128, Cranborne to Archbishop Hutton of York. See Coakley, 'Robert Cecil, 1603–1612', pp 218–45
40   Rymer, *Foedera*, vii part 2, pp 122–3, commission *ad Jesuitas exterminandos* to the privy council, 5 Sep 1604
41   Bruce, *Correspondence*, p 34
42   *ibid*, p 37
43   *ibid*
44   Peck, *Northampton*, pp 6–22; A J Loomie, 'A Jacobean Crypto-Catholic: Lord Wotton', *Catholic Historical Review*, LIII, 1967, 328–45; Lee, *Great Britain's Solomon*, pp 176–7. This much to the dismay of courtiers and councillors less well disposed towards Catholicism (Lake, 'Anti-popery', pp 87–8)
45   La Rocca, 'Who Can't Pray With Me, Can't Love Me', p 26
46   Dietz, *Receipts of Jacobean Exchequer*, pp 136–7
47   *Commons' Journals*, i, pp 144–5
48   La Rocca, 'James I and his Catholic Subjects', p 258n. For one example of the would-be application of this procedure see Nicholls, 'Sir Charles Percy', p 244
49   Loomie, 'Toleration and Diplomacy', pp 55–6
50   Caraman, *John Gerard*, p 199, or as Hugh Owen put it late in 1603 'I perceave there is no hope at all of amendment in this stinking king of ours. An ill quarter to look for righteousness: at the hands of a miserable Scot' (Loomie, *Spanish Elizabethans*, p 82)
51   Hatfield MSS 112/91, 113/54; PRO SP 14/216/124; Trevor–Roper, 'The Gentry', pp 38–9; Hurstfield, 'Gunpowder plot and the Politics of Dissent', pp 331–4; Loomie, 'Toleration and Diplomacy', pp 30–7; Bossy, 'English Catholic Community', pp 95–6; Wormald, 'Gunpowder, Treason, and Scots', pp 145–6, 150–7
52   Hatfield MS 190/93; *A Commotion of the Papists in Herefordshire* (STC 25232); Harrison, *Jacobean Journal*, pp 206–7
53   Hatfield MS 111/51, 'G D' to Sir Everard Digby, 11 June 1605
54   There is a vast body of literature on the events and significance of the conference. M H Curtis, 'Hampton Court Conference and its Aftermath', *History*, XLVI, 1961, pp 1–16 provides a summary, but see also Fincham and Lake, 'Ecclesiastical Policy of James I', p 171n
55   Fincham and Lake, 'Ecclesiastical Policy of James I', pp 176–9
56   *ibid*, p 179
57   PRO SP 14/8/17*

X

Councillor or courtier?

Investigating the treasons of 1603, the council clearly suspected the involvement of some more eminent figure. As it transpired there was no evidence which touched any nobleman other than Lords Cobham and Grey, and given the embryonic nature of their plots the search did not progress further. Yet at a time when the importance of men of rank and station within a well-ordered society was taken for granted, such suspicion was not unnatural, particularly since by June that year there were already signs of discontent among the English peerage. While at court James's position went unchallenged there were some already looking askance at the changes which he had brought about.

Quite suddenly, the relationship between James and Northumberland begins to show signs of strain. From May onwards, Beaumont's despatches are full of vague suggestions that the English are dissatisfied both with their new king and with favours granted to his Scots followers at the English court, and while the French ambassador nowhere mentions Northumberland at this time, the earl is probably still his first source of information.[1] On 8 June James visits Northumberland at Syon House amid great feasting and ceremony, and all, superficially, seems well.[2] Indications of tension, though, appear rather suddenly in various sources, and while none standing alone is decisive, taken together they begin to carry conviction.

The Percy family historians – apart from a tongue-in-cheek suggestion that the king thought little of Northumberland's passion for tobacco – blame the deterioration partly upon irreconcilable differences in the two men's personalities and partly on the disgust felt by the earl at the treatment of Ralegh and Cobham.[3] They suggest that Northumberland, seeing old friends tried and convicted on patently trumped-up charges, came to realise that his enemies had prevailed with the king and that the one course left to him was that of honourable retirement on his estates, in any case more congenial than remaining at a sycophantic court dominated by Cecilians and Scotsmen. The reality is, inevitably, far more complex. Northumberland made no move to defend Ralegh's actions, and although he sought James's mercy for the condemned men – which as we have seen was forthcoming – he did so in politic, sincere terms which could have given no offence.[4] The signs of discontent in any case considerably precede discovery of the plots.

We see them first in letters of the marquis de Rosny, Henri IV's special envoy sent to congratulate James on his accession. Although its credibility is marred by imaginative elaboration,[5] Rosny's account of his visit taken in conjunction with Beaumont's reports makes very interesting reading. After the earl had conducted him to and from his barge on the Thames during his first reception on 12 July, Rosny described Northumberland as an 'homme d'esprit, de credit et tenu pour vn des plus habiles, puissans et courageux Seigneurs d'Angleterre, assez mal content du Roy et du present gouuernement'. The earl, he wrote, had shown clearly that he 'n'aymer ny n'estimer pas trop le Roy son Maistre, et blasma vne grande partie de ses actions et deportmens'.[6] Rosny had cautiously welcomed these advances, and within days Northumberland had given him some tangible proof of his goodwill, sending him news of Spanish efforts to secure James's support for a joint invasion of France. While Rosny, ever cautious, chose to doubt these disclosures, he saw the very fact that they had been made as a most promising omen.[7]

But if Rosny seems to have then shared Beaumont's hopes of the earl, such optimism did not last long. After returning home he wrote a confidential minute for his king which gives us a rare glimpse of court factions at this period. Unsurprisingly seeing things primarily in terms of foreign policy, Rosny depicted four groups vying for influence at court. He placed in the first those closest to the new king: Lord Mountjoy, the Scottish peers Mar and Kinloss, and the gentlemen of the bedchamber. Rosny thought these men unlikely to dabble in politics to any great extent, since their prime ambition was to increase their share of royal favour. A pro-Spanish faction was represented by the Howard family, particularly by the earls of Nottingham and Suffolk, and Henry Howard. The third group – the core of the council – comprised the chancellor, Lord Ellesmere, the treasurer, Lord Buckhurst, Secretary Cecil, and others inclined to follow a traditional course of enmity towards France, wary peace with Spain, and a long-term desire to resurrect the old Burgundian state as a third power on the European mainland. These were all men who could be relied upon to support the status quo, but there was besides a fourth clique, dismissed in these terms:

Les autres comme la Comte de Northumbelland, de Sutenton, de Comberland, les Milords Cobham, Ralek, Griffin [Markham] et autres seront tousiours de toutes les factions qui voudront remuer mesnage ou dedans ou dehors leur Royaume, voire aucuns d'eux contre leur propre Roy et leur patrie.[8]

His conclusions should not be accorded too much weight, for Rosny had a fine Gallic opinion as to the general worthlessness of James's courtiers. It should also be remembered that he was in England for little more than two weeks[9] – an absurdly short time in which to have formulated such settled judgements. On the other hand, he had met Northumberland on more than one occasion, and had talked at length with the more experienced resident ambassador. Rosny may have exaggerated divisions in the English court, but it is difficult to escape a conclusion that by mid-June the earl was in some sort discontented, and that this discontent is best explained in terms of a clash of personalities.

Although highly untrustworthy sources, two papers in the Spanish archives at Simancas dating from July 1603 support this argument. Both were the work of Catholic Englishmen still hoping to secure foreign support, and if necessary military support, for their co-religionists. The first was written by a certain Robert Spiller who came to Brussels late in June on a mission from the Jesuit faction at home to solicit help both from sympathisers in the city and from the Spanish authorities. Spiller's *Auiso* comments on the religious and political sympathies of England's leading courtiers. He describes Northumberland as favouring peace with Spain 'with the condition that freedom of conscience be allowed and in no other way'. The earl's name is marked with a cross, apparently to indicate his potential support for the Catholic cause.[10]

An altogether more partial document is the memorandum drawn up by none other than Guy Fawkes. As we have seen, Fawkes, after several years' service with the Catholic forces in the Low Countries wars, had been sent to the Spanish court by his co-religionists in

Flanders to establish whether Philip III intended to honour pledges made by his late father that Spain would give military aid to an enterprise against the English regime. Writing with a mixture of honest personal conviction and politic manoeuvring, Fawkes launched into what was in effect little more than a polemic against king and Scots. He strove to convince his audience that Englishmen of all religious persuasions would welcome outside intervention to rid them of these hated northern parasites.

Fawkes did not write from first-hand knowledge. He had not been in England those many years and had been chosen for his mission principally through his mastery of French and Spanish. It is the anti-Scottish tenor of the document that strikes the reader today. Having dwelt at length on the king's personal shortcomings, he painted a vivid picture of an England already chafing at Scottish rule. Four prominent earls – Cumberland, Worcester, Shrewsbury, and Northumberland – were said to favour peace with Spain only if it was accompanied by guarantees that the English Catholics would suffer no persecution, the implication being that they were less than wholeheartedly behind the current regime. Northumberland's discontent was described in singularly graphic terms. The earl, according to Fawkes, had been the first to declare himself for the new king. At some stage he had also made plans to 'do something for the Catholics (as he told some persons later) but now finds himself discontented since the king has given him slight satisfaction'. Northumberland's own page had been killed by a Scottish royal page, and 'another Scot struck an Englishman in the presence chamber, yet they . . . merely excused him as insane'.[11] Such insults were not to be endured long – if ever a country was ripe for cleansing through invasion by a pure Catholic power, it was Fawkes's version of England in that summer of 1603.

Of course, the sanguine expectations of Fawkes – or the mysterious informant for whom he spoke – were based on little more than wishful thinking. While there were inevitably some disputes between Englishman and Scotsman in the court these were, as the Spaniards realised, in no way deep enough to suggest that all differences would not be buried at the first hint of invasion. Anti-Scottish feeling there most certainly was, and anti-English feeling too north of the border, but it was found among those with nothing to lose, the poor townsmen, the village topers who cursed in their cups.[12] In the narrow, claustrophobic world of the Stuart court, disputes remained on an essentially personal rather than on a nationalistic level. Two Englishmen, the earl of Southampton and Lord Grey, almost came to blows when in the queen's presence early in the reign,[13] while on 13 July Northumberland, encountering his old adversary and compatriot Sir Francis Vere, for some undisclosed reason spat in his face in full sight of James and the court, a *faux pas* which deeply offended the king.[14] For this action, the earl was promptly banished to the archbishop of Canterbury's summer palace at Croydon.

Given the simultaneous first disclosures of the Bye and Main treasons, Northumberland could hardly have timed his indiscretion more inopportunely. In a letter to the king sent via Cecil on 14 July he sought a swift release, fearing for his good name with so much talk of treason in the air.[15] Certainly the French ambassador was already anxiously putting two and two together, wondering also whether a growing affection that he had noticed between Northumberland and Queen Anne might lie at the root of the trouble, particularly since the queen was not well-liked at court.[16] The covering letter to Cecil shows that Northumberland felt very much on the defensive:

Perhaps I should haue knowen more of these matters if Rawleighe had not conceaued as he told me that I could keepe nothing from you. I am now glad of those thoughts in him and your freindship and mine, neuer stoode me in better steede if he haue done any thing that is not justifiable.[17]

By 18 July the storm, so far as the earl was concerned, had passed over. Beaumont's despatch that day states that Northumberland 'n'ayant été ni accusé ni reconnu coupable de tout ce dont l'on avoit fait courre le bruit ces jours passez, à eû congé du roy d'aller en vne de ses maisons proche de la cour de trois lieues'. With a touch of bravado, the earl told Beaumont that he had been preserved for some greater service, but the whole affair had clearly unsettled him. The ambassador, while hoping that he might yet prove useful, told Rosny that Northumberland would not now accept a proposed pension from France.[18]

The earl had reason to be cautious for his name had been mentioned by suspects during investigation of the plots. There was a suggestion by William Watson, who had himself received some form of assurance of toleration from the king in former days, that had the plot succeeded in toppling Cecil and his supporters, Northumberland would have been one of those who could have expected to prosper through the alteration – he would have been made a duke or marquess.[19] Watson was full of such grandiose and idle visions of a future England, but his words do suggest that Northumberland's current discontent was a matter of common knowledge.

So too does a remarkable and hitherto overlooked passage in the principal confession of Sir Griffin Markham, which survives only as an edited abstract. This preserves his claim that a fellow-conspirator George Brooke had advised him against recruiting the earl into the Bye because 'his discontent with a faire word was presently pacified and for feare of revealing yt to Rawley who had power to bewitch him'. The discontented man again.[20]

But one is entitled to ask why Northumberland should have been discontented, and in answering this question we move towards a truer understanding of the new world which James's accession was ushering in. It is at least possible that Northumberland, not for the last time in his life, was the victim of his own over-optimism; James had a host of other men to favour, advance, and repay. To an extent Northumberland did indeed, as his biographers suggest, retire from court to seek the seclusion of his country estates. On the other hand, another early chronicler of the Percy family concluded from the same scanty facts that the earl spent these years basking contentedly in royal favour, less of a statesman essentially by choice.[21] In November 1605 during the Gunpowder investigations, the earl himself urged the council to 'consider . . . the course of my lyfe, whether it hathe not leaned more of late years to priuat domesticall pleasures, then to other ambitions; examin but my humors in buildings, gardenings and my priuat expenses theas two years past'. Had there been no foundation for the claim it would never have been advanced at so dangerous a time.[22]

Such views are in any case simplistic. His discontent and his reaction to events that summer take a subtly different form. The years 1604 and 1605 see Northumberland, far from sulking in retirement on his estates, playing an important part in court life and adapting to a role as leading courtier outside the central councils of state. Evidence is admittedly sparse, but his attendance at meetings of the privy council does seem to be more intermittent after June.[23] In 1604 he was not appointed to the commission discussing the union of England and Scotland which met after the prorogation of parliament, nor did he help negotiate the peace with Spain.[24] Perhaps this only emphasises that there was disenchantment on both sides, for on James's part a man known to be both indiscreet and somewhat discontented was hardly one to be entrusted with vital matters considered the preserve of a privy council. It is, however, possible to see the strained relations between Northumberland and his king improve in the ensuing months. If personal disillusionment had underpinned the earl's discontent the king, to his credit, harboured no open grudges, and over the next two years Northumberland seems to have given no cause for further offence.

As for Cecil, he detested 'unsecrecy' above most other faults and would not have been blind to Northumberland's failings.[25] There were, in any case, quieter waters ahead; the situation had changed from the days of anxiety and uncertainty that had produced the secret correspondence. Ralegh and Cobham were helpless prisoners, James sat securely on his new throne, and Cecil himself had managed to increase his authority. Personal problems still remained unresolved: James's affection if not his respect for the Secretary was limited since they were men of very differing characters,[26] and the king, as Bacon had observed, was always more likely than Elizabeth to look favourably on the old nobility. But the Percies were not the only ancient family in England, and Cecil probably realised that the threat, if such it was, came not from Northumberland but from the increasingly influential Howard clan. Even then it was a problem for the future; most observers had fully expected favour to be shown to the Howards, such a 'policy' could have come as no surprise to Cecil. There is also not the slightest doubt that James – and the Howards, and other noblemen such as Worcester – recognised and appreciated Cecil's labours.[27] To the end of Cecil's life, Henry Howard relied on his support and looked to him for guidance.

Two political and administrative trends characterised the early years of the reign. One was a rapid expansion in the peerage to the extent that any political power inherent in a title was diluted. Although this continued throughout the reign, it was very much a two-stage process, and while it is true that the old nobility managed to maintain its standing and prestige among the large number of new creations in the 1610s and 1620s it is equally the case that those promoted earlier could boast excellent blood-claims to a peerage. On 21 July 1603, Henry Wriothesley was restored to the earldom of Southampton, Lord Thomas Howard created earl of Suffolk, and Lord Mountjoy was created earl of Devonshire following his triumphs in Ireland. On 13 March 1604 Thomas Sackville and Henry Howard became respectively earls of Dorset and Northampton. On the following 18 April, a second Thomas Howard was restored to his father's earldom of Arundel, and Robert Devereux, another son of an ill-fated father, received the earldom of Essex. In 1605, the Cecil brothers were elevated to the earldoms of Exeter and Salisbury, while Philip Herbert became earl of Montgomery. Indeed, these early creations probably should be seen as an overdue move to correct the 'abnormal' shortage of peers in the late sixteenth century. If he perhaps overdid things through undue generosity and extravagance, James well understood the benefits he derived from the use of patronage, and his actions in this line were, as is the way of human nature, only criticised by those who lost out in the race for favour.

Since membership was a valued and much sought-after honour, we also see a parallel expansion of the privy council to such an extent that there evolved a *de facto* inner ring of councillors responsible for the management of business. Although the privy council nearly doubled in size between 1603 and late-1605, there is evidence to suggest that its workload was carried by a group similar or perhaps even smaller in size to that operating under Elizabeth. With one or two exceptions, notably Northampton, it was a group dominated by the experienced men who had served Elizabeth, and there was no place for Northumberland, just as there was none for Exeter, or Cumberland, or the Scots.[28] One can see the decision as a studied and ungrateful rebuke to Northumberland's claims, but it might equally be portrayed as the successful continuation of an established system into which the earl himself found that he did not fit. Other signs of royal displeasure there are none.

Northumberland was soon freed of all restraint as it became clear that he was not directly implicated in the treasons committed by his friends. He was permitted to follow the royal progress that August.[29] Even then, the old ill-feeling between the earl and Sir Francis Vere smouldered on. During the progress, John Hercy wrote from Woodstock on 13 September to the earl of Shrewsbury:

On Satterdaye last . . . there was a fallinge out betwene Sir Francis Vere and a captayne whose name I cannot learne. His quarrel was susspected to be in the behalfe of the earle of Northumberland. The kinge had knowledge of this and was displeased therewith.[30]

But this time his displeasure was not, apparently, directed against the earl. In November Northumberland was among the peers who tried and convicted Lords Cobham and Grey of treason at Winchester.[31] He was present at most of the court's Christmas and new year celebrations, and there is nothing to suggest that he did not enjoy the experience.[32] At no stage, either, did he entirely neglect his responsibilities as a councillor, dutifully asking Cecil in one letter whether any council business had been planned for that day, as he 'woold not willingly be absent from the beginning of them'.[33]

These trends persist through the next two years. Northumberland continued to visit court[34] and to participate in the ceremonial there.[35] He was also conscientious in attending sittings of the 1604 parliament, playing a prominent, co-operative, if largely formal role in keeping with his position as a leading nobleman and privy councillor.[36] His scope for patronage, though less extensive than that of Cecil who was truly at the heart of affairs and though based more on his influence as earl of Northumberland rather than that inherent in his state or court offices, remained strong, far more impressive than anything which Northampton, for example, could manage. There is, though, no sign that it incorporated any sizeable number of grateful Catholics.[37]

Northumberland's household accounts show him regularly sending small tokens from his gardens to the king[38] and James visited the earl at Syon once again in October 1604.[39] Northumberland still received numerous royal favours – the freehold of Syon House being just one example[40] – and while the earl spent much time there, immersed in gardening projects,[41] it was one of the many attractions of Syon that it offered the comforts of a country retreat coupled with proximity to Hampton Court and easy access to London by river. Had the earl truly sought seclusion he could have retired to Petworth, in what is even today a somewhat remote corner of West Sussex, but Petworth was hardly visited in those years.

With Ralegh and Cobham removed from the scene, it is difficult to identify the earl's close companions. Household accounts show him exchanging gifts with other courtiers and acquaintances, many of whom, in the small world of the Stuart court, were relatives. Thus Lord Burghley might present him with a horse, the countess of Suffolk would give him a cheese, and Sir Thomas Throckmorton, sharing her concern for the inner man, might send him lamprey pies. Cecil's presents were more practical, especially bearing in mind the renovations at Syon. On 20 July 1604 three shillings were given in reward at the Custom House wharf in London, 'where his lordship had marbell stones that my Lord Cycell bestowed of him'.[42] Northumberland naturally reciprocated. An example may be cited from the Hatfield accounts of the previous year, when on 2 September his servant was rewarded for bringing grapes to Cecil.[43] Others who exchanged presents with Northumberland included the earl and countess of Shrewsbury, Sir Robert Wroth, Sir George More, and Sir William Slingsby. His 1604 accounts show him paying social calls on, among others, Burghley and Devonshire, who in his post of lord deputy in Ireland had proved a constant friend to more than one of the earl's brothers. Northumberland also stayed with Cecil at Theobalds and visited Copt Hall, home of the dowager countess of Southampton, the architect in search of inspiration.

But such presents and visits were simply courtesies of the age; nothing less can be expected from one living close to London and aware of his social responsibilities. Personal letters, those to Cecil apart, are scanty for 1604 and 1605, and taken out of their proper context, the few survivals are often merely obscure.[44] Of all the nobility, Northumberland perhaps felt closest to his uncle, Burghley. He was entrusted with Burghley's proxy during the parliament of 1601 – the only proxy he ever exercised – and when the earl's troubles began in 1605 Burghley was one of the first to whom he turned for help.[45]

Foreign ambassadors tacitly recognised that Northumberland was henceforth to be treated as a prominent courtier rather than a prominent statesman. Beaumont remained a friend: in February 1604 one of Northumberland's servants was sent to the ambassador's residence at 'Mouldsey' to view some horses. Beaumont lent his chef to teach Northumberland's cook some finer points of French cuisine, and if a 1603 precedent was followed the Frenchmen who served at Syon during the king's visit in October 1604 would also have been supplied by the ambassador for the occasion.[46] From summer 1603 onwards, though, the few direct references to the earl in Beaumont's despatches are in connection with rather trivial matters. At the end of 1603 the ambassador merely reported that James had not taken exception to a set of seasonal letters sent by Henri IV to various courtiers.[47] On 1 July 1604, describing how the earl of Southampton had recently offended the king, he wrote that Northumberland had spoken to the culprit on behalf of the council.[48]

Unable to match Beaumont's intimacy, Spanish envoys seemed quite unsure of Northumberland's role at court. On 28 June 1604 Juan de Tassis, count of Villa Mediana, put together a 'memorandum concerning the persons who ought to be kept satisfied in this kingdom', setting out firstly to assess the services rendered by various courtiers in finalising the impending peace treaty and secondly to predict what might be expected from them in future. Having considered Cecil, and the earls of Dorset, Nottingham, Devonshire, Northampton, and Suffolk, he turned his attention to

the Earl of Northumberland, member of the Council and one of the great Peers of this kingdom. He is not a friend of this peace as he believes the king will have greater need of him in other circumstances. He is considered a man of importance. I believe he is no more devoted to France than to us. I would consider it suitable to leave him under obligation so that he would be inclined to do more harm to them than to us. There should be a pension and a worthwhile present for his wife.[49]

This recommendation of a pension was, by comparison with others, rather half-hearted. It seems as if Villa Mediana and his colleagues sought to neutralise the earl's potential to make trouble, and while seeing him as an important figure they found it hard to define where his importance lay.

Nor were they sure of the earl's attitude to peace with Spain. In part this was because he had no direct role in the negotiations, but Northumberland may also have been genuinely undecided over the merits of such a treaty. In November 1605 he would remind the council that he had always been 'stiff for vppholdinge the [Dutch] states', but such support need not have extended to a conviction that it was worthwhile prolonging a tedious, unprofitable war.[50] Uncertain of their man the Spaniards eventually hedged their bets. The constable of Castile, having considered the recommendations made by his representatives in London, pruned their list when forwarding final pension-proposals to the Spanish court. He suggested that Dorset, Nottingham, Devonshire, and Cecil should each receive 3,000 *felipes* a year, besides jewels worth over 2,000 ducats a man. Northampton, a staunch ally to the Spaniard, was to have an annuity of 5,000 *felipes*, besides 6,000 *felipes* as a one-off payment and a jewel similar to those received by his fellow-councillors. Northumberland, in contrast, would have to be satisfied with a jewel worth 4,000 *felipes*.[51] The hope was that he would continue to refrain from direct involvement in deliberations over policy at this crucial time. But he was evidently considered insufficiently active in policy-making – or insufficiently friendly – to merit a regular pension.

It may be argued, then, that relationships between Northumberland and the king improved as they came to know each other, to understand each other's limitations. From the scanty figures that can be assembled it appears that the earl was beginning to play a slightly more active role in council by late-1605.[52] That, however, is not to suggest that past events had been wholly forgotten by either side.

For Northumberland there was, perhaps, only one cloud on an otherwise bright horizon, a recurring, hardly unusual problem that in all likelihood caused him little anxiety. Throughout the years 1602 to 1605 there was a continual flow of allegation and counter-allegation between his principal estate officers in the north. The most vociferous was John Carvile, Northumberland's solicitor. A sharp man with an eye for an insult, Carvile had a personal interest in the Yorkshire estates, leasing Nunmonkton – which would come to Northumberland in reversion – from the earl's stepfather Francis Fitton.[53] Perhaps because of this, he was especially critical of other Yorkshiremen, notably the auditor William Stockdale and Sir Henry Slingsby, the earl's cousin and his receiver in the county.[54] Both repudiated Carvile's charges of financial malpractice and answered him in kind, the dispute becoming increasingly acrimonious.[55] Referring wearily to allegations of mismanagement at Topcliffe, Northumberland noted in July 1604 that Stockdale was refusing either to show Carvile the relevant books or to confer with him about the earl's affairs.[56] While this particular dispute between the two men was patched up – after a fashion – the whole atmosphere was hardly conducive to enthusiastic or efficient estate management.[57]

But because an absentee landlord relied upon such information to warn him of incipient graft and peculation among local officers, Northumberland had to take this intense dispute seriously, and in so doing it is possible that he neglected the failings of others. In these bitter exchanges Thomas Percy, though mentioned, came away with his reputation comparatively undamaged. The earl did not, of course, trust him completely.[58] In his *Advice to his Son*, written some years later, he told Algernon that while petty cozenage was unavoidable, servants only succeeded in deceiving masters who were 'weak or careless by overbelieving'. 'It is the master's fault,' he wrote, 'if an evil and dishonest servant serve him long.'[59] Without the helpful information of other officers, though, it took an astute master to detect embezzlement at an early stage.

Percy, indeed, was a man whose information was listened to and acted upon, his support for informers prepared to testify against the local officials at Topcliffe either led to or helped instigate a major investigation there in 1603-4.[60] He gave the earl cause for satisfaction in his firm handling of some recalcitrant Northumbrian tenants, although his rather over-enthusiastic eviction of the lessee of Prudhoe Castle led to star chamber proceedings against him and his confederates.[61]

Inevitably, he had his enemies. William Wycliffe was at least suspicious of him, and the indefatigable Carvile found material to support accusations of malpractice.[62] Percy was, however, fortunate in being able to count on the friendship of William Stockdale. In March 1605 he sought and obtained the auditor's connivance in concealing some arrears by charging his debts on various bailiffs. The sums involved totalled between £200 and £350, and given the fate of earlier receivers in Cumberland and Northumberland, Percy was understandably keen that the earl should not learn of such 'temporary' debts. Stockdale agreed to the deception; there was nothing new in a receiver falling behind in his debt collections from the troublesome northern counties, indeed the sum involved was perhaps surprisingly small. There was certainly no real reason to suspect his friend of diverting the earl's money to some other purpose, especially since Percy had undertaken to remedy matters. 'If I liue but one yeare,' he had promised the auditor, 'I protest before god I will not owe him [Northumberland] one penny.'[63]

It must remain rather doubtful whether these sums were used in Gunpowder plot, since Catesby bore much of the cost before mid-1605.[64] They may even have represented genuine debts. It is, of course, almost impossible to estimate the extent of Percy's embezzlements from the evidence of contemporary estate accounts alone. After 1605, the earl's officers arrived at a figure of around £1,900, but, whatever his intentions regarding the Michaelmas rents, Percy does not seem to have had the chance to spend on so extravagant a scale and it is difficult not to suspect that the late auditor might have carried the blame for the negligence or knavery of those who had either held offices under him or who had owed him money.[65] For both counties, the figures on the receiver's accounts compiled before Percy's death increased steadily, but the figures were hardly remarkable, and in any case arrears alone were no indication of a receiver's honesty.[66] Any suggestions of malpractice before 1605 were effectively obscured by Stockdale's connivance, by debts remaining against previous receivers in the accounts, by the conflicts in Yorkshire, and by Percy's common sense. These conclusions are rather tentative given the unsatisfactory and incomplete nature of the financial records, but they may help explain why the earl's trust in Percy remained unshaken right up to the discovery of Gunpowder plot.

In Percy's letters to the earl that summer there is naturally no hint of any financial problem. He discusses the work of the border commissioners and current Anglo-Scottish tensions over 'debatable lands', parts of which were claimed by the earl.[67] In September and October he was busy in Cumberland and Northumberland collecting the rents, and while some in retrospect felt that the receiver had then been tense and unpredictable, his behaviour does not seem to have given rise to comment at the time.[68] This money collected, he began to bring it south. At Gainsborough he wrote letters dated 2 November, telling both Wycliffe and Stockdale that he had been unable to stay in York because the archbishop, having received malicious reports which had described Percy as a 'chefe piller of papistry' in Northumberland, had arranged to have him arrested if he showed his face in the city. He commented upon pressing estate business, outlined steps he was taking to guard the rent money, and assured both colleagues that on the following Tuesday – 5 November – he would meet them at Doncaster.[69]

But these letters were postdated; by the evening of that same day, 2 November, Percy had arrived in London,[70] and was busy at court studying the apartments and daily routine of Prince Charles.[71] Initially, he seems to have tried to keep his presence in the capital a secret from colleagues in the Northumberland household,[72] but on Monday 4 November he came into the open, visiting his master at Syon, dining with the earl and a few select companions.[73] True to character, Percy was playing the conspirator to the end.

Through September and October Northumberland remained in or near London. As a commissioner he attended the prorogation of parliament on 3 October,[74] and when the court returned to London at the end of the month his bed and some other possessions were moved from Hampton Court to Whitehall. On 29 October he attended the lord mayor's banquet in the city.[75] He supped with his wife at Syon on 2 November and, after dinner on the fourth, returned to Essex House.[76] To all outward appearances it was his intention to attend parliament the following day, his servant Henry Lucas bringing 'necessaries against the parlament' from court to the earl's London residence. All the dramatic events of 5 November leave but an indirect record in Northumberland's accounts: a footman's bill includes a claim for 'running charges the fyfte of november to Syon with a letter to my lady and backe againe'.[77] In the letter, Dorothy would no doubt have been told that a desperate plot to slaughter king, lords and commons together at the opening of parliament had been frustrated in the nick of time. She would also have learnt that John Johnson – the man taken red-handed in the cellars of Westminster – had already confessed that his master was Thomas Percy.

Notes

1 BL King's MS 123, fols 120, 142, 168v–9
2 Batho, 'Northumberland Household Accounts', pp 172–4; Nichols, *Progresses*, i, pp 165–6
3 Brenan, *History*, ii, pp 88–92; De Fonblanque, *Annals*, ii, pp 249–51
4 PRO SP 14/4/85. This letter is calendared under 18 November, but it was probably written after the trials of Cobham and Grey, 25 and 26 Nov 1603. De Fonblanque, *Annals*, ii, p 248
5 Rosny was later duc de Sully, the noted minister of Henri IV and Louis XIII; see Pfister, 'Les Economies Royales de Sully', pp 292–300 for an examination of Rosny's account; Sully, *Memoires*, ii, p 159
6 Sully, *Memoires*, ii, pp 163–4; BL King's MS 123, fol 253–3v
7 Sully, *Memoires*, ii, p 166
8 *ibid*, ii, pp 200–1
9 He left London on 25 June (*ibid*, ii, pp 229–30)
10 Loomie, *Spain and the Jacobean Catholics*, i, p 6. Loomie supplies a note on Spiller: he was a brother of Sir Henry Spiller and was reputed to be a 'domestic' of Henry Garnett
11 Loomie, 'Guy Fawkes in Spain', pp 61–3. Could his informant have been Spiller? The 'killing' might – if it had any basis in reality – have been an exaggerated account of the event described in John Manningham's diary under 9 April (Sorlien, *Diary of John Manningham*, pp 231, 398). The second incident sounds like Northumberland's own contretemps with Vere, in very garbled form. The story of the murdered page had reached Paris by the end of May. Carleton's correspondent St Saveur mentioned it along

with other tales of Anglo–Scottish hostility, adding that Northumberland was then thought to be at loggerheads with the earl of Mar (SP 78/49, fol 139v)

12   Wormald, 'Gunpowder, Treason, and Scots', pp 158–61

13   BL Cotton MS Caligula E X, fol 278; PRO SP 14/2/33

14   Sully, *Memoires*, ii, p 236; Syon MS U I 50(3); BL King's MS 123, fol 334; PRO (Transcripts) PRO 31/3/36, fol 169, Beaumont to Henri IV. He wrote to Villeroi with the news, expressing fear that the earl would be heavily punished for his *lèse majesté* (King's MS 123, fols 335–7). The queen does seem to have been friendly towards Northumberland. During his captivity after Gunpowder plot she helped his family, dining at Syon House in June 1607 (Syon MSS O I 2c, fols 22, 23; U I 50(4c))

15   PRO SP 14/16/41, undated, and calendared as relating to Gunpowder plot. But the earl was held at Lambeth on that occasion. Moreover, the letter is a copy in Carleton's hand (cf SP 14/2/71), and Carleton had left the earl's service by November 1605. After the Vere incident, it is possible that the earl was subjected to informal questioning by other privy councillors. In an undated letter to Cecil he declared that, although 'limited' to Syon, he intended to come to London in case he were sent for by the council. On the other hand, the summons might more probably have been to inform Northumberland of the king's pleasure with regard to his further restraint (Hatfield MS 188/25)

16   BL King's MS 123, fol 334–4v; PRO (Transcripts) PRO 31/3/36, fol 169, Beaumont's despatch of 16 July

17   PRO SP 14/2/71

18   BL King's MS 123, fol 337v. On 5 Aug 1603 Henri IV told Beaumont that he was 'tres marry de l'accident survenu au comte de Nortomberland et seray tres aise de savoir que il soit hors de peyne' (Laffleur de Kermaingant, *Mission de Christophe de Harlay*, part 2, pp 135–6). A letter of sympathy from Beaumont to the earl (PRO SP 78/52/353) formerly attributed to the time of Gunpowder plot, was probably written in 1603; Sully, *Memoires*, ii, p 238, Beaumont to Rosny, 12 Aug 1603 ns. Beaumont gives the earl an appropriate alias, 'le sourdaut', in this letter

19   PRO SP 14/3/16

20   PRO SP 14/3/54. It is possible that this was a transcriber's error. At Ralegh's trial Markham was said to have confessed that George Brooke had advised him for this very reason to avoid telling Cobham too much (SP 14/4/83, p 10). An alternative explanation is that Markham had misunderstood what Brooke had told him, and that subsequent comparison of their testimonies led to a recognition that a mistake had been made – the extract from Markham's confession is indeed lightly crossed out. But in either case one is entitled to wonder why Northumberland's name should have appeared at all in such a document, and one may wonder too at the suspicious thoughts that lay behind the error, if such it was

21   Bishop Thomas Percy in the 1779 edition of Collins's *Peerage*, repeated verbatim in the 1812 edition, pp 330–2

22   PRO SP 14/16/77

23   See appendix 3

24 Nor did his name appear among those named on the earl marshal's commission of February 1604 (PRO SP 14/6/51; 14/8/107; 14/10B; 14/12/82). He was included on only a few of the largest royal committees and I have found only one early instance where he was involved in the negotiations with Spain: on 13 January 1604, together with Cecil, Henry Howard, and Nottingham, he visited the Spanish ambassador to discuss a proposal that negotiations should be conducted in Flanders because of the constable of Castile's ill-health (Jones, 'Journal of Levinus Munck', p 250)

25 Handover, *The Second Cecil*, p 104

26 Marcham, 'Little Beagle Letters', pp 328–33

27 Wormald, 'Two Kings or One?', pp 201–3; Peck, *Northampton*, pp 24–30; Coakley, 'Robert Cecil 1603–1612', pp 47–73; Haynes, *Robert Cecil*, pp 206–9. James wondered publicly whether Cecil had served him honestly and Howard accused his old colleague of dishonesty while lord treasurer, but both waited until Cecil was dead before making their accusations (Spedding, *Letters and Life of Sir Francis Bacon*, iv, p 278; Peck, *Northampton*, pp 133–5)

28 See appendix 3; Marcham, 'Little Beagle Letters', pp 326–7

29 Syon MSS U I 3aa, Robert Delaval, declaration, 1 Apr 1603–25 Mar 1604; U I 3v, Henry Taylor, declaration, 25 Mar 1603–25 Mar 1604. These accounts give disbursements on riding charges and diet during the progress. See also PRO SP 14/3/61; 14/4/5, Carleton's accounts as comptroller of the household for the first eight weeks of the progress. For some reason these were sent to Cecil by Carleton

30 Lambeth MS 3203, fol 110–10v; Lodge, *Illustrations*, iii, p 24; Nichols, *Progresses of James I*, i, pp 261–2. The captain was possibly Edmund Whitelocke, see Bruce, *Liber Famelicus of Sir James Whitelocke*, p 10

31 Syon MS U I 50a(3), a book of foreign disbursements beginning 25 Mar 1603

32 *ibid*

33 Hatfield MS 103/28, undated, addressed to Lord Cecil

34 We can trace Northumberland's daily movements from household accounting documents, particularly Syon MS U I 10, a collection of bills presented to Henry Taylor. See Syon MSS U I 50(4a and b); U I 50a(3). See also Nicholls, 'Politics and Percies', pp 105–8

35 On 5 May 1605, for example, the earl and his countess played leading roles in the christening of James's daughter Mary (Nichols, *Progresses of James I*, i, p 512; Stow, *Annales*, p 863)

36 Munden has suggested that political tensions in the 1604 parliament were in some way fomented by privy councillors keen to ensure that James would oppose pressure for regular parliaments, but in this comparatively ill-documented session such suggestions are based on strong suspicions alone, and there is nothing to indicate that Northumberland engaged in activities of this kind (Munden, 'James I and "the growth of mutual distrust" ', pp 70–2; see also Munden's thesis, 'The Politics of Accession', pp 370–8). Northumberland was present at 62% of sittings, playing a full part in committees. Whereas the earl, when called upon to prove himself as a

statesman, betrayed his inexperience, the same cannot be said for his parliamentary work where eighteen years' acquaintance with the Lords allowed him to fulfil new obligations with some success

37   On patronage exercised by the earl 1603–5 see Nicholls, 'Politics and Percies', pp 132–8

38   He sent cherries to the king at Greenwich during June, and grapes from the Syon vines in September 1605 (Syon MS U I 10, fols 202, 117)

39   In Syon MS U I 50(2a), book of rewards given by Robert Delaval on behalf of the earl for the year beginning 25 March 1604, sums of money were given to the king's cook and bottleman 'his Majestie beinge at Syon the same daye' (3 October)

40   PRO C66/1648/27; Syon MS D XIV 10b, original letters patent, 4 July 1604; SP 38/7, fol 174, docquet. In March 1604 Northumberland joined the earls of Nottingham and Dorset as a third lord-lieutenant of Sussex (Syon MS V X 3, commission of lieutenancy)

41   Late in 1604, the earl of Shrewsbury drew a revealing contrast between Northumberland and Cecil when he wrote to the Secretary comparing Cecil's busy labours with those of Northumberland in his garden. The earl's work, wrote Shrewsbury, 'will busy and coste him more, till he can be hable to gather a poesie in hit, then it will doe in 20 yeares after, and yet I know he muste never leave planttynge, dyggynge, weedynge etc . . . continually, as occasion serves: but you have no leasure to becum a gardyner' (Hatfield MS 107/136)

42   Syon MS U I 50(2a)

43   Hatfield MS Accounts 6/31

44   eg PRO SP 14/9/85

45   *Lords' Journals*, ii, p 226; Alnwick MS 101, fol 12, dated 17 Nov 1605. Burghley had married Northumberland's maternal aunt, Dorothy Latimer

46   Syon MSS U I 50a(3); U I 3aa, Robert Delaval, declaration, 1 Apr 1603–25 Mar 1604; U I 50(4b), Henry Taylor's book

47   BL King's MS 124, fol 316v; PRO (Transcripts) PRO 31/3/37, fol 1

48   BL King's MS 126, fol 110; PRO (Transcripts) PRO 31/3/38, fol 184. For the earl of Southampton's troubles in 1604 see C C Stopes, *The Third Earl of Southampton*, London, 1922, pp 282–3

49   Loomie, 'Toleration and Diplomacy', p 53

50   Alnwick MS 101, fol 9v, Northumberland to the council, 14 Nov 1605

51   Loomie, 'Toleration and Diplomacy', pp 54–5

52   Appendix 3

53   See Syon MS X II 6 Box 12 bundle i, Carvile to the earl, 28 June 1608

54   Slingsby's mother was Mary Percy, sister of the seventh and eighth earls of Northumberland

55   There are many examples of, and papers relating to Carvile's charges. See for example Syon MS X II 6 Box 17 bundle f. Nor was he alone in making such accusations, Sir Thomas Leedes joined in (Syon MS Q I 14). In reply: Syon MSS P I 3g; Q I 16; Q I 17; X II 6 Box 11 bundle e. Slingsby's letter of 21 July 1604 is a particularly bitter self-justification, as are his and

Stockdale's letters of April 1605 in bundle e. For still further letters from Slingsby hostile to Carvile see YAS MSS DD 56/M/2/22 and 41

56 Syon MS X II 6 Box 18 bundle a, information about Topcliffe, with notes

57 It did bring about some tightening in accounting procedures, bailiffs being required in 1604 and 1605 to submit certificates of monies paid to principal officers (eg Syon MS X II 6 Box 27 bundle h, for Tadcaster)

58 When examined in 1605, Northumberland told the council that he had not placed great trust in Percy to begin with, joining him in commission with Wycliffe and other officers (PRO SP 14/216/113). This, however, was common practice (James, *Northumberland Estate Accounts*, p xxx)

59 Harrison, *Advice*, pp 77, 84

60 Syon MS X II 6 Box 12 bundle h, Thomas Percy's letter to Northumberland, 26 Jan 1603; X II 6 Box 18 bundle a, investigations at Topcliffe

61 PRO STAC 8/177/10; *History of Northumberland*, xii, pp 118–19

62 Evidence to illustrate Wycliffe's suspicions in 1602 is plentiful, see Syon MSS P II 2l and Q XI 2, but I have found no such complaints from Percy's fellow northern commissioner in 1604 or 1605; Syon MS X II 6 Box 11 bundle e, a memorandum of 'secret notes vnprouued', drawn up in 1605

63 Syon MSS C I 6, Stockdale's summary of northern receivers' accounts 1605; C II 2a, view of accounts for Northumberland; C III 9b, arrears on the receiver's account, 1606; Q I 12, Thomas Percy to Stockdale, 25 Mar 1605

64 Thomas Winter implied in November 1605 (Hatfield MS 113/54) that Percy had made no financial contribution to the plot before summer 1605

65 Syon MSS C I 6; C III 9b, arrears of Percy on the 1606 Northumberland receiver's account, Stockdale's summary of 1605; Alnwick MS Letters and Papers vol 7, fol 209; James, *Northumberland Estate Accounts*, pp xxxv, 168–70

66 The arrears for Cumberland were £268 in Michaelmas 1603, £412 in 1604, £450 in 1605. Those for Northumberland in 1605 were £1,338 (Syon MSS C I 6; X II 3 Box 10d; James, *Northumberland Estate Accounts*, pp 162–3, all figures to the nearest pound). Arrears could fluctuate according to problems in the cash-flow for any one year, thus Slingsby's arrears in Yorkshire for 1601 were about £100 and in 1602 were £1,058 (Syon MS X II 6 Box 12 bundle h)

67 Syon MS Q I 20; for the border commission see Galloway, *Union*, pp 85–6

68 PRO SP 14/17/16. Thomas Percy's movements in the two months preceding the plot were outlined in testimony, soon after and years after the plot, given by his erstwhile servants (SP 14/216/158; 14/87/5; 14/89/30)

69 PRO SP 14/216/4, 5, 223. Percy obtained a pass for post horses in late October 1605 from the northern commissioners (SP 14/15/106). He had apparently robbed Archbishop Matthew Hutton when the latter had

been dean of York, but had received a pardon for this misdemeanour (Hatfield MS 191/82, Sir Thomas Posthumus Hoby to Sir Edward Hoby, 26 Nov 1605)

70   PRO SP 14/216/59, examination of Josceline Percy, 9 Nov 1605. Josceline was Thomas Percy's nephew and was in the earl's service in London. The postmaster at Ware told Salisbury on 5 November (SP 14/216/8) that Percy had passed through the town bound for London on Saturday 2 November, although he had apparently told Northumberland's officer Thomas Fotherley that Percy had ridden through on the Friday (Alnwick MS 101, fol 1)

71   PRO SP 14/16/35, testimony of Agnes Fortun, a servant of the young prince

72   PRO SP 14/216/59; Hatfield MS 113/54

73   See below, p 160

74   *Lords' Journals*, iii, p 351

75   Syon MS U I 10, fols 62, 67, 80

76   *ibid*, fol 67

77   *ibid*, fols 28, 66; Batho, *Household Papers*, p 6

XI

'Clear as the day, or dark as the night'

Soon after the discovery of Gunpowder plot Northumberland was wakened by the earl of Worcester and, as we have seen, attended both that morning's meeting of the privy council and – after playing host to the earl of Sussex at dinner – the hastily prorogued session of parliament that afternoon.[1] As we have seen too, the council meeting ended in some uncertainty as to whether the earl should henceforth consider himself to be under house arrest, Nicolo Molin the Venetian ambassador relating how, in view of his continued mobility, a guard was placed on the door of Essex House to Northumberland's unconcealed disgust.[2] A man who knows himself to be innocent of a crime is sometimes slow to appreciate the depth of others' suspicions. It is also undeniably true that those under considerable stress do not always, in the heat of the moment, act in the most rational manner. Still later on 5 November the earl, recalling that Percy had expressed an intention to return north, sent off letters directing his Yorkshire officers to ensure the security of his Michaelmas rents, but apparently failing to stress that it was even more essential to apprehend the fugitive on a charge of high treason.[3] This was not the reaction expected of any loyal subject, let alone a privy councillor, and two days later – in a move superficially reminiscent of events in the summer of 1603 – the earl was confined to the archbishop of Canterbury's palace at Lambeth, in the custody of Sir William Lane, while investigations proceeded.[4]

Once the survivors of Holbeach had been brought to London the earl, still held at Lambeth, was examined at great length on 23 November. Transferred to the Tower four days later,[5] he underwent another examination – in the form of a list of questions which he was required to answer in writing – on 29/30 November, and a formal interrogation on 23 June, shortly before he at last appeared in star chamber. That much is the bare outline of the story; let us now look in detail at the examinations and other available sources to see how a case, however imperfect, was fashioned against him.

Early on, the evidence is unsolicited. While at Lambeth Northumberland naturally wrote several letters protesting his innocence, and although originals do not always survive, two entry-books at Alnwick supply the lacunae.[6] There are, however, certain problems in dating the letters contained in these books, since in instances where copies can be compared with originals the dates do not always correspond. The copy of the earl's letter of 10 November requesting that a good surgeon be sent to attend Percy – who was at that time reported wounded but alive – is dated accurately,[7] but that of 15 November in which Northumberland suggested as points in his favour the quiet and retired course of his recent life, his small store of weapons, and the dispersed nature of his stable, was dated 11 November in an entry-book.[8] Another letter, dated 16 November in copy, is dated 13 December on the original.[9] More reassuringly, though, the copies themselves are accurate when a comparison with the original is possible, encouraging us to trust the content of other copies, if not the dates they bear.[10]

Especially when one reflects that his kinship with Percy was – to begin with – the sole ground of suspicion, his letters make very interesting reading. Besides professing his innocence, Northumberland made several attempts to clear himself from particular circumstances then set against him, from which we are able to see how early some of these points arose. In retrospect, there is little doubt that he was unwise to do so, since the weight of circumstantial evidence was unquestionably the most telling point against him in the eyes of contemporaries. While such efforts are understandable, the feeling remains that he might have been better advised to go no further than a flat denial of any involvement in the treason, without embellishment, instead of adding fuel to already vehement suspicions.

Many observers placed a particularly sinister construction on the dinner party at Syon where Percy and the earl had met and talked the day before the intended explosion, and in a letter to the council on 8 November Northumberland developed an argument that Percy had only come to Syon because a servant had accidentally revealed his presence in London to members of the earl's retinue, so obliging the traitor to show himself openly in order to avoid unnecessary suspicion.[11] The surviving plotters' explanation of this visit, though different, also cleared the earl of direct complicity. Knowing by 4 November of the warning given to Monteagle, it will be remembered that they had agreed to allow Percy to put his head in the noose – if anything were known he would surely be arrested at Syon.[12] With Northumberland both a privy councillor and an acquaintance of Monteagle it was not unreasonable on their part to suppose that he would have been aware of any discovery. As we have seen, though, the argument had another implication which was in the end to turn not to Northumberland's advantage but to his disgrace.

To pursue this thread awhile, Robert Keyes testified on 30 November that he had been present when Percy had returned from Syon, and that he had then heard him declare either to Winter or one of the Wrights that he had used a fictitious story about a potential property purchase in Yorkshire to explain his visit, and that 'all was well'.[13] Northumberland, by implication, had heard nothing and had been left in ignorance. Nevertheless, for whatever reason, the visit had given new heart to the plotters. What stuck in the minds of the examiners was the simple fact that Percy had returned from Syon and had proceeded to give Fawkes the all-clear. Furthermore, human nature is such that they must have wondered whether Percy had really been taking a personal risk in going to Syon that day; might it be possible that he had felt safe with his master whether or not the plot had been discovered? The testimony of Winter and Keyes in any case did nothing to lessen the probability that Northumberland, for all his protestations that Percy had robbed and deceived him, had received a warning in general if not specific terms.

In another letter, the earl turned on those who cast doubt on his loyalty to the established religion, insisting that no one could seriously accuse him of being a papist. His household, he asserted, while it may have contained a few elderly family servants still clinging to old beliefs, was otherwise quite free of Catholics.[14] As for the current allegation that he had promised Catholics that he would stand by them, Northumberland maintained that

since the queens death that neuer any man liuinge harde me say such a worde. Before her majesties death vppon comaundement I receaued from the kinge if that commaundemente Percy brought me weare true, what I might saie to giue them conforte of tolleracions or that the kinge would be indifferent, or that I would doe them all the good I could to the ende to hold them firme to his majestie, suspecting by the generall oppinion and voyce that they affected the infantas title or might doe if they weare not held on with hopes, and to this ende shall you finde all my letters to his majestie in this sorte. And then perhapps I said that which would not haue byne well said now, yet I protest I remember noe perticulers

It was a point in his favour, he suggested, that when the Catholics had come to him in 1603 with their petition to James he had denied them his support and had counselled them against proceeding in this way. He even tried to make a virtue out of the fact that he had taken this petition to the king, suggesting that he had done so without the petitioners' permission and that he had also given their names to James and the council.[15] Whether it was his guilty conscience that moved him to touch on these matters, or the gossip of the town, or even some particular accusation, it is now impossible to say. Expressed in such a way, though, such vague protestations that all his dealings with the Catholics had been prompted only by a noble and disinterested desire to see James come peacefully into his inheritance, whatever their validity, would have been more likely to resurrect old suspicions rather than lay to rest new ones.

At the same time, the earl responded vigorously to suggestions that he had recently been in contact with his old friend Ralegh. He denied having written to Sir Walter since the latter's disgrace, and insisted that when Ralegh had written to him, his letters had been simply appeals to help the prisoner secure an early release. Once, Ralegh had sent him a letter supporting the petition for knighthood by one John FitzJames.[16] But that was all. Northumberland swore that he was withholding nothing. 'To be daintie', he wrote, 'I knowe breeds suspition yet often tymes forgettfullnes appeares to be dainties when it is not.' It was a reflection unlikely to cut much ice with men harbouring deep suspicions that the earl knew a good deal more than he was saying.[17] That the earl's old friendship should have at least been investigated was only natural. As we have seen, Fawkes named Ralegh as a potential sympathiser, and however much both sides may have denied any treasonous contact there was reason to suppose that they had been in touch recently through their mutual friend Sir Edmund Whitelocke, who was imprisoned in the Tower for a short time on the basis of such suspicions.[18]

On 19 November, in another letter to the council, Northumberland tried to rebut a further important circumstance that told against him. He enclosed some financial papers drawn together to show how Percy had robbed him of considerable sums while serving as his receiver. These papers, Northumberland argued, proved that he had not been 'soe nigh lodged in Percyes hart as the world might perhapps coniecture, or that his [Percy's] harte was soe tender that in a case of this nature hee would preferre my saftie before his purpose'. Assuming that the councillors were able to make sense of accounting papers set before them, and assuming that they were convinced that Percy had indeed been diverting funds, they could still have drawn several conclusions. The evidence certainly did not necessarily imply that Percy had decided against warning his master to stay away from parliament, and those inclined to suspect the worst might yet have wondered whether the earl had tacitly acquiesced to such a diversion of his revenues.

He might have helped undermine his cause still further when he claimed in a subsequent letter to have suddenly remembered two other guests at the dinner party of 4 November 'who I protest yesterday I had forgott'. The pair in question were Whitelocke and 'one Fitzharbart, a gentleman of myne'. Faulty memory was perhaps excusable, but so tardy a recollection would have done nothing to allay suspicions that Northumberland might yet have been harbouring more sinister secrets. This letter shows Northumberland also trying to explain away the origin of another current rumour – that he had actually intended to stay away from the opening of parliament. The earl put forward an ingenious theory: at dinner on 5 November, knowing that his fellow-councillors had 'suggested' that he stay in his house, he had expressed to his guest the earl of Sussex initial reluctance to go to Westminster that afternoon. Sussex was not a member of the privy council, and he or another then present might well have gone away with the idea that Northumberland had never planned to be present.[19]

The king, whom we see time and again taking an intense personal interest in Northumberland's case, asked Sussex for his version of events and passed on what the earl told him in a memorandum to Salisbury. Sussex's testimony gave some support to Northumberland's arguments, James writing that 'as for his purpose of not going to the parliament, he only saide at dinner that he was sleepie for his earlie rysing that daye, but soone after chainged his mynde and went'.[20] Northumberland's explanation, however, was itself implausible. Such gossip had probably developed out of a general suspicion that, like Monteagle, he had received some secret warning. That suspicion was, of course, a circumstance to which the earl could make no answer.

This letter provides one last example of the problems of dating letters in the two entry-books. In the 'Alnwick' copy Northumberland's letter is dated, very precisely, at six o'clock on 24 November, the day after the earl's well-documented examination at Lambeth. However, the undated copy in the 'Syon' entry-book has been endorsed by the earl himself: 'This letter was after my examination at my lord of Canterburyes 18 of Nouember 1605.' There is no other record of an examination on 18 November, and we may have here an instance of the earl looking back in later life and mistaking the date on which he was questioned. The balance of probabilities favours this hypothesis, since a covering note to Salisbury is also dated 24 November on the Alnwick copy.[21] Nevertheless, it would be well to establish before looking at the various interrogations that Northumberland may have been subjected to examination before the first for which we have a record. Written testimony was taken in order to obtain a signed admission which could be used in any future criminal proceedings. Consequently, it must not be supposed that at the examinations for which there are documentary records examinees were necessarily facing questions then posed for the first time.

Whatever their precise dates, the earl's letters from Lambeth suggest that he did not yet realise how vulnerable his position had become and how seriously he was threatened by the circumstances ranged against him. He appeared if anything more troubled by the possibility that the north-country landowner Sir Henry Widdrington, now appointed temporary custodian of Alnwick Castle, might take advantage of Thomas Percy's absence to remove valuable bonds from the traitor's study.[22] While obviously worried by the course of events, Northumberland seems to have believed that the storm would soon blow over, as it had in 1603, and that his fellow-peers would work to secure his freedom. Their failure to do so, coupled with his over-optimism, led to subsequent feelings of great bitterness towards 'unfaithful friends' which while understandable in an innocent man were hardly fair.

At his examination on 23 November, Northumberland was required to answer twenty-six questions apparently based on two lists of interrogatories drawn up by Popham and Coke. The drafting of these final questions provides a good example of how such lists were compiled, and their scope too is instructive, for they looked far beyond the recent treason, from the start embracing earlier events in the earl's political career. Popham suggested eighteen questions, of which fourteen sought to clarify the relationship between the earl and Thomas Percy, the obvious ground for suspicion:

How often and where was the said Thomas Percy with you sythens his last cumyng to London, and at what tymes of the day or night and who brought hym to you? . . . Did you send for the said Thomas to cum upp to you at his last being in Lundon upon what occasion dyd you so? . . . Dyd he receive your revenues how long hath he so don and by what means was he brught to do yt? . . . How many messages did you send after the said Percy and to what end now after hys last departure and where dyd you so send and at what tyme and what aunswer ys returned?

Understandably, he wished to know of all that had occurred at Syon on 4 November. Three questions worked away on the suggestion that, at or before James's accession, the earl had tried to ensure that English Catholics would look to him for leadership and guidance, while the last probed for an admission by Northumberland that he had been in recent contact with Ralegh.[23]

Coke sought enlightenment on a wider range of subjects, although like the lord chief justice he was naturally eager to know more about the traitor's career in the earl's service, and their meeting at Syon. He required Northumberland to explain why he had sent letters north on 5 November, and to declare how long he had known that Percy was renting the properties in Westminster. Coke's list contained just one question about the Catholics: he asked the earl to say what had moved him 'to affirme that his majesty nede not stand in feare of the Catholiques'. The attorney shared his colleague's suspicion that Ralegh might have been somehow implicated in the treason, demanding information on all recent communication between Northumberland, Sir Walter, and Lady Ralegh. Seeking clarification on a point that had apparently not occurred to Popham, he wanted to know if the earl had been aware that Whitelocke had come to the Tower on the morning of 6 November, clearly suspecting that he had been sent there by Northumberland after their meeting at Syon two days before. Breaking completely new ground, Coke also wanted to know how Northumberland had come to hear that James's nativity or horoscope had been cast in Paris, and why he had subsequently remained silent on the subject, telling no one what the prediction had been.[24]

None of these suspicions seems to have been allayed by the time that the final list of questions was prepared shortly before the examination of 23 November. Quizzed at some length on all these points, Northumberland's cautious, non-committal answers, while producing no damning evidence against him, did nothing to clear his name. He answered accusations concerning the Catholics by alleging that Percy, returning from one of his missions to Scotland, had said that 'the kinges pleasure was that his lordship should giue the Catholiques hopes that they should be well dealt withall or to such effect, and it may be that he hath tould so much as the king said, but remembred not to whom, but not since the kinges coming into England'. While he emphatically denied claiming that he could in any way direct the English Catholics, such vague words cannot have helped his cause.[25] The investigators must have doubted whether the earl could have forgotten so swiftly important matters that had taken place not three years earlier.

In addition, although Northumberland denied knowing that Percy rented property in Westminster 'vntill after the matter was discouered', his servant John Hippesley, examined on the same day, insisted that he had told his master about the lodging at least six weeks before.[26] As for the central question of his intimacy with Percy, Northumberland said that he had employed his kinsman for some ten years. He explained that Percy had himself suggested the mission to James, and that he had subsequently granted his enterprising messenger some moderate favour and advancement. With regard to the Syon meeting he said that they had spoken together in private before dinner, Percy having left at one o'clock. As to the subjects then discussed, he confirmed the story told by Percy to his confederates: 'There conference was concerning a guift of one Parkinson;[27] his coming downe into the countre the next sommer; and the entrie and taking possession of certain landes of Semer and Thurstanby in Yorkshire.' Nothing more. With regard to the king's horoscope, Northumberland recalled how in 1603 Dudley Carleton, then in his service, had told him that he had received a letter from a Parisian friend called St Saveur which had mentioned a prediction that 'the kinge should live many yeres'. This apart, Sir Robert Carr had informed him of another horoscope at about the same time, although he himself had never seen it. Moving to another point, he insisted that Whitelocke had told him only that he had been to the Tower and had then seen 'John Johnson'. He had rebuked Whitelocke for not waiting to be questioned there by the council, having been ordered to do so by one of Sir William Waad's men. Interestingly, there was no mention of Ralegh, either in the framing of the question or of the answer.

Besides an additional statement expanding on his knowledge of the second horoscope – perhaps in response to a royal directive[28] – that was the sum of his disclosures on the twenty-third. Given that the suspicions against him had hardly been dispelled by his answers, it is not so surprising that the decision was taken to transfer Northumberland to the Tower four days later. At the end of the month the further set of questions which he was required to answer in writing suggest that the range of suspicions was in fact widening. Seven questions covered the same ground as before: the wooing of the Catholics, the discussions with Percy on 4 November, and the casting of royal horoscopes – although on this occasion the examiners were trying to establish whether he had discussed such practices with Thomas Harriot, Nathaniel Torporley having by then admitted casting such a nativity at Harriot's request.[29] But the earl was also asked when and why he had 'increased' his stable with 'great horse', and also 'What was the last time that your lordship resolued to take phisick, and of whome, and to whome did you impart or give order for the same?'[30]

No answer to this interesting set of questions has survived, and Molin in his despatch of 12 December suggested that the earl had been extremely reluctant to say anything more. It is certain, however, that Northumberland did eventually reply, since in a letter of 13 December he added further information to an answer made to one interrogatory on the list. He had, so he claimed, only just remembered that Percy had raised the subject of the proposed articles of union between England and Scotland during the Syon dinner, although he could now remember no very precise details of the conversation.[31] Again the lords commissioners might have thought his forgetfulness suspicious. Sir William Lower, Northumberland's stepson-in-law, and another guest at the dinner, had already revealed during his examination on 2 December that the articles had been discussed at Syon, and assuming Northumberland had subsequently been informed of this, his own tardy 'recollection' could have been seen as nothing more than an attempt to cover himself in a matter that he would never have been the first to disclose.[32]

Of the added suspicions raised in these questions, the suggestion that Northumberland had planned to take physic rather than attend the opening of parliament was one of those allegations that could never be either proved or disproved, and it remained a topic of London gossip through the whole interval between the earl's arrest and trial. It was perhaps more significant that he was asked at the same time about purchasing fresh war horses for his stables. On 26 November, it will be recalled, Thomas Winter had revealed details of the Spanish treason, when the English negotiators had promised to supply such horses to an invading Spanish army.[33] It was later shown at Northumberland's trial that the earl himself had told the king about his efforts to buy horses at that time. Obviously James did not forget conversations so easily.

The king's attitude was clearly a vital, perhaps the vital element in this whole story. Besides the fundamental suspicion that Northumberland had been somehow designated protector of post-explosion England, James was clearly fascinated by other aspects of the case. He was intrigued by the earl's admission that he had known of occasions on which the royal horoscope had been cast, intrigued also to learn that Torporley and Harriot had themselves dabbled in such projects. Composing his memorandum to Salisbury, James personally drew up a list of questions that were to be put to Harriot on the subject, together with another set of questions for Carleton about the 'figure' cast in Paris. Both Harriot and Carleton were imprisoned for a time – Carleton in the Tower, Harriot in the Gatehouse – and Harriot's house at Syon was searched thoroughly for incriminating papers.[34]

While this was a subject that – not unnaturally – particularly interested the king, Northumberland's supposed taste for astrology formed no small part of the popular suspicion against him.[35] When, in the 1590s, the earl had first set about writing an *Advice* for his son, he had stressed the importance of such studies. Praising the science of astronomy, he had recommended the calculation of positional tables for the planets, because 'besides the inward satisfaction it hath yielded the best wits, rather admiring the beauty of the same than comprehending his whole secrets, [it] may withal embrace the doctrine of predictions, one of the highest points of human wisdom'.[36] The earl's reputation as a patron of the sciences grew considerably during his years in the Tower, and was exaggerated after his death, but the 'Wizard Earl' had nevertheless been supporting Harriot for some years, had been associated with Ralegh and other putative members of the 'atheistic' 'School of Night' about a decade earlier, and had certainly already gained a reputation as one who lacked religious conviction, maintaining that the love of scholastic enquiry transcended all other human emotions. It has even been argued, rather unconvincingly, that Shakespeare wrote *Love's Labour's Lost* to counter the tenets of the School of Night, as expressed in Northumberland's own unpublished 'Discourse on Love'.[37] The statement by Thomas Winter that 'for matter of relligion the earle troubled not much himselfe'[38] was not, so far as one can tell from the marginal and textual marks added by Coke, read at the earl's trial.[39] But the passage, while appearing to clear the earl of having held Catholic sympathies deep enough to ensure his support for Gunpowder plot, would certainly have been damning testimony itself in the eyes of contemporaries. In this matter as in all the other circumstances against him, credit and sympathy had been used up, and few were prepared to believe anything other than the worst.

No official, public explanation of the earl's confinement was forthcoming, and through November, especially before his committal to the Tower, his prospects for an early release seemed to alter day by day.[40] On 7 November, Chamberlain made some effort to be optimistic in a letter to Carleton, although his words could have given the recipient little comfort. Himself not particularly well-disposed towards the earl, Chamberlain saw grounds for suspicion all too clearly:

Not that your Lord (as I hope) can be any way toucht with this divelish conspiracie, but that neerenes of name, bloude, longe and inward dependance and familiaritie, cannot but leave some aspersion, that will not easilie or lightly be washt of without time.[41]

Molin was of course passing on any gossip that came his way. On 11 November he was in pessimistic mood:

The suspicion about the Earl of Northumberland goes on growing every day rather than diminishing, for it seems impossible that so vast a plot should have been hatched unless some great Lord were interested in it, and there is not the smallest indication against anyone except against this nobleman. Percy is his relation and his intimate, and as late as Monday last is known to have been in long conversation with him.[42]

Only two days later, though, the Venetian had been quite persuaded otherwise, believing that Northumberland was 'clearing himself more and more completely every day. It is thought certain he will be set free.'[43] The source of his information remains unknown, and most commentators inclined away from optimism. Pedro de Zuñiga briefed Philip III on 17 November about speculation linking Northumberland with the plot, wondering hopefully whether Beaumont, recalled to France less than a month before, might not also be under suspicion.[44] Nor was this simply ambassadorial wishful-thinking. Northumberland's friendship with Beaumont seems to have been common knowledge, and in a letter to Sir Thomas Edmondes on 19 November Sir Edward Hoby pointed out that if Northumberland proved to be guilty of treason there would be little doubt 'that Beaumont his hand was in the pye'.[45] The earl's prospects appeared all the more bleak once word got about that he had been questioned at Lambeth. On 26 November Philip Gawdy wrote that Northumberland had 'bene examyned this three days together'. Although not yet committed to the Tower, he was obviously 'in great daunger in the opinion of the world'.[46]

The casual observer, then, was clearly suspicious of Northumberland's motives and actions, a suspicion shared by those who would decide the earl's fate. Indeed, it appears that deep-rooted suspicion, based upon a mass of convincing circumstantial evidence which seemed to be growing day by day, finally saw the earl to the Tower. Commenting on this development, Molin expressed no great surprise, explaining that the earl was a known malcontent who had scarcely ever bothered to hide his feelings, that Salisbury was his bitter enemy, and that although 'the present earl seems disposed to adapt himself to the times', the Percy family had always been Catholic. Pessimistic once more, Molin saw nothing besides the obvious grounds for suspicion glaringly apparent to even the most ill-informed of Londoners:

There are evil prognostications for him, first because it seems impossible that in so vast a conspiracy, which had for its object to overthrow the kingdom and to set it in a blaze, there should not be at the head of it some nobleman, who aspired, if not to reign, at least to govern; as no one else has been discovered up to now, they think the Earl may be the man; that Percy was his relation gives a reasonable ground for suspicion, and it is considered a very lucky thing for the Earl that Percy is dead of the gun-wound.[47]

His opinion of the earl's good fortune was not, however, shared by Northumberland himself, who appreciated how Percy's testimony might well have helped to clear rather than condemn him. When he first heard rumours that his kinsman was but wounded in the attack on Holbeach, the earl had written to the council on 10 November asking them to examine Percy as soon as possible, and reminding their lordships that 'noen but he can shew me clere as the day, or darke as the night'.[48]

Notes

1 Hatfield MS 112/162; *Lords' Journals*, ii, p 355–6

2 *Calendar SP Venetian 1603–7*, pp 291–2, letter dated 7 Nov 1605. See also McClure, *Letters of Chamberlain*, i, pp 212–13, Chamberlain to Carleton, same day

3 Alnwick MS 101, fol 4. His messenger checked the money at Doncaster and, following orders, sent a colleague to find William Wycliffe – on his way home after the audit at York – so that Wycliffe could escort the money to London. Wycliffe heard the news at Leeming in north Yorkshire, hurried south to Doncaster via Wetherby, and had brought the money safely to London by 14 or 15 November (PRO SP 14/216/45; Syon MS X II 6 Box 30q, receiver's account for Yorkshire, 4 James I)

4 See above, p 143

5 Hatfield MS 113/50, Lane to Salisbury, 28 Nov 1605

6 Syon MS O I 2c; Alnwick MS 101. The Syon copies are damaged by fire. My quotes are almost solely drawn from the Alnwick volume. The earl has endorsed the Syon copies in places. Some flyleaves from the Syon series of letters, also burnt, are in Alnwick MS Letters and Papers vol 9

7 PRO SP 14/216/225; Alnwick MS 101, fol 6

8 PRO SP 14/16/77; Alnwick MS 101, fol 7

9 PRO SP 14/17/39; Alnwick MS 101, fol 11

10 Besides the earl's letters, the entry-books preserve a 'lost' letter from Thomas Fotherley to his master. Sent north by Northumberland on 5 November, Fotherley reported from Ware that the postmaster remembered Percy passing through on the previous Friday night, bringing with him three portmanteaux full of money. Two men had accompanied Percy, and though the postmaster had recognised neither, he judged that one had been a gentleman. This letter was recorded in Levinus Munck's 'Kalender' of papers relating to the treason (PRO SP 14/16/70), but was noted as missing by the mid nineteenth century (*Calendar SP Domestic 1603–10*, p 256 – the copy is Alnwick MS 101, fol 1, where it is dated on the night of Friday 7th [*sic*]. The date is there derived, probably, from a mistaken endorsement on the Syon copy (Syon MS O I 2c, fol 1v), which again suggests that the Alnwick copies were derived from the Syon set)

11 Alnwick MS 101, fol 4. See PRO SP 14/216/59, Josceline Percy's examination. See also SP 14/216/100, Fawkes's examination, 16 Nov 1605

12 Hatfield MS 113/54

13 PRO SP 14/216/126

14 See above, p 114

15 Alnwick MS 101, fols 9–10. This letter is dated in copy 14 November, and refers to a question at an examination on the day before. While the earl may have undergone some form of examination on 13

November, it is also possible that the date may have originally been 24 November, the error lying with the copyist

16   FitzJames was given permission to visit Ralegh in the Tower in January 1605, and the letter may have followed this visit (Hatfield MS 191/139). FitzJames's copy of an agreement over estates between himself and Ralegh, dated 26 May 1603, is among the archives at Alnwick (Syon MS X II 12 Box 2e). This must be one of the last surviving documents signed by Ralegh as a free man

17   Alnwick MS 101, fols 9–10. Fawkes mentioned Ralegh as a possible sympathiser (PRO SP 14/216/38, 54; see also SP 14/16/38). Ralegh too denied any recent contacts. He had only spoken to Whitelocke to find out how Northumberland was currently disposed towards him – getting no encouraging reply – and he had once given a present to the French Ambassador's wife via Whitelocke, the captain being in her entourage when she visited the Tower (Edwards, *Life and Letters of Ralegh*, ii, pp 387–8).

18   Hatfield MSS 112/160, 115/7, 191/43

19   Alnwick MS 101, fols 13, 14; Syon MS O I 2c, fols 10v, 11v. There is yet another copy, also burnt, in Alnwick MS Letters and Papers vol 7, fol 207

20   Hatfield MS 134/86. But James in addition reported that Sussex had raised a suspicious point: 'Sussexe sayeth that Northumberlande prayed him to dyne with him that fatall Tuesday and that thay being at dinner and discoursing of this great accident, Northumberland did aske some of his men hou and quhen Percy gotte that house, quho telling him that Percie had hyred it long agoe, Northumberlande suaire that he never knew before that Percie hadde it, so as ye maye nou see that it was not *lapsus memoriae* that maid him denye to the counsall his knowledge of Percies hauing that house, but only that purposlie he will not be thocht to haue any knowledge of the hyring of that house.'

21   Alnwick MS 101, fol 15

22   PRO SP 14/16/97, 112, Northumberland to Salisbury, 21 and 25 Nov 1605

23   PRO SP 14/16/100

24   PRO SP 14/16/101

25   PRO SP 14/216/112, 113, interrogatories and answers, 23 Nov 1605

26   PRO SP 14/216/115

27   As soon as 'Parkinson' had been mentioned, presumably in the course of earlier questioning, the council had ordered a search for men of that name in Yorkshire. Five unfortunates were rounded up. One of these, Cuthbert Parkinson, had a slight acquaintance with Percy but swore stoutly that he neither owned any land nor had held a serious conversation with the traitor for many years. They had, though, met on the highway recently (PRO SP 14/16/51; Hatfield MS 113/17; 191/88, three reports to Salisbury from Yorkshire and Northumberland, 11, 18, and 28 Nov 1605). The enthusiastic searchers also arrested Allan Percy of Beverley, Thomas's elder brother, and he was brought to London and imprisoned for a time in

the Marshalsea prison (BL Additional MS 12497, fol 372; PRO (Transcripts) PRO 31/6/1, fols 6–7; Hatfield MSS 191/76; 113/17)

28 PRO SP 14/216/113A

29 PRO SP 14/216/122

30 PRO SP 14/216/125, interrogatories of 29/30 Nov 1605

31 *Calendar SP Venetian 1603–7*, p 305; PRO SP 14/17/39

32 PRO SP 14/216/137, examination of Sir William Lower, 2 Dec 1605. One of Northumberland's footmen carried a letter from the earl to Lower, who had married Penelope Perrott, on 27 November (Syon MS U I 10, fol 66)

33 Hatfield MS 112/91

34 Hatfield MSS 134/86; 113/80, 92, 107, 141, 142; 114/40; 190/47; PRO SP 14/17/4; Shirley, *Thomas Harriot*, pp 340–4. Although imprisoned only for a short time, Carleton's career took years to recover. Early in 1607 Sir Allan Percy wrote to him suggesting that he take an opportunity to travel on the continent with the earl of Essex: 'if you only desire to ayre youre self for a tyme, I howlde this no smalle opertunety to shake of the gunpowder fume that yet hangeth vppon you for youre owlde masters sake' (PRO SP 14/26/9)

35 Shirley, *Thomas Harriot*, pp 336–57

36 Harrison, *Advice*, p 70

37 Yates, *A Study of Love's Labour's Lost*, *passim*; PRO SP 14/11/9

38 PRO SP 14/216/116, confession of 25 Nov 1605

39 It is not absolutely certain that the remark was omitted, since the omission marks may have referred to one of the other gunpowder trials. See Stonyhurst MS Anglia VI/62; below, p 196 n 47. According to Garnett in one of his confessions, Francis Tresham had expressed similar uncertainty over Northumberland's support for what Tresham understood as the Catholic cause (Hatfield MS 110/30, examination of 9 Mar 1606, see Gardiner, 'Two Declarations of Garnet', p 511). The prosecution, after all, was quite prepared to equate atheism with Catholicism

40 See, for example, PRO (Transcripts) PRO 31/9/113, fols 399–400, 402, 405, papers among Borghese transcripts

41 McClure, *Letters of Chamberlain*, i, pp 212–13

42 *Calendar SP Venetian 1603–7*, p 293

43 *ibid*, p 295

44 Loomie, 'Guy Fawkes in Spain', p 41. A friend to the last, Northumberland had given Beaumont his picture for a keepsake (Petworth MS 5726, unfoliated, Sir Edward Francis's book of payments, 1605; Gloucester Library, Smyth of Nibley papers, vol 7, fol 70)

45 BL Stowe MS 168, fol 232v

46 Jeayes, *Letters of Philip Gawdy*, p 164. Sir William Browne had certainly heard some very harsh judgements on Northumberland's conduct when he wrote from Flushing to Viscount Lisle on 2 December (Collins, *Letters and Memorials*, ii, p 316)

47 *Calendar SP Venetian 1603–7*, p 301. Similar views were also expressed about the same time by an unnamed party recalled in Vincent Earle's deposition (PRO SP 14/16/76i)

48 PRO SP 14/216/225

XII

Circumstances and time

In the absence of any clear statement on Northumberland's case several highly eccentric rumours were abroad. Molin, for example, reported on 28 November that the earl had for some reason sent his secretary to France a few days before the plot had been discovered, and that this man had already been examined by the council.[1] So far as one can extract a basis of truth to this story, it seems as if the ambassador was referring to Dudley Carleton, who had left the earl's service in March 1605 and who had subsequently been employed by Lord Norris in Spain and – latterly – Paris. As we have had cause to note, Carleton was recalled in November, partly because he had passed on information to Northumberland regarding the king's horoscope but also because he was thought to have assisted Percy in obtaining the lease of the 'gunpowder house' in Westminster.[2] Though unconcerned by talk of this kind, the government did think it advisable to disclose some details of the earl's case for circulation in foreign courts. At the beginning of December Salisbury wrote to all English ambassadors explaining the removal of Northumberland from 'honourable' confinement at Lambeth to the grimmer confines of the Tower:

Because Percy onely named him and Monteagle, whome hee would fore-warne, and that Monteagle had a letter of warning, together with the circumstance of Percyes inwardnes, and resorte vnto the earle, not 20 howres before the blow should haue bin geuen; the presumption hath bin thought sufficient like wise to commit him to the like place, and custodye, and thus much the rather, because the earle, vpon the death of the queene, and after, hath declared often to the kinge that the Catholikes had offered them selues, to depende vpon him, in all their courses, so farre as his majestie making him knowe his pleasure, he doubted not but to conteyne them from any extreamitye.

Salisbury thought that the earl might have received a warning of some kind, although there was obviously no way of telling whether or not he would have come to parliament. He concluded cautiously:

only this is his misfortune, that Catesby and Percy being dead, his innocencie or his guiltines must both depend upon circumstances of other persons and time.[3]

On 2 December the Secretary sent off a similar letter to the chancellor of Scotland, the earl of Dunfermline, in which he wrote that Percy was thought to have given his master some general warning, but to have said nothing of the plot itself.[4] There is no need to accuse Salisbury of hypocrisy in these letters. The earl's fate, as Northumberland himself realised well enough, would indeed have to depend upon circumstances, and all known circumstances up to that time hardly pointed to his complete innocence. No link had been traced between the conspirators and any other great nobleman. Northumberland had favoured Percy, Percy had dined at Syon on 4 November, Percy was dead and mute. Surely Percy would have warned the earl, just as Monteagle had been warned?

It was widely believed at this time that Percy had written the letter to Monteagle. Just why the conviction was so strong it is now a little difficult to say, but we have seen how in *King's Book* Monteagle no sooner heard Thomas Percy's name mentioned in connection with the Westminster vault than he suspected, by reason of Percy's 'backwardnes in religion' and their old friendship, that the letter had come from him.[5] Coke, at the trial of the plotters in January, explained how he 'assured himself' that Percy had written the letter.[6] Monteagle's financial obligations to Percy's wife and child could be seen as one good reason for the traitor to have done everything possible to save his life.[7]

But if Percy had so warned Monteagle, would he not also have warned his own kinsman and master, who had been so generous to him in years past? When Fawkes was asked on 6 November whether it had been Percy's intention to let the earl perish in the blast he had replied guardedly that in his opinion Percy 'would haue bene loth to haue done him hurt, bycause he was bounde vnto him', an answer hardly calculated to allay suspicion.[8] Fawkes subsequently confessed on 11 November that Percy had suggested both Northumberland and Monteagle might be warned to stay away from parliament. Repeating this statement on 30 November, he added that the plotters had agreed to warn various noblemen, expecting their assistance after the explosion.[9] Neither of these two last confessions survives in its original form so we cannot say in what precise context the statements were made. Inevitably, however, they blighted the earl's chances of clearing his name. Some points made in the examinations seemed to tell in his favour: thus on 16 November Fawkes recalled that Tresham too had been anxious to save Monteagle,[10] but with all warnings being left in the end to the individual initiatives of plotters,[11] it was apparent that none could ever be sure which noblemen had been warned, or by whom.

In his letter to Edmondes, Hoby also mentioned the rumour that Northumberland had received, and subsequently concealed, a letter similar to that sent to Monteagle.[12] With the two peers thus bracketed together in public suspicion, the earl could only suffer in the comparison. Even a man with Monteagle's dubious background had acted with diligent loyalty on receiving the obscure letter. What did that say for the actions of Northumberland, a privy councillor and captain of the king's bodyguard, who, supposing that he had also been warned by Percy, had either ignored or concealed the message?

So far as is known, Northumberland was not examined again by the commissioners until 23 June 1606, when all other major trials arising from Gunpowder plot had been concluded and the sentences all duly executed. Again so far as we know, he was not mentioned by name in any of these earlier trials. Witnessed and conducted by Lord Chancellor Ellesmere, the earls of Nottingham, Suffolk, Worcester, Northampton, and Salisbury, together with Popham and Coke, the examination of 23 June is, in the written record at least, shorter than its predecessors. The five set questions were notable only for the unoriginal nature of the subject matter. All five concentrated on clarifying what letters the earl had written to his estate officers in the north after the council meeting on 5 November, and on establishing the role which Northumberland had appointed Percy to play in transporting the Michaelmas rent money up to London. Northumberland replied by insisting that he had only written two letters that day, entrusting one to the post and the other to his official Thomas Fotherley, 'and the reason of his wrighting was because he heard of the lords of the councell what Percey had done, and was affraid that he would runne away with his money. And sayth that those letters conteyned no other matter but the safe keping of his money.' He told the examiners that Percy had controlled his revenue in Northumberland for 'about eight yeres'.

Subsequently, the earl answered some supplementary questions that do not appear on the original list, once again doing little to disperse the rumours surrounding his case. When asked whether or not he had spoken to Percy about his revenues at Syon on 4 November he replied that 'he remembreth not that he asked any such question of him at that time, but it might be he did and it might be he did not'. Contradicting his statement made on 23 November, the earl denied ever having given Catholics hopes that the king might ease their afflictions, and he also flatly denied having employed any go-between to the Catholics 'that they should be well dealt withall'. One new point, however, emerges from these additional questions:

Being demaunded when Percey was sworne a pencioner he aunswereth that it will appeare by the clarke of the checkes booke and that he gave ordre to some to giue him his othe and thinketh that ordre was giuen to the lievetenant and never asked his lievetenant whether he had giuen him his oth or no as he remembreth, but thought he was sworne because he sawe him beare the axe as he thinketh.[13]

When examined, the earl's brother Sir Allan Percy, his lieutenant of the pensioners, tried to help the suspect, insisting that he had indeed sworn in Thomas Percy. Unfortunately, those whom Sir Allan claimed had witnessed the ceremony flatly denied ever having been present when the traitor took his oaths.[14] Gardiner attached much importance to this particular failing in his analysis of the factors telling against Northumberland. The earl had, after all, received specific instructions from the king to see that all pensioners took the requisite oaths.[15] 'It is possible', Gardiner wrote, 'that the nature of this fault had not come to light till a short time before the trial, as Cecil, in a letter of March 3, does not refer at all to the omission of the oath.' He ventures so far as to suggest that it may have been 'the full discovery of the particulars of this transaction which turned the scale against the Earl'.[16]

Gardiner perhaps exaggerates his case, for it is hard to believe that the scale was exactly balanced before this point emerged. In addition, while Sir Allan had certainly been under no apparent suspicion earlier,[17] it is difficult to see this matter as a new discovery; the commissioners seem to have known of Percy's failure to take the requisite oaths long before June 1606. On 25 June, Chamberlain wrote to Carleton with news of Northumberland's recent examination,

mentioning current rumours that the earl would soon follow
Mordaunt and Stourton to star chamber. He went on to say that
their mutual friend Sir Allan – himself one of Carleton's regular
correspondents – had also been examined and committed to the
Tower. Chamberlain was at a loss for an explanation, 'but some say
yt is about the old matter of Percie that he was not sworne when he
was admitted pencioner; others, for conveyenge some letters lately to
my Lord'.[18] Sir Allan did indeed join his brother in the Tower for a
short time, and his examination, probably taken there, was used as
evidence in the earl's trial. When the proceedings in star chamber
were over, though, imprisonment was soon replaced by house arrest,
and letters to Secretary and privy council ensured his release by
mid-July. Not surprisingly, though, he lost his lieutenancy of the
gentlemen pensioners.[19]

Chamberlain must be allowed the privileges of the world-weary
Londoner, for whom virtually all news, particularly that which
astonishes miserable rustics, is stale. But in some ways this
undoubtedly was an 'old matter'. In December 1605 the professional
decipherer Thomas Phelippes, then a prisoner, had written to Hugh
Owen supplying him with information which he claimed to have
received from a reliable source 'who should seeme to knowe some
thinge in state matters'. Northumberland, he wrote, was suspected
because he was thought to have known long before that Percy had
hired a house in Westminster, because his intention to take physic on
5 November had been disclosed by his 'apothecarye', and – most
significantly in the present context – because he had admitted Percy
to the place of a pensioner without making him take the oath of
supremacy.[20] Another letter from Phelippes to Owen written in the
following month expressed an opinion that Northumberland would
soon be censured for his 'soolen contumacye' in star chamber.[21] The
significance of this evidence is extremely hard to assess. For one
thing, there are no original letters; all that we have are summaries of
their contents set down by the man who helped Phelippes by making
final copies from the rough drafts. Another complication is that
Phelippes, essentially a loyal servant of the government, was writing
to Owen hoping to draw secrets from him and so restore his own
reputation.[22] In so doing there is no need to doubt that he gave free
rein to his imagination, including in his letter the wildest gossip. All
the same, he probably did not pluck the stories about
Northumberland out of thin air.

Knowing Percy's religious persuasion, it would surely have been natural for the council to have made enquiries about the oath at an early stage. Perhaps it was then felt that evidence of deeper guilt might yet emerge. Rather than this point being either fully appreciated or rediscovered in June 1606, it was probably then resorted to by the prosecution as one of the few certain facts to back a host of suspicions, and it was probably brought up at the pre-trial examination precisely because the earl had not yet conceded this dereliction of duty in a written confession. That, perhaps, is the most likely explanation, but it might be allowed that in this one instance at least, public speculation may have successfully moved ahead of the official enquiry.

In December 1605, and then throughout the first half of 1606, the earl's prospects remained the subject of some imaginative but still uncertain public speculation. On 12 December 1605, according to rumours passed on by Molin, the earl was not only refusing to answer questions, but was also demanding trial by his peers. The same gossip had it that when Salisbury told him that his late brother-in-law had never remained stubbornly silent in that way, Northumberland had retorted that this was quite irrelevant, since at the end of his life Essex had simply lost his wits. Dorothy, wrote Molin, was working hard to secure her husband's release and was in good spirits because the king was treating her kindly, but general opinion, so far as the Venetian could tell, was far less optimistic, given Salisbury's hostility and the notorious fact that, once a great man entered the Tower of London, he was unlikely to re-emerge – at least with his head still on his shoulders.[23] Molin had learnt one lesson from his cursory study of English history, and this gloomy reflection was seldom far from his mind when ruminating on Northumberland's case.

Early in the new year the earl's prospects again seemed somewhat brighter, and Zuñiga wrote that as a result of the death of Percy – from whom they had hoped to learn 'grands cosas' – the council had insufficient evidence to make a case against Northumberland.[24] On 15 January Molin, now joined in London by his successor Zorzi Giustinian, gave support to this view, claiming that the earl was successfully countering Salisbury's hostility, steadily proving his innocence, and so might soon be set free.[25]

Such optimism again proved groundless, and in fact it seems that Northumberland had been destined for an earlier appearance in star chamber until the capture of Garnett brought a halt to proceedings against the suspect noblemen while the new prisoner was examined, not least on what he could say about their part in the plot. Originally, king and council seem to have intended only the briefest of intervals between the trials of the Gunpowder plotters and those of the noblemen. Star chamber would thus be used for a purpose made increasingly familiar over the past century – as a means to correct the misdeeds of overmighty subjects. On 12 February, however, the earl of Shrewsbury wrote to Edmondes from Whitehall telling him that, while the council had intended to summon some of the suspect lords in the Tower to star chamber on the following day, their cases had now been deferred until Easter term.[26] Garnett's capture had other consequences too: Northampton argued successfully in the House of Lords for a delay in proceedings of attainder against the plotters, since the new prisoners could almost certainly supply new pertinent information.[27] Nevertheless, the very proposal to try the suspect noblemen in February itself suggests that the government held no great hopes of ever catching the principal Jesuit suspects.

In Northumberland's case there was another possible inducement for a postponement. On 15 November 1605 the professional informer Ralph Radclyffe informed Salisbury that he had learnt at third-hand how Christopher Harris, a Cornishman allegedly long favoured by the earl, had spoken privately to Northumberland during the previous summer. During their conversation the earl was alleged to have said:

I dare tell you the kinge will speake to me: and say I ame an honest man, but he loves me not, no more doth he men of the sworde and Mr Harrys I may saye to yow we have a discontented state, many lords and noblemen are troubled in mynde, and as the state nowe stands yt cannot howlde, and that will shortly appeare.[28]

Salisbury endorsed this document with the date 'February 1605', perhaps reflecting the original plans for a trial that month. Such testimony was, to say the least, unimpressive, but in looking for facts where nothing but circumstances and suspicion existed the prosecution was prepared – as it did when the trial finally took place – to use anything that came to hand. Radclyffe, though, proved a reluctant witness. When summoned to testify in star chamber he begged to be excused, declaring – quite truthfully – that all he had said was nothing more than hearsay.[29]

Also in February 1606, one of Salisbury's informants, the part-time alchemist Henry Wright, took time off from his search for the philosophers' stone to inform the Secretary that, so far as Northumberland was concerned, there were in his opinion 'not passing three or fower persons which can say much against him now that Percy is gone, but I presume (upon some good grounds) that those three or fower can say something to the purpose'. Wright suspected that the Jesuit Thomas Strange, captured in Warwickshire during the previous November and then being re-examined, was one of those 'three or fower'.[30] Strange, it soon transpired, could say nothing which might incriminate the earl, and given all the circumstances a postponement of the trial was probably felt to be in order.[31]

There is nothing in Salisbury's correspondence from this period to suggest satisfaction at the downfall of a potential rival. The letter of 3 March referred to by Gardiner was sent to Henry Brouncker, lord president of the council in Munster and a brother-in-law of Lord Monteagle.[32] In this letter, Salisbury was at pains to point out that the king had to restrain Northumberland; in a case like this there could be no question of taking chances. Nevertheless, considering

the greatnes of his howse, and the improbability that he should be acquainted with such a barbarous plott, being a man of honor and valour, his majesty is rather induced to beleeue, that whatsoeuer any of the traytours haue spoken of him, hath ben rather their vants then vpon any other good ground; so as I think his liberty will the next terme be granted vpon honorable and gracious termes.

He concluded the letter with an unsolicited testimonial: 'though ther hath neuer ben any extraordinary deerenes between vs, I wish [his release], because this state is very barren of men of great blood and great sufficiency together'. Gardiner considered this to have been the opinion of a sincere man and there was certainly no particular reason for Salisbury to have made so personal a remark in such a letter. Six days later, the Secretary noted that James had decided to have three lords tried in star chamber, but it is not clear to which three of the four peers then in custody he referred. In any case, it is very likely that the king did indeed take the final decision, and that these plans were but postponed until Garnett had been arraigned for treason.[33]

As time went on, and the earl remained a prisoner, optimism gave way to more realistic appraisals of the situation. Writing in April, Sir Allan Percy described how he had been given permission to visit his brother in prison, how no mention had been made of the earl at Garnett's trial, although 'there was a shew as thought [sic] they could say more then they would', and how one or two small favours had left the earl anticipating an early release. 'His course for living at Petworth,' he wrote, 'is altered, and Harry Tayler is gone to day to Sion to lay in beare.' But privately, Sir Allan felt that his brother was building his hopes too high, and that Garnett's trial would only prejudice the earl's cause, keeping Gunpowder plot at the forefront of public attention. If pressed to write honestly, he could not see the beer being drunk.[34] On 8 May Giustinian, an altogether more astute man than his predecessor, made what turned out to be a rather accurate prediction when he suggested that the earl was too powerful either to be condemned or to be set free.[35] The many suspicions remained unanswered, and after Garnett's execution almost all those who might have been able to speak concerning the earl's guilt or innocence had been silenced forever.

This must have been a worrying, trying time for Northumberland as he awaited some action about his cause, even though the conditions of his imprisonment were by no means harsh – as soon as he was sentenced the council gave orders that he be confined more strictly.[36] A book of disbursements kept by John Hippesley in the first half of 1606 gives us some idea of what the earl's life was like.[37] He received cheeses regularly from Sir William and Lady Waad; a reward was given to the countess of Suffolk's gentleman usher when he brought the earl a pair of gloves to mark the young earl of Essex's wedding. At least Northumberland ate well, consuming large quantities of figs and almonds – 'gelly', hares, gammon, cockles, cherries, possets, and apples were all delivered to him. Boredom must have been the worst hardship, and this was lightened by gaming, playing with 'shittelcockes', taking a look at the 'lyons' of the Tower, listening to a 'blind harpor' and watching the antics of 'tomfoole'. Apart from a brief list of rewards and two entries for 'works', the final entries in the book – the only dated entries – were for one shilling spent on a pen and inkhorn, and one pound given in reward to the warders that waited on him on 27 June, the day on which he was at last escorted to star chamber for his trial.

Notes

1   *Calendar SP Venetian 1603–7*, p 301
2   PRO SP 14/216/39, Susan Whynniard's examination, 7 Nov 1605.

Baron Hoboken, ambassador from Spanish Flanders, related the same rumours, and told how it was thought that Northumberland had confessed to participating in the plot (Brussels, Archives Générales du Royaume, PEA 365, fol 62v, despatch of 7 Dec 1605 ns)

3 PRO SP 84/65, fol 122, Salisbury to Winwood, 1 Dec 1605; BL Stowe MS 168, fols 264v–5, Salisbury to Edmondes, 2 Dec 1605

4 PRO SP 14/17/2

5 *His Majesties Speach*, sig G2v

6 Bodleian MS Add C86, fol 7

7 Hatfield MS 113/91. Waad discovered this point in December 1605 – a very late, clumsy arrangement if the authorities had indeed been manipulating the plot all along!

8 PRO SP 14/216/16A

9 Bodleian MS Tanner 75, fol 203; *Archaeologia*, xii, p 211*

10 PRO SP 14/216/100

11 PRO SP 14/216/146. Winter had said earlier (Hatfield MS 113/54) that as many noblemen as possible were to be warned. See also the vague reply that Catesby allegedly gave to Ambrose Rookwood when asked what had been done to preserve some Catholics 'and diuers other friendes' (SP 14/216/136). Catesby had assured Digby that all those lords worth saving would be warned 'and yet knowe not of the matter' (SP 14/216/135)

12 BL Stowe MS 168, fol 232v

13 PRO SP 14/216/220

14 Cheshire CRO De Tabley MS DLT/B 8, p 172

15 See above, p 129

16 Gardiner, *History of England*, i, p 285

17 PRO SP 14/20/4, Sir Allan Percy to Carleton, 1 Apr 1606

18 McClure, *Letters of Chamberlain*, i, p 228

19 Alnwick MS 521, p 139, list of Tower prisoners; Hatfield MSS 192/103; 116/135, letters to Salisbury and to the privy council, 5 and 7 July 1606; PRO SP 14/22/53 and 67*, letters to Carleton, 16 and 31 July 1606

20 PRO SP 14/17/61

21 PRO SP 14/17/62

22 Williamson, *Gunpowder Plot*, pp 98–9, thought that both were probably forgeries made by the copier Thomas Barnes at the direction of Salisbury. The Secretary, he suggested, had employed Phelippes to forge a confession of Thomas Winter and was arranging to have him safely out of the way when Winter was tried. It is difficult to see why – the deposition would not have been subjected to scrutiny at a trial. See also Hatfield MSS Petitions 248; 117/82

23 *Calendar SP Venetian 1603–7*, p 305. See also PRO (Transcripts) PRO 31/9/113, fol 406

24 Simancas E2585/2, 3, Zuñiga's despatch, 7 Jan 1606

25 Calendar SP Venetian 1603–7, p 315. Towards the end of February a diarist noted similar optimism, but subsequently cancelled the passage from his journal (Roberts, *Diary of Walter Yonge*, p 3)

26   BL Stowe MS 168, fol 327v. See also fol 353, a letter from the earl of
Northampton to Edmondes, 2 Mar 1606
27   *Lords' Journals*, ii, p 370
28   Hatfield MS 113/9
29   Hatfield MS 114/112, undated. A similar situation arose in August
1606. One Biller claimed to have seen the earl at several masses, but later
denied everything, arguing that he had been drunk when making these
accusations. (Hatfield MS 117/64) One report around this time claimed that
Northumberland had produced 'una scrittura' in his defence (PRO
(Transcripts) PRO 31/9/114, fol 238, Borghese *avviso*), but there is now no
trace of such a document
30   Hatfield MS 110/8
31   Hatfield MS 113/34, list of interrogatories for Thomas Strange. One
asked whether he or some other principal Jesuits had not 'made certain
account' that the earl of Northumberland would 'stand surely for the
Catholic cause when time served'. This line of questioning was based on
information concerning discussions between Hugh Owen and William
Baldwin in Brussels, passed on by the spy John Ratcliff. The discussions were
supposed to have taken place the year before. Strange was examined on
some of these questions in December and February (PRO SP 14/17/12, 32;
14/18/109) but there is no record of an answer that even mentions
Northumberland. See also SP 14/16/116, questions prepared around the
start of December 1605, for an earlier indication that this matter was under
consideration. See also Hatfield MSS 190/35; 109/160, Popham and Sir
Thomas Challoner to Salisbury, 1 and 5 Feb 1606, about searches made for
Ratcliff's reports. In 1610 Baldwin was brought to England for questioning,
and Ratcliff was produced to confront him with the same accusations –
apparently without result (HMC, *Downshire*, iii, p 16)
32   PRO SP 63/218/21
33   As has been seen, with Garnett dead, the trials of the suspect lords
were delayed no longer, Mordaunt and Stourton being arraigned within five
weeks, and Northumberland within two months of his execution
34   PRO SP 14/20/4. The earl's application to see his brother was
mentioned by Sir William Lane in an undated letter to Salisbury (SP
14/22/21)
35   *Calendar SP Venetian 1603–7*, p 350. Cf PRO (Transcripts) PRO
31/9/114, fol 245, Borghese *avviso*
36   BL Additional MS 11402, fol 112v, privy council to Waad, 30 June
1606
37   Alnwick MS 790

XIII

Northumberland in star chamber

All the pent-up suspicion in high places was at last expressed openly at the earl's trial.[1] When he was brought to star chamber on 27 June it was to take a central role in one of the most public of public trials during that busy year. Far from being the shamefaced, secret affair that some have described,[2] this was a major showpiece, Coke's final appearance as attorney-general, and there was intense competition to be present.[3] John Hawarde, an experienced observer of proceedings in the court, wrote that 'a greate scaffold was erected for the courtiers and other men of great account',[4] but the spectacle attracted a host of lesser men too, certainly more than the court could comfortably hold. One eyewitness did not commit himself to reporting events strictly according to the 'meathod then observed, because the presse of people was soe greate and out of order' that he 'could not make due observacion of all particulers as they weare oppened'.[5] In a letter to Salisbury, another spectator wrote of being 'somewhat wearied with presse', and described how those at the back of the crowd had not been able to hear the sentences and had been obliged to ask 'such as had stood nearer and were passing by outwards at what somme the earl was fyned?'[6] The mix of some sympathy, much interest in the fall of a great man, and a prospect of further disclosures about Gunpowder plot proved for many a difficult blend to resist.

Watched by this eager throng, the trial began. As with Mordaunt and Stourton, Northumberland was held to have admitted in his examinations the actual offences laid against him, since proceedings *ore tenus* in star chamber could in theory only follow upon a confession of guilt by the accused.[7] The attorney-general was present simply to recite the earl's undisputed indiscretions so that the lords of the privy council could pass sentence. Coke, however, no doubt in compliance with instructions from the council but also following the habits of a lifetime, considered that the occasion was right to say more. He felt it necessary – as he had done in the earlier trial of the Gunpowder plotters – to justify Northumberland's treatment during the past seven months. No one, he noted, had been asked any specific question about the earl in connection with the Gunpowder treason; all information now presented that had been taken from the testimony of other men had been gathered from general questioning alone.[8] Once again feeling himself obliged to excuse the delay in bringing the prisoner to trial, Coke resorted to the same explanation, drawing upon the dark and complex nature of the crimes involved. It had seemed likely to investigators of the treason that the 'venom thereof had infected farther then could bee easilie or so speedily discovered'. He reminded his audience that two Gunpowder conspirators – Robert Winter and Stephen Littleton – had only been captured in January, and that the arrest of Garnett had subsequently again delayed the due process of law. For the king, he said, had decreed that the suspect noblemen were to be tried in star chamber, and such 'mild and mercifull courses' could not be followed until the manifest traitors had all been attainted by parliament.[9]

Because the king, respecting his peerage, jibbed at the thought of spilling noble blood, he had decided that Northumberland, like Mordaunt and Stourton, should face trial for contempts alone, although the attorney could not resist expressing his own strong opinion that by this decision substances were 'made circumstances, bodies shadowes',[10] implying that he felt the evidence quite sufficient to sustain a capital charge. If circumstances alone were to tell, however, Coke had no intention of omitting anything that might help his case. He remarked at the outset that there was 'matter of a higher nature' uncovered by the investigations which, although the earl could not be punished for it in star chamber, had to be mentioned as it was inextricably tangled with the charges he intended to pursue.[11] It is hardly necessary to add that this 'matter' consisted of numerous heavy hints that Northumberland had been directly involved in both Gunpowder plot and the Spanish treason of 1602–3.

True to his word, Coke then proceeded to weave into his description of the earl's 'verye greate and highe Contemptes, Mysprisons and Offences' a large number of these grave but circumstantial matters.[12] Technically, Northumberland was being censured for three contempts, everything else being, in the words of one commentator, 'circumstances and probabilityes tendyng to aggrevacions for his cencure'.[13] As presented, he was inescapably guilty of all three. Firstly, the earl had sought to 'wynd and worke' himself into a position where the Catholics of England would come to depend upon him as a means of obtaining relaxations in the penal statutes. It was alleged that he had advised James to dissimulate over his future religious intentions – a course of action 'hatefull to god' – and that he had chosen to disregard what James considered to have been a plain disavowal of any intention to grant religious toleration, set out in letters to Northumberland during 1602.[14]

Secondly, he had made Thomas Percy – whom he well knew to have been a 'jesuited recusant', a gentleman pensioner in the summer of 1604 – very soon after Percy had joined in Catesby's enterprise.[15] Much was inevitably made of this unhappy coincidence, and the earl's failure to ensure that the requisite oaths were taken was seen as a very serious offence, one which had been compounded by deceit: 'there was a shewe and a coullour made to have him [Percy] sworne by Sir Allen Pearcye knight brother of the saide earle but in truthe he was never sworne at all whereby he was the more at libertye to execute his detestable treason, or anie other villanye'.[16] Even if the earl had not known that Percy was a Catholic – which was extremely unlikely – 'the disposition of the man otherwise' had made him an unsuitable candidate for so responsible a post.[17]

The third offence had been committed by the earl when he had sent messengers north to secure his money from Percy's rapacious hands while confined to his house on 5 November. Coke held this to be a threefold fault, suggesting not only that it had been done without the consent of the rest of the council, and without ordering Percy's apprehension but also that it had been intended as a 'watche worde' to the traitor, had he indeed fled back into his native country.[18]

The exact course of proceedings in trials of this period is seldom clear, since reports – for the sake of clarity – invariably rearrange evidence to a greater or lesser extent. Northumberland's trial is no exception. It does, however, appear that besides being allowed to address the court after Coke had finished speaking, Northumberland was given permission to answer each contempt individually.[19] To the first, he argued that he had never written to the king suggesting that Catholics should be encouraged with promises of toleration. He conceded that, based upon the king's *verbal* reply as conveyed by Percy, he had encouraged some hopes of better days ahead, but denied having done so for any selfish reason. He insisted with the obstinate passion born of desperation that he had written to James out of loyalty alone, and that his advice in those letters had been 'to noe other end but to make his [James's] enterie more easie and quiet'. In support of this argument he produced the king's own letter.[20] To the second and third charges, though, he made no real defence, merely denying any ill-intent to the king and suggesting that any man might be unlucky in his friends and could hardly be called to account for their misdeeds.

It was, perhaps, the aggravating circumstances that made most impression on the audience. They were effectively unanswerable. Coke pointed out that the earl had apparently set about befriending the Catholics at the very time that those same Catholics, through Winter and Fawkes, had opened negotiations for an invasion from Spain.[21] The attorney on such an occasion naturally saw no reason to draw distinctions between the various Catholic factions – to his mind a Catholic was a Catholic, all equally culpable of treasonous intent. He reminded the court that, when plans had been drawn up for this invasion, it had been realised that success would depend upon a supply of horses and a safe place to land. Winter had confessed that he and his colleagues had guaranteed both, and it was to say the very least curious that the earl had been busy at the same time buying new horses for his stable. Indeed, he had been so brazen as to admit this move quite openly to the king himself.[22] What was more, Northumberland had controlled Carew Castle, the key to Milford Haven which Sir Walter Ralegh himself had once suggested as an ideal landing-place for an invading army. Completing a very satisfying chain of suspicion, Coke pointed out that Ralegh and Northumberland had at that time been 'very inwarde and secrett freindes'.[23]

Turning to later events, Coke noted that Northumberland had passed on the Catholic petition to James when the king stayed at Theobalds on his journey south to London in 1603. It was also recalled that William Watson had proposed a presumably sympathetic Northumberland for a marquessate or dukedom should the Bye plot have succeeded.[24] As with the point regarding Carew Castle, Coke's homework on the treasons of 1603 was here used to full effect. Yet one of the most suspicious points of all, in Coke's eyes, was the known fact that Percy had visited his master at Syon on 4 November. Was not Percy the likely author of the Monteagle letter, and had not Percy also declared that his master would curse him were the plot to fail?[25] It was surely only too likely that he had warned Northumberland, and while the charitable might suppose that his warning had been veiled, the earl had nevertheless chosen to conceal it.

Coke then turned to the issue preoccupying king and council. The 'saide traytors have amonge them allsoe confessed that suche of the popishe nobilitye as should have bene saved should of themselves have chosen a protector' for one or other of James's children. Surely, the attorney argued, if Northumberland had survived the blast, none would have been so suitable as he.[26] And, of course, there was no way of ever knowing for certain that he would have attended parliament on 5 November. One unreliable report on the trial maintains that the court was told how the earl had 'absentted himselfe from the parliment by leaue before the daie as to take phisicke, but in the morninge the matter beinge knowen, as to cleare himselfe came to the parliment'.[27] While this account is alone in portraying Northumberland's indiscretions as 'bodies' rather than 'shadows', and while it is virtually certain that no such accusation was made, it is a clear indication both that the fine distinctions were not fully appreciated by the audience, and also that suspicions clearly remained on this important and insoluble matter. Northumberland was all along quite aware that much depended on this point, at one stage telling Salisbury that, if such was ever proved to have been his intent, he would willingly confess to all the crimes alleged.[28]

Given James's personal interest in the subject, it comes as no surprise to find Coke also referring to the earl's knowledge of attempts to cast the king's nativity. He argued that Northumberland's covert awareness of such matters provided obvious grounds for suspicion, although it was reassuring to the good Christian that such dubious pastimes had profited him little in the end. Some of the privy councillors subsequently echoed the attorney's views, declaring that these calculations represented an 'vnlearned learneinge and deceaveable doctrine'. Certain wits among them gravely pointed out to Northumberland that 'the Starrs could not informe him that hee should now bee tried in the Starr chamber'.[29]

Nor was that the end of the circumstantial evidence. Also

mentioned was the report received from an informant in Flanders, Sir Thomas Challoner, that Hugh Owen had been overheard to tell the priest William Baldwin in Sir William Stanley's camp how he was wholly confident of Northumberland's support for the Catholic cause when time should serve. With Owen, Baldwin, and Stanley all suspected of involvement in the treason, this not particularly sensational evidence – known for some months[30] – was at least felt worthy of comment.

Coke was hardly covering new ground and the judges eventually felt that they had heard enough about the aggravating circumstances, especially since these 'inclined to offences of higher nature then this courte could judge of'.[31] Coke therefore brought his information to a close with a final recapitulation of Northumberland's 'many great misfortunes'. At the end, he did not fail to make capital out of suggestions that the earl had been 'discontented'. Discontent, he argued, could arise either through want, disgrace, or ambition. The prisoner was clearly not impoverished, 'his estate was equall to the best subiect in this land', nor was he in disgrace, for James had showered him with favours. The attorney was therefore forced to conclude, not without much regret and horror, that Northumberland's discontent had come about through ambition alone.[32]

There was really very little that Northumberland could say in reply. He apologised for any errors and contempts that he may, inadvertently, have committed, and concentrated on repudiating insinuations that he had been involved in the Spanish and Gunpowder treasons. Referring to the former, he argued that 'if traitors pretendinge anie manner of practize (to countenaunce theire owne proceedinges) would giue out that some men favoured theire cause, yt followed not that the same must needes bee true, and if theise did soe, yt could take noe more hould of him, then of others'.[33] With regard to Carew Castle he pointed out that he had obtained its lease after Ralegh's plot had been foiled[34] and that in any case he knew very little about the place. On the subject of horses, he again insisted that at the time of the Spanish treason he had owned 'not many more then hee kepte ordenarilie'. Furthermore, those horses that had then filled his stable had been intended for the king's service, should James have ever required them.[35] Turning to Gunpowder plot, he strove to show that Percy had in all likelihood never even considered warning him to stay away from parliament. Percy, he insisted, had been wont to 'raile on the earle', he had even 'pretended himselfe to be of the elder howse . . . which shewed that he thirsted after the earldome'.[36] It was all one man's word against the suspicions of others, and as such no evidence for a court even to consider.

But his constant stance did him little good. After summarising his speech, an official account declared that

the matter of whiche excuse bothe by all the matter preceedent and otherwise fell out directlie against him, vizt that the said Pearcye was obliged to the said earle by manie bondes of duetye bothe in respect of bloodd and exceedinge and contynuall benefytt and therefore moste inwardlye trusted by him, soe as he was made to understand by the courte that those his allegacions beinge without grounde of probabilitye did rather tende to the farther accusacon then excuse. The saide earle in the end perusinge his former confession under his owne hande concerninge the severall mysprisons, contempts and offences wherewith he was uppon his owne confession chardged and nowe offered to the judgement and sentence of this honorable courte confessed his errors therein, and humblie submitted him selfe to the censure and judgement of this moste honorable courte.[37]

As was customary, each of the nineteen judges present – in ascending order of seniority from John Herbert the second secretary to Archbishop Bancroft and Lord Chancellor Ellesmere – then suggested sentences appropriate to the charges confessed. Unfortunately, the sources are found somewhat wanting at this point, and all that can be said for certain is that a large majority favoured imprisonment at the king's pleasure, a fine of thirty thousand pounds, and loss of all public offices held by the earl.[38] Hawarde, who at least tells us something about the councillors' speeches, gives us only very brief and sometimes-obscure shorthand notes. In his account, the judges differed solely in the relative importance they attached to Northumberland's three offences. For the lord chief baron and Sir John Popham the earl's failure to supervise in person the administering of the oath to Percy had been particularly reprehensible. Ellesmere, by contrast, disliked most his endeavours to lead the Catholics, considering it a 'dangerous thinge to raise a pryuate man's name aboue or neere the kinge's name'. Lord Zouche was moved to declare that two religions could not stand together, for Percy 'either had no feelinge of religion, or was a knowne papiste, before he was a pentioner'. Richard Vaughan, the bishop of London, pondered gravely on the theme 'non minuit delictum dignitas personae'.[39] In only one report of the trial is there a suggestion that the councillors criticised Northumberland in anything like a hostile manner – it has Popham say that he would personally petition the king that the earl 'might never come forth for it could not be but his lordships handes was as deep as any other in the powder treason though it did not as yet evidentlie appeare'.[40] By contrast, in all other reports the councillors expressed ostensible consideration and even some sympathy for the prisoner.

This is certainly true of the two best-reported speeches, those of Salisbury and Northampton. In Hawarde's account, the former said:

I haue taken paines in my nowne harte to cleare my lorde's offences, which now haue leade mee from the Contemplation of his virtues; for I knowe him vertuous, wyse, valiaunte, and of vse and ornamente to the state. The more perylous wyse men's actions be, there the more industrye they vse to gouerne them. Actions doe conteigne *euidenciam operum*. The Cause of this Combustion [was] the papistes seekinge to restore there religion. *Non libens dico sed res ipsa loquitur.*[41]

Another report helps clarify what the Secretary said:

My lord of Salisburie my lord of Northampton and others of the lords vsed him with great respect and comisseration omitting no commendations that was due vnto him but acknowledgeing his noble birth and virtues in verry ample manner . . . This (saith my lord of Salisburie) must I doe as a judge, but if the king ask my aduice as a councellor I shall in tyme convenient and when I may dar be an humble suitor to his majesty for a mittigation, and to that end spoak my lord of Northampton also.[42]

Northampton, as might have been anticipated, in fact spent most of his customarily long speech flattering the king: '*solem e mundo non cum mundo* a kinge most gracyous, clemente, sweete and worthye prince that euer was. Many greate princes haue suffered for lesse faultes.' All the same, he did find time to consider the earl's predicament and 'agreede with Salisberie'.[43] The lords accepted that the sentence might appear harsh, but they explained that it had been so designed in order to allow the king full scope for clemency. Thus 'where sin had abounded grace might superabound'.[44] Despite Hawarde's description of conciliar unity, one judge, Lord Knollys, held out for a fine of just twenty thousand pounds. As the sum was apparently calculated on the basis of ten thousand pounds for each offence, it seems either that Knollys considered one contempt to have been insufficiently serious to merit such a fine, or, more likely, that as Countess Dorothy's uncle he feared the effects on Northumberland's family were the full penalty ever enforced.[45] In one manuscript list of the suggested punishments, eleven judges wanted the earl imprisoned during the king's pleasure, eight – Salisbury and Northampton included – favoured 'perpetuall imprisonment'. But whatever the legal niceties involved this division was hardly significant in practice; as Ellesmere observed, brushing aside an argument over semantics, 'perpetuall imprisonmente and ymprisonmente duringe lyfe was all one'.[46]

The earl seems to have had the last word, for at the end of the proceedings he solemnly declared himself a true protestant.[47] Nevertheless, the trial had obviously been a terrible ordeal for a frightened man. One who was present for part of the proceedings was told 'by some that were ther from the beginning that he [Northumberland] answered very weaklie and discouered great distresse not onlie of mynde but also of bodie by imperfection both of speach and heareing'.[48] The range of circumstances laid to his charge, particularly by such a master of the prosecutor's art, had clearly shocked him; writing to James on 7 July Northumberland admitted that, having heard all of Percy's actions outlined at his trial for the first time, he could understand only too well how his own fidelity had come under suspicion.[49]

It was this lingering uncertainty, fuelled by a poor reputation, rather than the personal animosity of Salisbury or other councillors that blighted Northumberland's cause. After his sentence, no voice was raised to denounce the verdict.[50] One diarist wrote laconically that the earl had been punished 'for the fact of the 5th of November'[51] and even among Catholics he was 'not much pyttied'.[52] His erstwhile association with Ralegh and reports that he 'troubled not much himselfe' over religion hardly brought him popularity, and it is not really that surprising to see Boderie, the newly arrived French ambassador, predict the earl's sentence quite accurately in a despatch written on the eve of the trial.[53] By that time the authorities would have decided on their course of action, even though the case was still regarded as unsatisfactory and incomplete.

Notes

1   The principal sources for Northumberland's trial are: BL Harley MS 589, fols 111–34, published in De Fonblanque, *Annals*, ii, pp 600–6; and by Gardiner in his *History of England 1603–16*, London, 1863, ii, appendix 1 (omitted from the complete 10-volume 1603–42 history). This is a draft prepared for entry into the now-missing decree books of the court of star chamber. However, a copy of the decree itself survives at Alnwick (Syon MS

N I 19, see HMC, *6th Report*, appendix, p 232a); Hawarde, *Les Reportes*, pp 292–9 (the Hawarde MS is now in the Carl F Pforzheimer Library, New York, MS 36); Cheshire County Record Office, DLT/B 8, pp 168–74, two reports among the collections of the seventeenth-century antiquary Sir Peter Leycester, see HMC, *1st Report*, appendix, p 48a; YAS MS DD 56/R/4, report in the Slingsby family collection, formerly at Scriven Hall (NRA 12891); BL Additional MSS 5495, fol 30–30v; 30305, fols 19–22v, two further reports, the former in the form of a letter dated 3 July 1606 to an unnamed lord, copied in a commonplace book purchased by the British Museum from a Mr Hasted in 1816, the latter among papers once belonging to the Fairfax family of Denton, like the Slingsby family Yorkshire neighbours of Northumberland; Bodleian MS Perrott 7, fols 200–8, copy of a report on the trial in a miscellaneous commonplace collection of the early seventeenth century, published in Nicholls, 'Wizard Earl in Star Chamber', pp 177–88. With the exception of Hawarde's report, and the official 'Decree' which was drafted by William Mill, clerk or registrar of the star chamber, all these sources are anonymous and give every indication of having been independently composed. Besides these, several documents set out the charges laid against the earl, and his sentence, the inconsistencies between them reflecting some public ignorance of the judicial process being followed, for example Stow, *Annales*, p 884; BL Cotton MS Vespasian C XIV, fol 451; Additional MS 22591, fol 261v. From a comparison of these sources, the exact order of the proceedings remains slightly obscure, but it is unlikely that anything of moment has been omitted. See also Jardine, *Criminal Trials*, ii, pp 113–14

2   eg Shirley, *Thomas Harriot*, pp 352, 357

3   BL Additional MS 5495, fol 30

4   Hawarde, *Les Reportes*, p 292

5   Bodleian MS Perrott 7, fol 202v

6   Hatfield MS 119/151, John Wodenothe to Salisbury

7   Hudson, *Collectanea Juridica*, ii, p 63 wondered at the legality of the proceedings, 'for it was *ore tenus*, and yet not upon confession'

8   There was a direct question on the earl's support for the Catholic cause in a list of questions prepared for Fawkes and Winter around 1 December 1605 (PRO SP 14/16/116) but no answers survive

9   Bodleian MS Perrott 7, fol 202; Nicholls, 'Wizard Earl in Star Chamber', p 179

10   Cheshire CRO DLT/B 8, p 168. See also Bodleian MS Perrott 7, fol 202

11   Syon MS N I 19, fol 1

12   *ibid*. It is not clear whether Coke presented the aggravating circumstances completely separately from the contempts, or whether he added them to each contempt as he presented it. The latter is more likely, but the distinction was in any case probably blurred by Coke's loquaciousness. The various accounts differ on the point: 'First De Tabley' and 'Slingsby' are edited versions which clearly rearrange charges and contempts for the benefit of the reader. The Harley-Syon 'Decree' follows each contempt with the relevant circumstances and adds circumstances which do not fit any

particular contempt at the end, but this too would have been an edited, formal presentation of events. 'Perrott', an eyewitness, places most of the contempts first, but the author notes specifically that he might well be mistaken about the 'meathod' of presentation

13 BL Additional MS 30305, fol 21

14 Syon MS N I 19, fol 7; Bodleian MS Perrott 7, fol 204–5; Nicholls, 'Wizard Earl in Star Chamber', p 183

15 Syon MS N I 19, fol 18

16 *ibid*, fol 20

17 BL Additional MS 30305, fol 20v

18 Syon MS N I 19, fol 25

19 This is not quite certain, but there is no doubt that the earl was given every opportunity to speak for himself. 'Perrott' writes that the lord chancellor 'willed him to take his owne time for hee should bee hard' (Nicholls, 'Wizard Earl in Star Chamber', p 186)

20 Cheshire CRO DLT/B 8, p 173; Bodleian MS Perrott 7, fol 205

21 Doubtless extracts from their examinations were then read: Cheshire CRO DLT/B 8, pp 171–2; Nicholls, 'Wizard Earl in Star Chamber', pp 188–9

22 Nicholls, 'Wizard Earl in Star Chamber', p 181

23 Syon MS N I 19, fol 12

24 YAS MS DD 56/R/4, fol 1; PRO SP 14/3/16

25 Bodleian MSS Tanner 75, fol 203; Perrott 7, fol 204

26 Syon MS N I 19, fols 30–1; Bodleian MS Perrott 7, fols 203v–4; Hawarde, *Les Reportes*, p 296. Garnett confessed this to have been the plotters' intention as it had been related to him by Tesimond (Hatfield MS 110/30; PRO SP 14/20/44, 9 Mar and 25 Apr 1606)

27 Cheshire CRO DLT/B 8, p 174. See above, pp 167–8. It may not be wholly irrelevant to note here that J Dade's popular *Almanacke* for 1605 (at sig C2) recommended 5 November as a 'good daye of sympathie' for physic

28 Alnwick MS 101, fol 14

29 Bodleian MS Perrott 7, fol 203v

30 Hatfield MS 113/34, list of interrogatories for Thomas Strange (see above, p 184 note 31)

31 Syon MS N I 19, fol 33

32 YAS MS DD 56/R/4, fol 3. Of all the plotters, only Fawkes seems to have referred to the earl's 'discontent'. No deposition as such survives, but his assertion that Northumberland was discontented appears as a line added to the list of questions for Fawkes and Winter prepared by Coke (PRO SP 14/16/116)

33 Bodleian MS Perrott 7, fol 206v

34 Or his countess had, and she had made the castle over to her uncle Lord Knollys (PRO C66/1653/39, dated 25 Feb 1605; SP 14/60, p 36, 29 Feb 1605) to hold for her in trust. In 1606 these lands were leased to provide a regular income for the countess (Syon MSS X II 14 Box 4d and k)

35 On the question of horses, it may be of interest that Garnett – in his letter of 4 April 1606 to Tesimond – claimed that Winter and his associates

had never intended to seek the help of noblemen in obtaining them (Hatfield MS 115/154)

36   Cheshire CRO DLT/B 8, p 173

37   Syon MS N I 19, fols 35–6

38   YAS MS DD 56/R/4, fol 3v; Nicholls, 'Wizard Earl in Star Chamber', p 189

39   Hawarde, *Les Reportes*, pp 298–9

40   Cheshire CRO DLT/B 8, p 173. Not to be outdone, Ellesmere is supposed to have said that the earl's censure 'was not a full punishment for all his offences but for those knowne and if hereafter any other thinge should appeare his lordship should answere it elswhere in a higher nature'

41   Hawarde, *Les Reportes*, pp 298–9

42   BL Additional MS 5495, fol 30v

43   Hawarde, *Les Reportes*, p 299

44   BL Additional MS 5495, fol 30v

45   YAS MS DD 56/R/4, fol 3v; Bodleian MS Perrott 7, fol 207v; Nicholls, 'Wizard Earl in Star Chamber', pp 188, 189

46   Hawarde, *Les Reportes*, p 299

47   BL Additional MS 5495, fol 30v. Coke is said to have conceded that Northumberland was no papist, suggesting that he did not trouble himself with any religion, bringing in Winter's confession to telling effect (Stonyhurst MS Anglia VI/62, Richard Blount to Persons, 1 Aug 1606). See, however, the doubts as to whether this confession by Winter was ever read at the trial (above, p 169 – the confession is not included in the list given in the De Tabley MS)

48   BL Additional MS 5495, fol 30v. Both this author and the author of the Perrott MS admitted that they had not been present throughout the proceedings and had not heard all the circumstances laid against the earl. At some point during the trial it was apparently stated that Northumberland had employed a footman formerly in the service of Francis Tresham. This was considered suspicious. The earl wrote to Salisbury on 28 June that the man had been with him for two years before November 1605 and that therefore he could not have been infected with Tresham's treasons (Hatfield MS 192/100). At another stage in proceedings Northumberland had spoken to his officer, Sir Edward Francis. This action was subsequently censured, the earl having to send Salisbury a note admitting full responsibility (Hatfield MS 193/33)

49   Hatfield MS 116/137

50   Although the purpose of John Wodenothe's letter was to inform against a stranger who had asked him at the earl's trial 'if it be a law that men may be called into question for their lives without proofes vpon probabilities and presumsions who shall be safe?' – very much a voice in the wilderness, it seems, from Wodenothe's reaction (Hatfield MS 119/151)

51   Roberts, *Diary of Walter Yonge*, p 9

52   Stonyhurst MS Anglia VI/62

53   Boderie, *Ambassade*, i, p 182

XIV

The eternal suspect

Any appraisal of the official investigation into Northumberland's case must needs differ from an examination of the treason's other facets in one particularly significant way. When weighing the earl's guilt or innocence we must take into account the interrelationships of the privy councillors themselves, with one of their number suspected if not accused by others of the highest crimes imaginable. For that reason, there is a temptation to explain developments in terms of personal conflicts, all the while assuming that there was no criminal mystery demanding investigation and that councillors consequently had the leisure to indulge in such vendettas. The attraction of this approach is that it inevitably furnishes a part of the truth. It would be absurd to suggest that personal feeling has no place in this story, just as it is absurd to argue that it colours every move of accusers and accused. Problems begin when the case remains unresolved, the leading characters pass away, and the evidence for personal relationships becomes distorted by the perspectives of history.

If circumstantial evidence helped convict the earl, some have felt since that other apparent circumstances clear his name and show that his sole 'crime' was to have fallen victim to Salisbury's machiavellian intrigues. Thus one historian of the plot wrote of Thomas Percy:

By Lord Northumberland he was enrolled one of the royal gentlemen pensioners, but without swearing the usual oath. On the discovery of the plot, the crafty and unscrupulous Cecil seized upon this trivial circumstance as an excuse to imprison the innocent Northumberland in the Tower, and to impose upon him a colossal fine.[1]

A subsequent commentator thought that 'Cecil was doing his

utmost to implicate Northumberland all along, and finally threw him into the Tower for fifteen years on the flimsy excuse that Percy's visit to Sion [sic] House that Monday made Northumberland guilty of misprision of treason.'[2] In still more recent times Thomas Harriot's biographer uncompromisingly sees Salisbury behind most of the earl's troubles.[3] Even those who are by no means convinced that there was hostility between the two men – something assumed with monotonous regularity by those antagonistic to Salisbury – tend to leave the cause of Northumberland's disgrace an open issue, generally accepting that Salisbury 'doubtless benefited' from Northumberland's downfall.[4] There is, certainly, a lot of suggestive evidence which can be made to support these suspicions. There are the letters of Molin already mentioned, there are similar sentiments expressed by Boderie, the new French envoy, who had also picked up gossip that Salisbury was bent on crushing a rival.[5] Some have felt it significant that the Secretary did not, at times, do all that he might have done to clear the earl's name. George Blacker Morgan, for example, noticed that, when asked by Northumberland to 'talke and examin the auditor how this last year I cald on for his [Percy's] accounts, and how they betwene them iuggled of the matter', Salisbury made no perceptible move to interrogate Stockdale.[6] He never even appears to have mentioned Percy's financial chicanery in public – though the evidence could have helped blacken the traitor's character.

All such arguments, however, do not really ring true. Salisbury's failure to do everything in his power to clear the earl need not imply that he contrived Northumberland's downfall. The Secretary may well have wondered how the earl could have failed to notice the loss of two thousand pounds, even if Stockdale had helped Percy conceal a small part of the theft.[7] He might indeed have suspected that Northumberland had perhaps consented to a diversion of his rents, but in any case the issue hardly affected the three charges and the circumstances laid against him. As for the apparent reticence over Percy's embezzlements, it is worth remembering that Percy – a manifest traitor – was not the man on trial. Morgan was perhaps nearer the mark when he suggested that Salisbury might have feared Northumberland's potential as a focus for trouble – and in this he was not, perhaps, alone.[8] Given the earl's past career, the Secretary was disinclined to make strenuous efforts to save him from the damning circumstances. This need not imply enmity, the fault rather lay in Northumberland's earlier actions which had somehow earned him a reputation for discontent.

It is in any case impossible to talk about the relationship between Salisbury and Northumberland as something immutable. Like all relationships, it developed over time. When Algernon, Lord Percy married Ann Cecil in 1628, both families accepted that Northumberland held the girl's grandfather to have been his greatest enemy. During negotiations for the match, he wrote to Ann's father, the second earl of Salisbury, explaining that, while he bore the girl and her family no ill-will, he could not forget the wrongs that Salisbury had done him; the thought of them still caused him pain, even after all those years.[9] It is said that he so disliked the idea of this marriage that he believed the blood of Percy and Cecil would never mix, not even in a 'bason'.[10] But this is all very late evidence, and may in part reflect Northumberland's endeavours to obtain a favourable marriage settlement. During Salisbury's lifetime, indeed, Northumberland and his countess never ceased to pin their hopes on him as the surest means of winning the earl his freedom. Northumberland was obviously affected by rumours of Salisbury's hostility, yet he only seems to have given them serious consideration when his prompt release was not forthcoming. On 30 July 1606 he thanked the Secretary for passing on a letter to James 'being soe farre from suspecting that yow woold not doe it sincerely as I protest I beleue yow woold doe me any good were in yowr poore, if I be deceaued the faulte is not myne, for there be many reasons to perswade me to it, as well as reasons to thrust me from it'.[11]

At the same time, Sir Allan Percy's letters show clearly how Northumberland's partisans were beginning to doubt that *any* of the earl's fellow peers would champion the prisoner's cause. Early in 1606, the earl of Suffolk had agreed to present Northumberland's new year gift to the king. That July, however, he returned it, saying that he had waited to see what would happen to the earl, 'and fawling forthe as it doth, hee must pardon hym for hee thinkes it not fit the king showld take, or hee offer to deliuer it'. As far as the disillusioned Sir Allan was concerned, this simply confirmed 'the opineon wee had of his loue', but it is very hard to see what else Suffolk could have done – he seems to have acted honestly in a difficult matter.[12]

That September, the earl was obliged to apologise to Salisbury for the frequency with which his countess had been requesting a reduction in his fine.[13] Dorothy had certainly not been idle. Earlier in July, according to Sir Allan Percy, she had asked Salisbury to speak to the king on Northumberland's behalf. The result was unpromising. Salisbury,

after hee had taken some deliberation and set one a graue countenance towlde her shee had no reason to expect such a fauor from hym, who was neither hys brother nor kinsman, and therefore hee woulde not vndertake that which hee knew would not bee pleasing to his majesty. In the end she fell to chiding, and did vntill the[y] were frendes agayne and so parted.

Here, perhaps, Sir Allan touches on the real problem – neither Salisbury nor any other councillor was likely to press for anything so alien to the king. When Dorothy plucked up her courage and approached James directly she got a far more abrupt answer.[14]

Later that year, Salisbury lay seriously ill with a suspected ulcer in the bladder, and Sir Allan, for all his earlier cynicism, expressed nothing but sorrow upon hearing the news, 'for I feare all thinges will goe worse with us then they doe if hee miscary, if worse may bee'.[15]

When Salisbury died in 1612, however, both Northumberland and his wife, in common with many others, do seem to have felt that a malign influence had been removed from the scene. The explanation for this change in attitude, though, lies more in the events of 1611–12 than in those of 1603–6. Upon the Secretary's death, Dorothy immediately petitioned the king once again, seeking either the release of her husband or at least some substantial reduction of his fine.[16] Her plea, though, had no immediate effect, for royal suspicions, recently reinforced by disclosures made by that most dangerous of creatures, a discharged household servant, remained strong, even after Salisbury's death. The allegations made by Timothy Elks, in the words of Sir Walter Cope, raked up again the embers of the powder treason.[17] Elks's charges covered all those points left unresolved five years earlier: the circumstances surrounding the admission of Thomas Percy as a pensioner, the hiring of the cellar, and the earl's own plans for 5 November. Elks maintained that Northumberland had confided many secrets in his old friend Edmund Whitelocke. Once when Whitelocke quarrelled with his patron, he had declared angrily that he knew of evidence which would, if disclosed, allow the authorities to prosecute a far more serious case against the earl. The increase of Whitelocke's pension from forty to sixty pounds a year appeared to Elks as nothing less than a bribe to ensure the man's silence, though the thought inevitably occurs that if Whitelocke had really enjoyed so strong a hold over the earl he might have felt that an extra twenty pounds was poor return for keeping his counsel.

In any case, Whitelocke, like Thomas Percy in earlier proceedings, was dead. To prove his case, all Elks could suggest was that some of those who had known the deceased, Northumberland's brother Sir Josceline Percy among them, might have shared in his secrets.[18] It was, though, no more possible to prove the earl's guilt in 1611 than it had been five years earlier, and by 27 November Chamberlain was announcing that the whole affair had blown over.[19] Elks, increasingly paranoid and fearful for his own safety, left England in the following year.[20] His allegations though, however specious, had quite naturally disturbed Northumberland. One summer's morning he was visited by a group of councillors and re-examined on old matters which he must have hoped had long been forgotten. Northampton, who had been among the visitors, told Viscount Rochester afterwards that the earl had changed a great deal in a short time, 'his conceite beinge excedingly bluntid and his spirites weakenid. We found him more ready to awnser and with lesse frowardnesse then we lookid for but with so great caution and consideration entermixid with doutes and distractiones as might expresse both a great fear and a very great vncertainty'.[21]

And not without reason: Northumberland had lived with this for five years. Knowing himself an innocent man, he could only have seen in these renewed investigations more harassment and persecution. Such developments would inevitably have encouraged his growing suspicions that some of his fellow-peers were conspiring to keep him in prison rather than doing what they could to secure his release. Other circumstances would, by then, have strengthened these suspicions. Although they too had been sentenced to imprisonment during the king's pleasure, Mordaunt and Stourton had left the Tower long since; these new allegations were now brought forward to vex him alone. To the earl, it all began to smack of betrayal, secret enmity, the working-out of malice. After the Elks affair, moreover, renewed efforts were made to collect his fine, with the result that the earl's suspicions focused on Salisbury, lord treasurer since 1608. If any one thing explains his change of attitude by 1612 it is probably this. For the first time he wrote Salisbury a bitter and reproachful letter, reminding him that star chamber sentences were imposed *ad terrorem* not *ad ruinam*, reminding him also that men were put into the king's hands 'that they may vse mercie, not rigor of sentence, and this hath ben your lordships owne conceite of that court, as unwilling farther then duty commaunded to be there, where nothing was to be pronounced but lashinges and slashings, fynings and imprisonings'. Salisbury might respond that he was only carrying out the king's orders, but Northumberland expressed a touching confidence that James would listen to reason if only he were made aware of the savage, unparalleled nature of the fine. He implied that Salisbury, for all those fair words used at the trial years earlier, had failed him in this; royal grace had never been given the chance to 'superabound'. Tactlessly he reminded Salisbury, then a very sick man, that it was the lot of all mortals to die and that everyone would choose to be remembered for charitable rather than for unjust actions.[22]

But was he justified in seeing the treasurer's hand behind these renewed investigations? Northampton's real purpose in writing to Rochester had been to relay the latest developments in the case, through the current favourite, to the king. James's interest was as deep as ever – he carried out some investigations of his own, discovering that Whitelocke was thought to have been poisoned and that he had been visited by Northumberland's physician before his death.[23] Rumours of his deeper guilt had persisted ever since the earl's trial, all the while helping to fuel James's anxieties. In 1607, the government arrested the Jesuit archpriest George Blackwell, causing the Venetian envoy to wonder whether the subsequent interrogations 'may have revealed something against the Earl in regard to the late plot'.[24] At about the same time Sir Charles Cornwallis reported that the Spaniards had planned to 'make use' of Northumberland before his imprisonment.[25]

Furthermore, if it had achieved little else, the investigation of Elks's charges had at least won from the earl a confession that he had, at Percy's request, asked his brother to dispense with the oath at his admission to the band of pensioners. Hitherto, Northumberland had always denied having done so. In 1611, he also claimed to have forgotten whether or not he had, after his arrest, asked Sir Allan to accept responsibility for this dereliction of duty.[26] Such disclosures can only have confirmed the investigators in their suspicions that secrets still lay hidden, and that the earl – who had at no time been totally frank with them – might on balance consider himself fortunate rather than hard done by.

Finally, it is worth remembering that Salisbury's position at court had been at least partially undermined by 1611 after the collapse of the Great Contract.[27] It may also be worth noticing the decidedly hostile tone of Northampton's letter. At this stage it is doubtful whether Salisbury alone could have persuaded James to release Northumberland, especially with the king's own suspicions unallayed and Elks's recent, unanswerable, insinuations fresh in the mind.

Of course, the strongest evidence to show that Cecil was working to encompass Northumberland's disgrace comes from the earlier events of 1601–3, but it can be argued that those were abnormal times, that Howard's vicious attacks did not always reflect Salisbury's views, and that things had changed by 1605. One can emphasise again that Cecil's own uncertain position in those years would have made him none too careful of other men's reputations in his own search for favour from James. He had spent so much of his life involved in court faction opposed to Essex that with Essex suddenly, one might almost say providentially, removed, it was surely natural that he should see other potential Essexes – potential rivals for power – even where they did not exist. This may go a long way to explain his dealings with Northumberland. By 1605, the latter's failings as a statesman were obvious and the two men were on perfectly correct, even cordial terms.[28] Of course, the new earl of Salisbury might have been acting in a duplicitous fashion, but he was not a man to waste his energies, and the truth of the matter is that he really did not have to bother.

In 1601 Cecil might have worried about the earl's overture to James. In 1627, looking back, remembering the frustrating years after 1606, the earl might have seen Cecil as his greatest enemy. Yet in the crucial period between 1603 and 1606 there is no clear evidence of hostility. As Salisbury himself admitted, there was never any 'extraordinary dearness' between them. But while the oft-repeated expressions of affection might have been conventional posturing – Salisbury, though less reluctant to express his feelings than his father had been, seldom wrote a bitter word – their relationship seems amicable enough.

It has already been suggested that the conventional picture of early-Jacobean politics writes up the role of Salisbury at the expense of other members of the privy council. It would be quite possible to suggest that, had the various members of the Howard 'clan', for example, petitioned James for the earl's release, their approach would have had as much impact as one made by Salisbury alone. That they did not do so is again, surely, due in part to their own reluctance to exert themselves on Northumberland's behalf, and in part to their recognition that such a move would, as Salisbury pointed out, 'not be pleasing' to the king. It is unnecessary to look for any more personal motives.

We might suggest that the writer of the secret correspondence would have been quite as likely as Salisbury to block the release of a man he professed to despise. But the argument again lacks supporting evidence. The fear and dislike so evident before 1603, had, even with a man like Henry Howard, probably been replaced by more settled, rational emotions. Howard, now earl of Northampton, enjoyed the certain favour of the king by the time of Gunpowder plot, and he was using his alliance with Salisbury to establish himself at the centre of English political affairs.

If he had seen Northumberland as a personal rival in 1602, the situation had surely altered by November 1605. Although evidence is scanty, Northampton seems to have reassured and comforted Northumberland during his troubles. When the earl had first been committed to the Tower, Northampton had eased very real fears by assuring the prisoner that he for one would never consent to his execution. In January 1607, Northumberland thanked him for the sympathy that he had shown since, begging him to help in any way that he could.[29] A year and a half later, while seeking Northampton's furtherance of his countess's latest petition, the earl suggested that his correspondent was well qualified to sympathise with him in his troubles. 'The blacke oxe', he wrote, 'hathe trode vppon yowr foote heretofore as well as it doeth now vppon myne and therefore yow know the nature of afflictions.'[30] Northampton was ever the 'subtile serpent' and would have been a treacherous ally at best, yet there is some evidence to show that Northumberland's petitions directed to him and to Salisbury did not go wholly unanswered. Another point may be considered here: if Northumberland had not fallen under suspicion, was it so improbable that another, genuinely Catholic peer, from one of England's greatest and most turbulent houses, might have been suspected instead? Northampton, in quiet moments of reflection, may have offered up sincere thanks for the grace of God.[31]

Jacobean justice, although imperfect in many ways, was not the arbitrary monster sometimes portrayed. It is easy to forget when examining personal rivalries that a strong circumstantial case existed against Northumberland, and justice had to be seen to be done. For all Northumberland's continuing appeals, his case always turned upon two considerations: could the weight of circumstantial evidence be ignored in law, and if it could, was it possible for the king to forget his own suspicions of the earl? Whenever James pondered the matter, those same, deep suspicions would doubtless have led him to the same conclusion, and if the king was determined to keep Northumberland under restraint were Salisbury, or Northampton, or any of the other lords really in a position to change his mind? So it was that Northumberland remained in the Tower, comfortably, it is true, for James was not one to countenance unnecessary cruelty, until 1621.

With Algernon still young, there was indeed little incentive to return to a greatly changing world.[32] On 22 December 1614 Chamberlain thought him 'so well inured to a restrained life, that were yt not that the world takes notice that he is in his princes displeasure, he wold not seeke to chaunge'.[33] Northumberland might have been able, had he wished, to secure his release through the good offices of James Hay, who married his younger daughter Lucy in 1617. But he disapproved of the match and refused to contemplate accepting his freedom as a gift from the king to one of his Scottish favourites. The fate of Ralegh – who had remained a friend throughout their years in the Tower[34] – and the death of his countess both affected him deeply, perhaps encouraging him to accept continued imprisonment with equanimity. When Dorothy died in August 1619 he took her passing so much to heart that, according to Chamberlain, it became necessary for friends to remind him that his married life had been anything but harmonious.[35] Nevertheless, the earl's grief was touchingly genuine, for all the scornful misogynism expressed in the pages of his *Advice*.[36]

Northumberland ultimately owed his release to the combined efforts of Hay (by then Viscount Doncaster and soon afterwards created earl of Carlisle), George Villiers, marquis of Buckingham, and the lord keeper, John Williams.[37] He was set free in an amnesty to mark the king's fifty-fifth birthday, his release being marked by a discharge of cannon,[38] and it was reported that the Tower porters were very upset at the prospect of losing so generous a prisoner.[39] Northumberland had probably been at last persuaded that his freedom would enhance Algernon's prospects at court, for while neither James nor Charles ever showed an inclination to visit the father's sins upon the son it would have been natural for the earl to have done all in his power to ensure that his heir, now nineteen years old, would not be handicapped by reminders of his family's unhappy past.[40] With Algernon's good in mind he buried his differences with Hay and cultivated the current favourite Buckingham. As early as 6 August 1618 he had asked Hay to assist Algernon on his European travels. 'I am growne olde,' he wrote, 'and good for little. I shalbe gladd to leaue in him some argument off my faith and loyaltye (howsoeuer it hath bene misconstrued) he beinge soe nighe me as he is.'[41]

The earl had long expected great things from his son, devoting much time and effort to his education and clearly hoping that the boy would in time be able to restore the family's tarnished image.[42] It must be said that Algernon, by and large, lived up to those expectations. Even so, a bad name is not easily lost. The Percy line was ancient and noble, yet it had a reputation for turbulence and treason which was only strengthened by the connections with Gunpowder plot. Years afterward, the historian William Sanderson recalled a favourite saying of Sir Josceline Percy which may serve to sum up the enduring contemporary opinion on the family: 'Seldom Treason without a Piercy'.[43]

Northumberland lived on for eleven years, in quiet retirement at Petworth, Bath, London, and with his daughter Dorothy at Penshurst.[44] He never attended another session of parliament.[45] In old age, the earl is glimpsed reading Heylin's *Life of St George* late into the night, day-dreaming of the grapevines at Syon, keeping abreast of events in the Thirty Years War, looking after his estates, and corresponding with old acquaintances, including Dudley Carleton.[46] When he died, appropriately enough on 5 November 1632, his friends consoled themselves with the thought that he had enjoyed a full span of years and a tranquil old age. As John Pory noted in his newsletter to Viscount Scudamore, Northumberland had been 'the antientest knight of the garter when hee took his leave of this worlde'.[47]

Later bitterness on the earl's part suggests his own over-optimism, which heightened the sense of betrayal when in 1611 and 1612 Lord Treasurer Salisbury, rather than striving for his release, seemed much more interested in extracting from him the full, severe, fine.

What it need not suggest is that the sense of betrayal was well-founded. Northumberland would have found it difficult to swallow injustice in silence. But there remains a feeling that, finding the real target of his wrath was above criticism, he had to redirect it against one who had been genuinely unable to help him. All this does less than justice to Salisbury, but it also obscures the very real truth that in building the case against one of the greatest subjects in his realm, James himself played an obvious role. A recent commentator founds his belief in the theory of Salisbury's secret hostility to Northumberland on the grounds that only Salisbury could have 'manoeuvred King James from his position of complete trust to that of complete distrust of one of the most stable members of his Privy Council'.[48] But his premise is faulty; the other man who could have achieved this end was Northumberland himself. It was James who in the end decided the fate of the suspects, and it was left to James to decide just how long imprisonment 'at the king's pleasure' should be. Surely it is most significant that Northumberland was not freed for sixteen years. The king, by birth, by inclination, and by experience, was a cautious man.

Notes

1   Sidney, *A History of the Gunpowder Plot*, pp 41–2
2   Durst, *Intended Treason*, p 111
3   Shirley, *Thomas Harriot*, pp 329–30
4   Coakley, 'Robert Cecil 1603–1612', p 132; Coakley, 'Robert Cecil in Power', p 75
5   Boderie, *Ambassade*, i, p 182
6   Morgan, *The Great English Treason*, ii, pp 33–4; PRO SP 14/16/97. The auditor was in London, staying at the Talbot in the Strand (Syon MS X II 6 Box 30q), so it would not have been too difficult to have him questioned
7   We have seen that Stockdale confessed to concealing smaller sums at Percy's request in earlier accounts (Syon MS C IV 3, Stockdale's note of c Nov 1605, see also above, p 151). But as he later observed, the manner of accounting on the Northumberland estates did not make negligence or theft immediately perceptible (Syon MS Q I 31, Stockdale to Northumberland, 26 July 1608. See also Batho, 'Percies and Alnwick Castle', pp 59–60). Even accepting the high figure set on his embezzlements, if most of Percy's thefts had occurred in the half year prior to the 1605 Michaelmas audit, the fact that they had not come to light by that November could hardly be blamed on Stockdale. For methods of estate accounting see James, *Northumberland Estate Accounts*, pp xxv–xxxiv
8   Morgan, *The Great English Treason*, ii, pp 33–9
9   Hatfield MS 200/11

10   The quote apparently originated with Osborn, *Traditionall Memoyres*, pp 67–8

11   Hatfield MS 192/112

12   PRO SP 14/22/67*

13   Hatfield MS 117/104

14   PRO SP 14/22/53. When Dorothy wrote to Salisbury in the autumn of 1606 seeking his help in securing her husband's release, she told him that he should do so for the sake of justice, even if he 'did not love' her husband (Hatfield MS 108/153). This may again suggest that the two men had never been close, but Dorothy was only too susceptible to rumours that the Secretary was her husband's enemy. Earlier, she too had expressed hopes that Salisbury would show himself a 'true noble friend' (Hatfield MS 114/99)

15   PRO SP 14/23/12; Gardiner, *History of England*, i, p 93

16   Alnwick MS Letters and Papers vol 10, fols 43–4

17   PRO SP 14/65/83, Cope to Carleton, 20 Aug 1611; Elks was apparently ìirst recommended to the earl as a tutor for Algernon during his restraint in the Tower awaiting trial (Hatfield MS 114/64, letter of Sir William Lane, undated, endorsed '1605')

18   PRO SP 14/66/28i–iv, enclosures in letter from Elks to Thomas Lumsden, 28 Sep 1611

19   McClure, *Letters of Chamberlain*, i, p 318. For a time the accusations had appeared very threatening and rumour outran fact. The Venetian envoy mentioned a report that the earl had been executed in the Tower (*Calendar SP Venetian 1610–13*, p 185; see also HMC, *Downshire*, iii, p 109, John More to William Trumbull, 18 July 1611 for varying rumours)

20   PRO SP 14/66/93; 14/72/16, letters from Elks to Lumsden. Elks's final accusations may have appeared in a tract hostile to the earl apparently published by Francis Burton in 1612 (Alnwick MS Letters and Papers vol 10, fol 19)

21   PRO SP 14/65/26, written c 19 July 1611. Investigations concentrated on the extent to which the earl had connived in Percy's acquisition of the lodging at Westminster (SP 14/65/83i)

22   Alnwick MSS Letters and Papers vol 10, fols 12–13; 101, fols 51–2, 2 Feb 1612. Not surprisingly, Salisbury took offence at this letter (Alnwick MS 101, fol 71, Northumberland to Northampton, 23 Aug 1613)

23   Hatfield MS 129/114, Rochester to Salisbury, undated

24   *Calendar SP Venetian 1607–10*, p 15

25   Sawyer, *Winwood Memorials*, ii, p 321

26   PRO SP 14/65/26. Salisbury told both Winwood and Buisseaux, the French ambassador, that Northumberland had been questioned in order to make plain the justice of his censure in star chamber, admitting that this had been called into question by some (Sawyer, *Winwood Memorials*, iii, pp 287–8; PRO (Transcripts) PRO 31/3/42, fol 91–1v)

27   Lindquist, 'Last Years of Salisbury', esp pp 33–41, insists that we should not exaggerate Salisbury's 'decline'

28   See Nicholls, 'Politics and Percies', pp 112–16 for evidence of the apparently cordial relations between the two men 1603–5

29   Syon MS O I 2c, fol 15. See also fol 16, a letter to Northampton dated 2 Feb 1607 (Alnwick MS 101, fols 31–2)

30   Syon MS O I 2c, fol 50; Alnwick MS 101, fol 41

31   Birch, *Memoirs*, i, p 227, Lady Bacon to Anthony Bacon, 14 Apr 1595; Hatfield MS 126/121, undated letter from Dorothy thanking Salisbury for services rendered; Batho, 'Payment and Mitigation of a Star Chamber Fine', p 45. I have found only one – very late – rumour implicating Northampton in the affair (HMC, *Downshire*, iv, p 351, Sir Thomas Leedes to William Trumbull, 27 Mar 1614; McClure, *Letters of Chamberlain*, i, pp 508–9, Chamberlain to Carleton, 17 Feb 1614)

32   The earl had his own apartments, cook, and walk along the Tower walls which he maintained for private recreation (HMC, *Ancaster*, p 378). Besides being allowed the company of congenial friends (BL Additional MS 11402, fol 128v, council order of Aug 1607), he had his son with him for much of the time. See also G R Batho, 'The Wizard Earl in the Tower', *History Today*, VI, 1956, pp 344–51; J W Shirley, 'The Scientific Experiments of Sir Walter Ralegh, the Wizard Earl and the three Magi in the Tower, 1603–17', *Ambix*, IV, 1949, pp 52–66; Shirley, *Thomas Harriot*, pp 358–79; Batho, 'Education of a Stuart Nobleman', pp 132–40

33   McClure, *Letters of Chamberlain*, i, p 566

34   Edwards, *Life and Letters of Ralegh*, ii, p 362, Ralegh's letter to his wife, 22 Mar 1618. See also PRO SP 14/103/74; Powell, *John Pory*, ii (microfiche), p 47, Pory to Carleton, 7 Nov 1618). Ralegh was executed in 1618 after the failure of his expedition to South America, the sentence passed in 1603 being finally carried out

35   McClure, *Letters of Chamberlain*, ii, p 257

36   Harrison, *Advice*, pp 88–106

37   Aikin, *Memoirs of the Court of James I*, ii, pp 252–3; Gardiner, *History of England*, iv, pp 136–7; McClure, *Letters of Chamberlain*, ii, pp 389–90. Recording his release, the Venetian envoy described him as the richest nobleman in England (*Calendar SP Venetian 1621–3*, pp 91–2)

38   Hughes, *A Complete History of England*, ii, pp 657–8, 18 July 1621

39   McClure, *Letters of Chamberlain*, ii, p 390

40   Algernon was made a knight of the Bath in 1616, but especially noticeable was the favour shown to him early in Charles's reign. He carried the king's train at his coronation, February 1626, and was Queen Henrietta's master of horse (HMC, *11th Report*, appendix 1, p 84, Florentine newsletter, 2 Oct 1626)

41   Alnwick MS 93A/8. Northumberland welcomed Carlisle back from an embassy in France in June 1625 and asked him to keep the new king well-disposed towards both him and his son: 'forgett not Aulgernoun if yow may doe him any good' (National Library of Scotland MS 578, art 110)

42   See Batho, 'Education of a Stuart Nobleman', pp 134–43

43   Sanderson, *Compleat History*, p 334

44   Dorothy was married to Sir Robert Sidney, later second earl of Leicester

45   He was ordered to absent himself from more than one session in the 1620s (Syon MS P I 3n, fols 18 and 22v, Northumberland's letters to the

bishop of Lincoln, 14 Feb 1624 and 25 Apr 1625. See also McClure, *Letters of Chamberlain*, ii, p 546, Chamberlain to Carleton, 21 Feb 1624) and made regular use of Hay, Buckingham, or his son and heir – from 1626 sitting in the Lords as a baron – as his proxy (*Lords' Journals*, iii, pp 4, 431, 491, 685; iv, p 3)

46   PRO SP 16/184/86; 16/149/53; 16/150/90; 16/164/73
47   Powell, *John Pory*, ii (microfiche), p 323, 10 Nov 1632
48   Shirley, *Thomas Harriot*, p 329

Conclusion

The tradition: Gunpowder plot reconsidered

Fear hath a hundred eyes that all agree
To Plague her beating heart; and there is one
* (Nor idlest that!) which holds communion*
With things that were not, yet were meant to be.

Wordsworth

At the trial of the Gunpowder plotters, Coke confessed that there would always be those ready to doubt whether so heinous a crime had ever really been projected. Future generations, reflecting on 'a treason *sine nomine, exemplo, et modo*' which had 'intended the destruction of the frame and fabrike, name and nation', might well wonder 'whether it were a facte or a fiction'.[1] As was only to be expected in so sensational an affair, his words were a response to an existing rather than a theoretical problem. Early in December 1605, a letter-writer in London blamed Salisbury for the whole business: 'Those that have practical experience of the way in which things are done, hold it as certain that there has been foul play, and that some of the council secretly spun the web to entangle these poor gentlemen, as did Secretary Walsingham in other cases.'[2] By 13 November Dudley Carleton, who would soon discover to his cost how seriously the affair was being treated, had heard reports in Paris that 'there was no such matter, nor any thing neere it more then a barrell of powder fownd neere the court'.[3]

There is, naturally, not the slightest evidence to show that the anonymous author of the first letter himself had any 'practical experience of the way in which things are done', and Carleton was certainly in no position to know the truth. But rumour ever thrives on ignorance, and in complex investigations into involved crimes its scope will inevitably be wide. For nearly four centuries Gunpowder plot, an unsuccessful treason planned by a mere handful of men, has been the subject of bitter religious and academic debate, media controversy, popular speculation, and the wildest of gossip. As we have seen, many historians, while making allowance for the excessive flattery of the king found in *King's Book*, have argued for the 'traditional' story.[4] Just as in 1605, however, others still beg to differ, questioning much if not all of the received version, and they too follow in a very old tradition. Since those first suspicions expressed immediately after the discovery there has always been someone prepared to argue that the treason had either been fashioned or encouraged by Salisbury as a means of discrediting the English Catholics, tightening the recusancy laws and bolstering his own position with the king. In recent times, few works do not pay lip-service to the possibility that Salisbury knew of the plot long before October 1605,[5] and such views have found perhaps their most determined and skilful advocate in Father Francis Edwards, who suggests that the leading conspirators were *agents provocateurs*, that those conspirators tried and executed in January 1606 went to their deaths confident that, having carried out Salisbury's orders, the Secretary would ensure their last-minute reprieve.[6]

Faced with these arguments, an investigator can only look at the minutiae of the affair. Within the all-embracing controversy over the plot's origins and nature, many smaller puzzles have proved no less fascinating down the years, and often lie at the heart of cases made by those who seek to prove government involvement. The author of the letter to Monteagle, for example, has never been conclusively identified, although many names both probable and improbable have been suggested: Salisbury himself,[7] the Jesuit Father Edward Oldcorne,[8] Thomas Phelippes,[9] Thomas Winter,[10] Anne Vaux,[11] and Francis Tresham's servant William Vavasour[12] being just a few, quite apart from the still most likely candidate, Francis Tresham himself.[13] Such small problems, however, can often be solved, and their solution all the while helps shed light on other aspects of the mystery. The reconciliation of many apparent inconsistencies lessens the likelihood of official manipulation and increases the probability that, far from shaping events, the authorities were very much being led by them.

At a superficial level there are admittedly some rather strange aspects to our story. Why were the lords commissioners apparently so slow in determining the sources of the gunpowder? Perhaps none had ever really been collected, for gunpowder manufacture was, after all, a government monopoly and its sale was thus surely regulated closely.[14] Then we are told that Catesby was known to have been at Salisbury's London home shortly before the fifth, and that Percy had been seen emerging from the back door of the same house at dead of night.[15] Similar suggestions of government involvement abound.[16] At various times we have been asked to consider suspicious its apparent failure to order that Catesby and Percy be taken alive. According to Bishop Godfrey Goodman, Salisbury had given 'special charge and direction' to those sent after the midlands rebels: 'Let me never see them alive', he is reported to have said, fearing that if the traitors were not silenced they might reveal 'evil counsel given'.[17]

Why, when Tresham died in the Tower, were the government in such a hurry to bury him? Goodman suggested that he had been poisoned.[18] The same author recalled also how John Whynniard, Percy's landlord at Westminster, 'as soon as ever he heard of the news what Percy intended . . . instantly fell into a fright and died; so that it could not be certainly known who procured him the house, or by whose means'.[19] Father Edwards has suggested that if Whynniard died suddenly on 5 November, it could have been 'because he stumbled prematurely on something he was not supposed to know'.[20] Although a surprisingly large number of records and depositions survive, the very fact that a number are missing, or exist only as copies, has produced theories – argued at great length – that some may well have been forged.[21] Several men claimed subsequently to have given the authorities advance notice that a plot was being planned.[22] Surely, it is argued, all this affords an impartial investigator ample grounds for doubting the official version of events?

In fact, none of these 'doubts' will bear close scrutiny. The monopoly did not extend beyond London, and gunpowder was not that difficult to acquire, especially as the conspirators had well over a year in which to make their purchases. Before he was admitted to the plot, Ambrose Rookwood supplied Catesby with four barrels of gunpowder, later transferred from the conspirators' house at Lambeth across the river and into the Westminster lodging.[23] With so many other more pressing questions to ask, it is not surprising that the authorities paid little attention to this matter. There was certainly gunpowder in the vault: on 7 November, according to the ordnance records, eighteen hundredweight of 'corne powder decaied' was transferred thence to the Tower.[24]

It is, as we have also seen, quite wrong to suggest that no order was given for Percy's apprehension: royal proclamations of both 5 and 8 November specifically directed that he should be preserved for questioning, and the latter offered a reward which, were the man who brought Percy in himself a traitor, would still be worth one thousand pounds at least, in addition to a pardon.[25]

Since the unfortunate Tresham died of a strangury it is unnecessary to look beyond the nature of his ailment for an explanation of his swift burial. While there are some who have suggested that his death was 'staged' to cover the exile of an *agent provocateur*, the long-undiscovered testimony of his manservant and government plans to exhibit his head alongside those of Catesby and Percy in the following February must surely afford the impartial investigator sufficient proof of his death.[26] As for John Whynniard, far from dying on 5 November he signed his last will three weeks later on the twenty-sixth, bequeathing his Westminster properties to his wife Susan who had apparently looked after them and who had been examined about the leases to Percy earlier in the month.[27]

Allegations made later in the seventeenth century that Salisbury was the instigator of the plot, that the king had even been moved on occasion to refer to 5 November as 'Cecil's holiday', deserve no more respect than do the equally groundless rumours circulating in Rome late in the eighteenth century after the suppression of the Jesuit order that evidence existed there to prove conclusively Garnett's complicity in the treason.[28] As for the suggestion that Percy and his colleagues were *agents provocateurs*, it is hard to believe that Fawkes, as he witnessed the ghastly deaths of his colleagues on 31 January, really thought that he could expect any mercy,[29] yet even then he gave not the slightest sign that his part in the plot had been other than that of a committed and genuine conspirator.

Evidence for Salisbury's clandestine meetings with Percy and Catesby is particularly flimsy. Catesby was so accused years afterward, in a deathbed confession made by one of his former servants, while the charges against Percy were laid, according to Goodman, by Francis Moore, whom the earl of Northumberland had employed as a barrister. Much of the tittle-tattle which fuels these slender allegations is taken from the pages of Goodman, an undeniable gossip, who was in any case writing many years after the events he described. Even assuming the integrity of the informant and the absence of any embellishment by the author, Gardiner pointed out that the streets of London were dark, and that under such conditions identification could hardly have been very accurate.[30] It is Paul Durst, not normally one to play down such a mystery, who reminds us that on

5 November several trustworthy witnesses claimed to have seen Percy, in broad daylight, making his escape from London – and that according to these accounts he had headed north, south, and east simultaneously.[31]

Regarding the loss of some original documents, including, regrettably, some important depositions made by Fawkes and Winter, it is important to remember that these documents were used at four trials, were afterwards lent to Robert Abbot so that he could draw on them for his *Antilogia*, were in some cases carried about by Coke in a 'buckram bag' for upwards of eleven years, and were thereafter stored in increasingly unsuitable conditions down to the early nineteenth century, which should leave us surprised only that so many – in contrast to those relating to the Bye and Main plots – have survived.[32] Documents have also disappeared which it would have been in nobody's particular interest to destroy, and the scrappy nature of original testimony, with its underlinings and erasures, makes it only too understandable that a copy would have been more suitable for preservation as a record.

The question of forgery has been long discussed, and there is little good reason to dwell on the matter here, beyond referring the reader to the discussion on Winter's confession above[33] and reflecting that those who propose forgery are often those who also find sinister the absence of original documents. Vanished testimony can be reconstructed from accounts of those most public of public trials which none of the accused saw fit to contradict.

As for those men who claimed to have uncovered the conspiracy long before, not one of them could boast an honest character. Thomas Coe, for example, was a prisoner in the Counter gaol. Before the plot he had passed on to the government some form of vague warning that had come to him in a dream. After the discovery, he naturally suggested that his former information had been nothing less than a disclosure of the conspirators' intentions, revealed in the only manner then safe for him to use. Our old acquaintance Henry Wright, the part-time alchemist, claimed simply to have rendered assistance in 'discovering of villanous practises' when he petitioned in 1606 for funds to help him in his research.[34] Like William Udall, another informer with a similar claim, Wright waited until Salisbury was dead before suggesting that he had played any more specific part in foiling the conspiracy, and even then Udall admitted that Salisbury, who had good reason to doubt this informer's mental state, had laughed at his 'disclosure' at the time.[35]

We must also rule out of court at this stage the argument dear to so many authors that, because we have evidence of government manipulation of plots in Elizabethan times, Gunpowder plot must necessarily have been known to the Cecilian intelligence network and must also have been shaped by government undercover activities. What Walsingham could do, Cecil could do also, and better. While flattering to the Secretary, this attractive argument loses its strength under anything more than a passing scrutiny: we have evidence for this involvement in earlier conspiracies, we have precisely nothing worthwhile in the case of Gunpowder plot. In addition, the much-vaunted Cecilian 'intelligence' service so beloved of the 'conspiracy within a conspiracy' school[36] was in reality no more than a group of men such as Udall, Southwick, and Wright, untrustworthy at best, and at worst dangerously unreliable, who would offer their services as a means of earning a scarcely honest penny. Cecil's foreign information network extended to no more than eight or ten men through Europe, who would pass on the gossip of court and tavern with little discrimination in return for retainers which came out of the Secretary's own purse, and which he seriously considered reducing as uneconomic from time to time.[37]

Such resources were in point of fact woefully inadequate: when in 1612 Archbishop George Abbot of Canterbury, increasingly interested by the Jesuits' part in the treason, asked a Briton abroad for news of Gerard, he assumed that the Jesuit had only recently fled overseas, whereas in fact he had done so in 1606.[38] We are today painfully aware that for all its sophistication, modern counter-espionage is at best a business of chance, a game in which the odds against failure are lengthened by persistence, meticulous and thorough work, and the employment of large resources. It is axiomatic that the obvious is never obvious until it has occurred, and the counter-espionage resources of early-modern England were certainly no more sophisticated than government itself, quite as capable as today's extensive and costly intelligence services of overlooking a small but well-organised and dedicated terrorist plot.

It is surely more realistic to see the treason as one of the greatest challenges that early-modern English state security ever faced, and to accept that it remained in the minds of the authorities through the reign of James I precisely because the mystery was never fully cleared up. Hence the determination to obtain Hugh Owen's extradition, the anger at the favour shown to Owen by the Spanish court which time and again refused his extradition and even granted him an increased pension in 1607, hence the bungled and humiliating attempt to kidnap him in 1608, and the premature elation at the successful extradition of William Baldwin in 1610.[39] Hence too the continuing animosity towards Northumberland. Treason, as Coke once observed, was like a tree with poisoned roots, roots which lay 'secret and hid within the earth'.[40] The protracted investigations into Gunpowder plot had seen the tree felled, but might there not still be life in those roots? Fears like these allowed county animosities to be played out on a national stage for years to come, with John Yorke of Nidderdale[41] and Roger Widdrington of Northumberland[42] both being accused in the 1610s of complicity in the treason. And they were similar fears which ensured that some attention was paid to quite absurd stories in 1615 that kinsmen of the plotters, lurking amid the Welsh hills, were at work on a plan of revenge.[43] At the start the reader was asked to assume that the plot came as a surprise to its intended victims – it may now be argued in conclusion that the long labours of investigation, the evident interest in and direction of the same investigations by a perplexed, frightened monarch, and the important questions which remained unanswered years after 1605, themselves provide evident proof of the hypothesis.

While on a material level the sequestered property of the traitors gave rise to disputes years afterwards,[44] the plot's significance soon acquired a less-tangible dimension. By 1613, Catesby and his associates were already passing into legend as 'martyrs' to a cause, their names being found inscribed on bones in the possession of John Cotton of Warblington, Hampshire.[45] Soon the legends grew, of the plotters assembling on Hampstead Heath to watch the results of their handiwork, of the plotters' wives waiting in the gatehouse of Coughton for news of their menfolk, and then the November celebrations of the plot took over and merged with other, older ceremonies marking the onset of winter.[46] Nowadays, perhaps, the reveller on an early November night is happier in the ancient traditions than he is with the younger anti-Catholic element to the ritual.

We have perhaps been apt to exaggerate the significance of Gunpowder plot. When all is said and done it was really just another in a long line of 'intended treasons' which came to nothing as, to quote Robert Winter in one of his confessions, 'most things of this nature dothe'.[47] But even if the old religious animosities that helped perpetuate the commemoration of 5 November have died away, the sense that the plot stands for something important in our religious and social history remains, even among those who play down the political importance of the affair. Some see it as an end, the 'last fling of the old Essexians, the idiot fringe of the indebted gentry', or the 'last fling of the Elizabethan tradition of a politically engaged Catholicism'.[48] For others it marked a beginning, albeit of something that would prove harmful or stultifying to the development of the English nation. Hurstfield, for example, saw English Catholics carrying 'the inherited taint of the plotters' guilt' for centuries after.[49]

But to argue, as Hurstfield did, that the government in the years immediately following 1605 actively continued to keep a dead issue alive to secure harsher penalties against the Catholic minority is to fly in the face of evidence. In the relatively relaxed religious climate of Jacobean England, the issue of Gunpowder plot kept itself alive, an unresolved issue, its last remaining secrets irredeemably lost. Only afterwards, with the Catholic scares of the mid and late seventeenth century, was the by now only half-remembered story called to mind and used again for criticism and reproach. The argument over the strengths and weaknesses of these anti-Catholic crusades is interminable and essentially circular, for of course they offered the strengths of unity and brotherhood and the weaknesses of blinkered bigotry to those who urged their concerns on an often complacent government. The plot was in any case used at all times as a warning not necessarily against Catholic perfidy, but against over-confidence among the 'righteous'. To gloat, to be complacent was to tempt God, both sinful and dangerous. When the protestant writer warned that 'these busie bodies take no rest' he warned against the moral backsliding of his own kind as much as against the dangers posed by others.[50]

Although no longer provoking the same extremes of emotion, Gunpowder plot is remembered today because of its use for three centuries in the religious conflicts that course through Britain's history, a symbol both of the perfidy of Roman Catholics and the unwarranted repression of a largely obedient minority by an intolerant authority. The *Book of Common Prayer* itself ensured that nineteenth-century Anglicans, like their predecessors two hundred years earlier, thanked God on their knees for the deliverance of their faith from the agents of Darkness. Yet perhaps it should also be remembered, more modestly, as one of the most interesting official investigations into a criminal conspiracy against the established church and state ever undertaken by an English government. It is an aspect of the affair which, in all the heat and fire of religious controversy, has been sadly neglected down the years.

Notes

1 Hawarde, *Les Reportes*, p 252

2 Quoted by Gerard in *What was the Gunpowder Plot?*, p 43

3 PRO SP 14/16/69

4 For example, Jardine in *Narrative of Gunpowder Plot*, Gardiner in *What Gunpowder Plot Was*, Hurstfield in 'Gunpowder Plot and the Politics of Dissent', and Thomas Coakley in 'Robert Cecil 1603–12'

5 For example, Gerard in *What was the Gunpowder Plot?*, Morgan in *The Great English Treason*, Williamson in *Gunpowder Plot*, Durst in *Intended Treason*, Parkinson in *Gunpowder Treason and Plot*, and Haynes in *Robert Cecil*

6 Edwards, *Guy Fawkes*, pp 56–60, 197, 225–8

7 Edwards, *Greenway Narrative*, pp 247–9, reprint of an article by the graphologist Joan Cambridge in *The Observer*, November 1967, which points to similarities between the Monteagle letter and examples of Salisbury's handwriting, conveniently overlooking the fact that similar parallels could be drawn for many other letter-writers of the age

8 Spink, *The Gunpowder Plot and Lord Monteagle's letter*, *passim*. Spink, a lawyer, creates a huge structure of circumstantial evidence based, unfortunately, on erroneous foundations

9 Haynes, *Robert Cecil*, p 153

10 Simons, *Devil of the Vault*, pp 132–40

11 Jardine, *Narrative of Gunpowder Plot*, pp 84–6

12 Morgan, *Identification of the Writer of the Anonymous Letter*, *passim*, see particularly p 28

13 One candidate, Dame Dorothy Selby of Igham Mote who, according to an old rhyme, by her art 'disclosed' the treason, can now be ruled out. Sir Edward Harrison in 'A note on Dame Dorothy Selby and the Gunpowder Plot' (*Archaeologia Cantiana*, XLII, 1930, pp 177–8) showed this to be a reference to a needlework depiction of the plot executed by Dame Dorothy. The old story is, however, still repeated in connection with an alleged haunting at Igham (Andrew McLeod, *Who Betrayed Guy Fawkes?*, London, 1980)

14 Durst, *Intended Treason*, pp 281–90

15 Corpus Christi College Oxford MS 297, fol 33; Goodman, *The Court of James I*, i, pp 104–5

16 See, for example, Gerard, *What was the Gunpowder Plot?*, pp 42–53; Foley, *Records*, iii, pp 498–9; iv, p 119n

17 Goodman, *The Court of James I*, i, pp 106–7

18 *ibid*, i, p 107. Durst suggests that henbane could have been the poison (*Intended Treason*, p 313)

19 Goodman, *The Court of James I*, i, p 107

20 Edwards, *Greenway Narrative*, p 86n

21 See above, pp 28 and 32

22 See Huntington Library MSS EL 5739, 5744, depositions of Thomas Coe; Lodge, *Illustrations*, iii, pp 173–6; Harris, 'Reports of William Udall', p 283; SP 14/216/237, a petition from Henry Wright written in the 1620s during Conway's secretaryship. In fact, Wright did not really claim to have uncovered the plot, rather he maintained that he had 'had a hand in the discovery of the practises of the Jesuites in the powder-plott, and did reveale the same from tyme to tyme to your majestie, for two yeares space almost, before the said treason burst foorth'. He had passed on information about 'the said Jesuiticall practises, their metings, and trayterous designes in that matter'

23 PRO SP 14/216/126, 136, examinations of Keyes and Rookwood, 30 Nov and 2 Dec 1605. Rookwood admitted that he had bought some of the gunpowder. See also Parkinson, *Gunpowder Treason and Plot*, pp 53–4

24 Roger, 'Ordnance Records and the Gunpowder Plot', p 125

25 Larkin and Hughes, *Stuart Royal Proclamations*, i, pp 123, 127–8

26 Wake, 'Death of Francis Tresham', pp 40–1; Hawarde, *Les Reportes*, p 257

27 PRO PROB 10/238; 11/107, fols 74v–6, John Whynniard, Feb 1606; SP 14/216/39, examination of Susan Whynniard, 7 Nov 1605

28 BL Additional MSS 35402, fol 129; 35839, fols 351–7, Hardwicke papers of 1773–4

29 See Parkinson, *Gunpowder Treason and Plot*, p 82

30 Gardiner, *What Gunpowder Plot Was*, p 117

31 Durst, *Intended Treason*, p 319; SP 14/216/7, 9, 14, 234, letters from Bancroft, Popham, Waad, and a maidservant of one Cole, reporting sightings of Percy

32 *Antilogia* was but the most historically significant volume in a long and acrimonious controversy regarding Garnett's guilt, see Milward, *Jacobean Religious Controversies*, pp 87–9; for the 'buckram bag' see Jardine, *Criminal Trials*, p viii

33 See above, p 28

34 Lodge, *Illustrations*, iii, p 174; PRO SP 14/19/83, Henry Wright concerning his 'theorike', 26 Mar 1606; Gardiner, *What Gunpowder Plot Was*, pp 173–5

35 Harris, 'Reports of William Udall', p 283

36 See Williamson, *Gunpowder Plot*, for a particularly exaggerated example

37 The best account of the Cecilian secret service remains arguably that found in H V Jones's Harvard (1950) thesis 'The Rise to Power of Robert Cecil', pp 374–7

38 HMC, *Downshire*, iii, pp 257–8, Abbot to William Trumbull, 20 Mar 1612, see also *ibid*, iv, pp 144, 292 for further moves against Gerard

39 HMC, *Downshire*, ii, p 346, De Villiers Hotman to William

Trumbull, 24 Aug 1610. Baldwin remained in an English prison for eight years, the authorities quite unable or unwilling to bring a charge of treason against him; Edwards, 'Attempt in 1608 on Hugh Owen'. See also HMC, *Downshire*, ii, pp 117, 128, 148, 151, 158, 162, 179; HMC, *De L'Isle*, iii, pp 248, 261 for English efforts to extradite Owen and Baldwin in the years following Gunpowder plot

40   Howell, *State Trials*, ii, col 167; *True and Perfect Relation*, sig D4

41   Izon, 'New Light on the Gunpowder Plot', pp 245–50. Yorke and Sir William Ingleby, uncle of the brothers Winter, were accused by their neighbour Sir Stephen Proctor of Fountains Abbey of full complicity in Gunpowder plot. They were arrested on charges of high treason in 1611, the archbishop of Canterbury declaring confidently that the new revelations would at last 'give us light to the Powder Treason'. Such high expectations were soon dashed when witness after witness eventually turned against Proctor, alleging bribery and manipulation of evidence. Izon argues strongly, though, that the accused might after all have been fortunate to escape justice

42   Forster, 'The Real Roger Widdrington', pp 196–205

43   PRO SP 14/81/66, 66i, 103

44   For example the squabble over Percy's goods in 1623 (PRO SP 14/149/115)

45   HMC, *Downshire*, iv, p 152, Sir John Throckmorton to William Trumbull, 21 June 1613

46   See C S Burne, 'Guy Fawkes' Day', *Folk-Lore*, XXIII, 1912, pp 409–26

47   PRO SP 14/216/176

48   Trevor-Roper, *Historical Essays*, p 109; Bossy, 'English Catholic Community', p 95

49   Hurstfield, 'Gunpowder Plot and the Politics of Dissent', p 347

50   Wiener, 'Beleaguered Isle', p 50

Appendix 1 The Percy family: earls of Northumberland

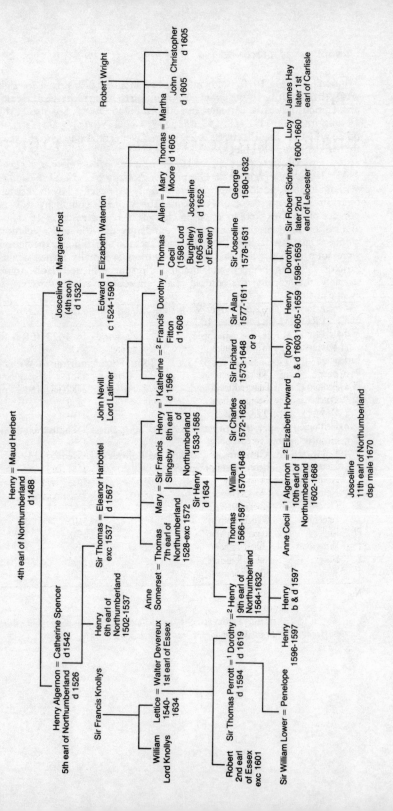

Appendix 2

English marquesses and earls at the accession of James I

	Title	Name	Date of birth	Inherited title
Marquessate:				
	Winchester	William Paulet	1560 (before)	1598
Earldoms:				
P	Bath	William Bourchier	1557 (before)	1561
PE	Bedford	Edward Russell	1572	1585 (July)
	Cumberland	George Clifford	1558	1570
	Derby	William Stanley	1561 (c)	1594
	Hertford	Edward Seymour	1539	1559 (created)
P	Huntingdon	George Hastings	1540 (c)	1595
P	Kent	Henry Grey	1541	1573
	Lincoln	Henry Clinton or Fiennes	1539 (after)	1585 (Jan)
	Northumberland	Henry Percy	1564	1585 (June)
†	Nottingham	Charles Howard	1536	1597 (created)
P	Oxford	Edward De Vere	1550	1562
	Pembroke	William Herbert	1580	1601
PE	Rutland	Roger Manners	1576	1588
†	Shrewsbury	Gilbert Talbot	1552	1590
E	Sussex	Robert Radcliffe	1573	1593
†	Worcester	Edward Somerset	1550 (c)	1589

Notes: E   Essex rebel
             †   Privy councillor
             P   Peer entering a proxy at the 1601 parliament (playing little part in political life)
Sources: *Handbook of British Chronology; Lords' Journals*, ii, p 226

Appendix 3

Privy council registers

The privy council registers for the period January 1602 to May 1613 were apparently all destroyed in a fire at Whitehall in 1619. Nevertheless, thanks to the survival of a contemporary abstract of their contents (BL Additional MS 11402) and a large number of original or copied letters in various collections, it is possible to learn something of council business during the early Jacobean period. It must be noted from the outset that for such a purpose these sources are far from ideal. Only a small proportion of individual letters and orders has survived, and certain types of letters – for example those sent to the officials of several different counties – are more likely to have been preserved than others. The abstract is selective and omits all record both of attendances at council meetings and signatures on council letters.

The following table is based on letters and orders found in the course of research for this book; a more single-minded search for such material would, no doubt, add substantially to the collection. It shows the number of letters and orders signed by each councillor in each month between mid-April 1603 – when the great council ceased to function – and 5 November 1605. When two or more letters of the same date have identical signatures, only one has been counted. Where, however, the signatures differ, all such lists have been included. There are very obvious difficulties in interpreting the results: the total number of letters and orders thus considered is rather small, and the fact that a councillor signed an order does not necessarily imply that he was present at a particular council meeting, he might have signed the order later, prior to despatch. Nevertheless, even in such cases a subsequent council meeting would have been the most convenient occasion for signing prepared letters, and the overall totals here provided do perhaps show which councillors were most active and which seldom played a part in affairs of state.

Appendix 3 Table

	(1602–3)									Un-dated 1603	1603	(1604)												1604	(1605)									O–N (5th)	Un-dated 1605	1605	Total
	A	M	J	J	A	S	O	N	D			J	F	M	A	M	J	J	A	S	O	N	D		J	F	M	A	M	J	J	A	S				
*Abps. Canterbury	5	2	0	0	0	0	0	0	0	0	9	2	0	2	4	0	1	0	4	0	3	3	0	8	3	5†	2	4	0	0	1	0	0	2	0	2	172
*Ellesmere	5	3	1	2	2	1	1	1	4	0	23	2	2	3	6	1	3	2	1	3	3	3	4	33	2	7	3	6	2	0	4	0	1	2	1	36	92
*Dorset	5	4	3	2	4	3	0	1	4	0	23	3	5	3	6	2	5	3	0	2	2	2	7	43	5	5	5	6	0	0	4	1	0	2	1	44	110
*Nottingham	5	3	6	4	3	3	1	0	2	0	24	5	2	5	4	3	1	2	1	4	2	2	6	29	3	9	3	1	1	1	0	2	1	1	1	12	65
Suffolk	5	1	4	4	5	5	1	1	7	1	38	3	9	3	5	2	1	0	0	3	1	3	8	43	3	3	3	2	1	0	3	1	1	1	1	33	114
*Salisbury	4	4	7	4	6	5	3	1	8	1	39	3	9	3	5	2	3	1	1	5	3	3	9	46	5	9	3	8	1	1	5	1	4	4	1	50	135
*Worcester	4	4	2	1	0	3	2	0	4	0	22	3	3	3	4	2	1	0	1	3	2	5	5	40	3	9	3	4	0	0	5	3	3	3	0	23	85
Lennox	3	4	2	0	0	1	2	0	0	0	6	1	1	0	1	1	0	1	0	1	1	0	4	7	1	1	1	1	1	0	1	1	3	0	1	17	30
Northumberland	3	4	1	4	0	0	1	0	3	0	16	2	5	0	1	1	1	1	1	4	2	2	4	17	5	5	0	1	1	1	0	1	0	1	1	27	60
Northampton	0	1	0	3	2	2	3	0	6	0	18	1	6	2	4	0	2	1	4	0	3	5	7	38	6	6	1	4	0	0	10	4	0	2	1	39	95
*Shrewsbury	0	0	4	0	1	1	0	0	0	0	11	0	0	1	1	0	1	0	0	0	0	5	0	15	1	0	0	0	0	0	0	0	0	0	0	0	26
Cumberland	0	0	0	0	0	0	0	0	0	0	2	1	0	2	0	0	1	0	0	0	0	0	0	4	1	1	2	2	1	0	0	0	1	0†	0	7	13
Devonshire	0	0	3	3	1	1	2	1	3	0	17	2	2	1	3	0	1	1	0	4	1	1	2	21	2	1	0	0	0	1	9	0	1	1	1	25	63
Mar	0	0	3	2	2	2	0	0	1	0	11	1	1	1	0	1	0	0	0	0	1	0	1	3	0	2	0	0	0	0	0	0	0	0	0	2	16
*Knollys	5	3	7	2	2	2	1	0	3	1	25	2	2	1	2	0	1	0	1	5	1	2	6	30	2	8	4	2	2	1	11	1	2	2	1	26	81
*Wotton	6	1	5	3	3	4	2	0	7	0	30	2	2	1	6	1	2	0	0	2	0	0	6	22	5	5	1	0	1	1	6	1	1	1	1	27	79
Bruce	2	2	0	0	0	0	0	0	0	0	4	1	1	0	1	0	0	0	0	0	0	0	0	5	1	1	0	0	0	0	0	0	0	0	0	12	21
*Fortescue	4	2	2	0	2	1	0	0	4	1	6	1	0	0	2	1	1	0	0	1	1	0	1	2	0	4	2	2	1	0	7	0	0	2	1	18	26
*Stanhope	6	0	4	2	3	4	1	0	4	0	27	1	4	1	0	0	1	0	0	0	2	0	4	17	4	1	3	2	1	0	4	0	0	1	0	17	61
*Herbert	0	0	0	1	0	0	0	1	0	0	1	3	3	1	2	1	0	0	0	1	2	0	3	13	2	0	1	3	0	0	5	4	2	2	1	20	34
Zouche	3	3	1	1	0	1	1	0	0	0	8	1	2	1	0	1	1	0	0	0	3	2	4	11	0	1	0	0	0	0	0	0	4	2	1	7	26
Exeter											5	2	2	0	0	0	1	1	0	2	2	2	0	10	3	0	0	0	1	1	2	0	0	2	0	7	22
*Popham	2	2	0	0	0	1	2	0	0	0	5	0	0	2	0	0	0	0	0	0	2	0	0	5	2	0	2	1	0	0	3	0	0	0	0	8	18
*Hunsdon	0	0	0	0	0	0	0	1	1	0	0	0	0	0	0	0	0	0	0	0	0	0	1														0
Berwick	0	2	1	0	3	1	1	0	1	0	8	1	0	0	0	0	0	0	1	1	1	0	1	3	1	0	1	0	0	0	0	1	1	0	0	2	13
Balmerino	0	2	5	5	6	5	3	0	1	0	7	1	2	0	1	0	0	0	0	0	3	5	8	5	0	0	0	0	0	0	0	0	5	0	0	2	12
	(6	5	7	5	6	5	3	1	8)	(1)	(47)	(3	9)	3	5	2	3	1	5	5	3	5	9)	(53)	(2	7)	3	8	1	8	13	4	5	4)	(1)	(53)	(153)

Notes: The councillors are referred to by their titles in November 1605

( ) Maxima

† Councillor died

* Councillor under Elizabeth

Sources:

PRO SP 14/1/28, 30, 37, 40, 41; 14/2/12, 17; 14/4/46; 14/6/61; 14/7/35; 14/9A/5, 17, 55; 14/12/24, 41; 14/13/33; 14/14/55; 14/15/66; 14/190, fol 136v; 15/36/48, 70; 15/37/18, 44; 46/67, fol 174; 78/51, fol 307–7v; E407/56, fols 88–91, 99, 101, 103, 105, 107–9, 196–7; *APC 1601–4*, p 495; Huntington Library MSS EL 1438, 1760, 6212, 6223; STT 899; HA 13778; BL Additional MSS 5752, fols 126, 131; 5753, fols 231, 234, 303; 5755, fols 167, 188, 193, 194; 12507, fols 5, 375; 18675, fol 15; 32092, fol 207; 41527, fols 27–8v, 29v–30, 31v–2, 33v–4; 41613, fols 47v–9; 48591, fols 156, 159–60, 171–1v; Cotton MS Vespasian C IX, fols 118v–20, 209v–10v; Egerton MS 2644, fol 133; Harley MS 703, fols 132v–3v; Lansdowne MS 160, fol 230; Stowe MS 150, fol 194; HMC, *Laing*, i, p 104; Edinburgh, Laing MS II 636, 2; Lewes, East Sussex CRO De La Warr MS 533; Glynde GLY 293; Rye Corporation MSS Rye 47/64/19; 47/67/3; 47/68 unnumbered; 47/69/1, 2; Lambeth MSS 3201, fols 91, 153, 179; 3203, fols 235, 269; 3204, fol 384; Hatfield MSS 101/140; 111/42; 112/37, 162; 187/95, 142; 188/78; Sawyer, *Winwood Memorials*, ii, pp 2, 10, 12, 21, 25, 33, 36–7, 58; *Calendar SP Irish 1603–6*, pp 77, 192, 199–200, 209, 215–16, 265–6, 268, 269, 298, 324, 336–7, 590, 591; Bodleian MS Tanner 75, fol 241; HMC, *7th Report* appendix, pp 591, 667 (Loseley MSS); Alnwick MS Letters and Papers vol 7, fol 64; City of Coventry MS A 79/91D; Washington, Folger Shakespeare Library MSS L a 746; X d 30(43, 44); Murphy, *Hertford Lieutenancy Papers*, pp 24, 43–4; Chelmsford, Essex CRO MSS Q/SR 165/18; 171/58; 173/116, 117; Rutter, *Documents of Rose Playhouse*, pp 216–17; Cambridge University Library MSS Add 60 (8), fol 13; Mm I 40, p 384; Jeayes, *Berkeley Castle Catalogue*, p 336; *Sir Henry Whithed's Letter-Book*, pp 25, 31–2; Oxford CRO, Oxford Diocesan Papers C264, fols 1–2; Carlisle, Cumbria CRO D/Pen/216 (Muncaster MS border commissioners' letter-book), fols 2, 4, 9v, 11, 12, 12v, 16, 22, 35v, 43; Plymouth, Devon CRO MS 1392 M/L 1605/1; *Register of the Privy Council of Scotland*, vii, pp 472–3

Bibliography

A Manuscripts

Alnwick Castle
  Alnwick MSS
  Syon MSS
Brussels
  Archives Générales du Royaume
    Papiers d'Etat et de l'Audience
Cambridge
    University Library MSS
Carlisle
  Cumbria CRO
    Muncaster MSS (D/Pen)
Chelmsford
  Essex CRO
    Quarter Sessions Rolls (Q/SR)
Chester
  Cheshire CRO
    De Tabley MSS
Chichester
  West Sussex CRO
    Petworth House MSS
    Petworth Parish Register
Coventry
  Coventry Libraries, Arts and Museums Department
    City of Coventry MSS
Edinburgh
  National Library of Scotland MSS
    Advocates' (Adv) MSS
  University of Edinburgh
    Laing MSS
Exeter
  Devon CRO MSS

Gloucester
  City Library
    Smyth of Nibley Papers
Hatfield House
  Salisbury (Cecil) MSS
  Accounts
Leeds
  Yorkshire Archaeological Society
    Slingsby MSS
Lewes
  East Sussex CRO
    De La Warr MSS
    Glynde MSS (GLY)
    Rye Corporation MSS (RYE 47)
London
  British Library
    Additional MSS
    Cotton MSS
    Egerton MSS
    Hargrave MSS
    Harley MSS
    King's MSS
    Lansdowne MSS
    Royal MSS
    Sloane MSS
    Stowe MSS
  Farm Street, English Province of the Society of Jesus
    Stonyhurst MSS (transcripts)
  Inner Temple
    Petyt MSS
  Lambeth Palace
    Carew MSS
    Shrewsbury MSS
  Public Record Office
    Records of Chancery (C)
    Records of Exchequer (E)
    Indexes (IND)
    Transcripts (PRO 31)
    Prerogative Court of Canterbury, Probate materials (PROB)
    State Papers (SP)
    Records of the Court of Star Chamber (STAC)
Oxford
  Bodleian Library
    Additional (Add) MSS
    Ashmolean MSS
    Carte MSS
    Perrott MSS
    Rawlinson MSS

Tanner MSS
Wood MSS
Corpus Christi College MSS
Oxfordshire CRO
Oxford Diocesan Papers
Queen's College MSS
San Marino, California
Henry E Huntington Library
Ellesmere Papers (EL)
Hastings MSS (HA)
Stowe (Temple) MSS (STT)
Archivo General de Simancas
Sección de Estado (E)
Warwick
Warwickshire CRO
Aylesford MSS (microfilm)
Washington DC
Folger Shakespeare Library MSS

B   Printed sources

Abbot, Robert, *Antilogia adversus Apologiam Andreas Eudaemon-Ioannis Iesuitae pro Henrico Garneto Iesuita Proditore . . .*, London, 1613 (STC 45)

Acts of the Privy Council of England, New Series, eds J R Dasent and others, 46 vols, London, 1890–1964

Akrigg, G P V (ed), *Letters of King James VI & I*, Berkeley, 1983

Bain, Joseph (ed), *The Border Papers: Calendar of Letters and Papers Relating to the Affairs of the Borders of England and Scotland . . .*, 2 vols, London, 1894–6

Barlow, Thomas (ed), *The Gunpowder-Treason, with a Discourse of the Manner of its Discovery . . .*, London, 1679 (reprint of official accounts of events in 1605 and 1606, but including on pp 229–63 letters and papers of Sir Everard Digby, discovered in 1675)

Barlow, William, *The Sermon preached at Paules Crosse, the tenth day of Nouember, being the next Sunday after the Discouerie of this late Horrible Treason*, London, 1606

Batho, G R (ed), *The Household Papers of Henry Percy, Ninth Earl of Northumberland (1564–1632)*, Camden Society, 3rd Series, vol 93, London, 1962

Berger de Xivrey, J (ed), *Recueil des Lettres Missives de Henri IV*, 9 vols, Paris, 1843–76

Birch, Thomas (ed), *Memoirs of the Reign of Queen Elizabeth, from the year 1581 till her death*, 2 vols, London, 1754

The Court and Times of James the First, (based on Birch's collection of letters, edited by Robert Folkestone Williams), 2 vols, London, 1849

Boderie, Antoine le Fevre de la, *Ambassade de Monsieur de la Boderie en Angleterre sous le regne d'Henri IV et la minorité de Louis XIII, 1606–11,*

5 vols, np, 1750

Braunmuller, A R (ed), *A Seventeenth-Century Letter-Book: A Facsimile Edition of Folger MS V a 321*, Newark NJ, 1983

Bruce, John (ed), *'Liber Famelicus'* of *Sir James Whitelocke*, Camden Society, Old Series, vol 70, London, 1858

   Correspondence of King James VI of Scotland with Sir Robert Cecil and others in England . . ., Camden Society, Old Series, vol 78, London, 1861

Calendar of State Papers, Domestic Series, ed Mary Anne Everett Green, vols 3 and 8 (1591–4 and 1603–10), London, 1867, 1857

Calendar of State Papers relating to Ireland, of the reign of James I, eds C W Russell and J P Prendergast, vol 1 (1603–6), London, 1872

Calendar of State Papers relating to English Affairs . . . in the Archives and Collections of Venice, eds H F Brown and A B Hinds, vols 9, 10, 11, 12, 17 (1592–1603, 1603–7, 1607–10, 1610–13, 1621–3), London, 1898–1911

Camden, William, *History of the Most Renowned and Victorious Princess Elizabeth, late Queen of England*, 3rd edn, London, 1675

V Cl Camdeni et illustrium virorum ad G Camdenum epistolae, [ed Thomas Smith], London, 1691

Caraman, Philip (ed), *John Gerard: The Autobiography of an Elizabethan*, 2nd edn, London, 1956

Carswell, Donald (ed), *Trial of Guy Fawkes and Others (The Gunpowder Plot)*, Notable British Trials Series, London, 1934

Coke, Sir Edward, *The Reports* . . ., eds J F Thomas and J F Fraser, 6 vols, London, 1826

Collins, Arthur (ed), *Letters and Memorials of State* . . ., 2 vols, London, 1746

Devon, F, *Issues of the Exchequer*, London, 1836

Edwards, Francis (ed), *The Gunpowder Plot: The Narrative of Oswald Tesimond, alias Greenway*, London, 1973

Fisher, F J (ed), 'The State of England Anno dom 1600, by Thomas Wilson', *The Camden Miscellany XVI*, Camden Society, 3rd Series, vol 52, London, 1936

Foley, Henry, *Records of the English Province of the Society of Jesus*, 7 vols in 8, London, 1875–83

Gardiner, Samuel Rawson (ed), 'Two Declarations of Garnet relating to the Gunpowder Plot', *The English Historical Review*, III, 1888, pp 510–19

Hailes, David Dalrymple, Lord (ed), *The Secret Correspondence of Sir Robert Cecil with James VI King of Scotland*, Edinburgh, 1766

Hardwicke, Philip Yorke, 2nd Earl of (ed), *Miscellaneous State Papers: From 1501 to 1706*, 2 vols, London, 1778

Harris, P R (ed), 'The Reports of William Udall, Informer, 1605–1612', *Recusant History*, VIII numbers 4 and 5, 1966, pp 192–284

Harrison, G B (ed), *Advice to his Son by Henry Percy, Ninth Earl of Northumberland (1609)*, London, 1930

Les Reportes del Cases in Camera Stellata, 1593–1609, from the original Manuscript of John Hawarde, ed William Paley Baildon, London, 1894

Hill, L M, 'Sir Julius Caesar's Journal of Salisbury's First Two Months and Twenty Days as Lord Treasurer: 1608', *Bulletin of the Institute of Historical Research*, XLV, pp 311–27

His Majesties Speach in this Last Session of Parliament . . . Together with a discourse of the maner of the discouery of this late intended Treason, ioyned with an Examination of some of the prisoners, London, 1605 (STC 14392); commonly known as the *King's Book*

Reports and Calendars issued by the Royal Commission on Historical Manuscripts:

First and Second Reports with Appendices, London, 1874

Third Report with Appendix, London, 1872

Fifth Report with Appendix, London, 1876

Sixth Report with Appendix, London, 1878

Seventh Report with Appendix I, London, 1879

Eighth Report with Appendices, 3 vols, London, 1881

The Manuscripts of Henry Duncan Skrine, esq: Salvetti Correspondence (Eleventh Report Appendix I), London, 1887

Report on the Manuscripts of the Earl of Ancaster, (formerly) preserved at Grimsthorpe, London, 1907

Calendar of the Manuscripts of the Marquis of Bath, preserved at Longleat, Wiltshire, 5 vols, London, 1904–80

Report on the Manuscripts of His Grace the Duke of Buccleuch and Queensberry, KG, KT, [formerly] preserved at Montagu House, Whitehall, 3 vols in 4, London, 1899–1926

Report on the Manuscripts of Lord De L'Isle and Dudley, preserved at Penshurst Place, 6 vols, London, 1925–66

Report on the Manuscripts of the Marquis of Downshire, (formerly) preserved at Easthampstead Park, Berks, 4 vols in 5, London, 1924–40 [1942]

Report on the Laing Manuscripts, preserved in the University of Edinburgh, 2 vols, London, 1914–25

Report on the manuscripts of Lord Montagu of Beaulieu, London, 1900

Calendar of the Manuscripts of the Most Honourable the Marquis of Salisbury . . . preserved at Hatfield House, Hertfordshire, 24 vols (called parts), London, 1883–1976

Report on the Manuscripts in Various Collections, 8 vols, London, 1901–14

Howell, T B, and others (eds), *A Complete Collection of State Trials and proceedings for high treason and other crimes and misdemeanors*, 34 vols, London, 1809–28

Hudson, William, 'Treatise on the Court of Star-Chamber', in *Collectanea Juridica: Consisting of tracts, relative to the law and constitution of England . . .*, 2 vols, London, 1791–2 (Hudson's treatise is in vol 2)

James, M E (ed), *Estate Accounts of the Earls of Northumberland, 1562–1637*, Surtees Society, vol 163, Durham, 1955

Jeayes, I H (ed), *Descriptive Catalogue of the Charters and Muniments . . . at Berkeley Castle*, Bristol, 1892

Letters of Philip Gawdy of West Harling, Norfolk, and of London to Various Members of his Family, 1579–1616, London, 1906

Jones, Howard Vallance (ed), 'The Journal of Levinus Munck', *The English Historical Review*, LXVIII, 1953, pp 234–58

Journals of the House of Lords, vols 2–4, London, [1767–71]

Journals of the House of Commons, vol 1

Laffleur de Kermaingant, Pierre P, *L'Ambassade de France en Angleterre sous Henri IV: mission de Christophe de Harlay, Comte de Beaumont, 1602–5*, Paris, 1895

Larkin, James F, and Hughes, Paul L (eds), *Stuart Royal Proclamations*, 2 vols, Oxford, 1973–80

Laughton, John Knox (ed), *State Papers relating to the Defeat of the Spanish Armada, anno 1588*, 2 vols, Navy Records Society, Publications, vols 1 and 2, London, 1894

Lodge, Edmund, *Illustrations of British History . . .*, 2nd edn, 3 vols, London, 1838

Loomie, Albert J (ed), *Spain and the Jacobean Catholics*, vol 1, Catholic Record Society Records Series, vol 64, London, 1973

McClure, Norman Egbert (ed), *The Letters of John Chamberlain*, 2 vols, Philadelphia, 1939

Maclean, John (ed), *Letters from Sir Robert Cecil to Sir George Carew*, Camden Society, Old Series, vol 88, London, 1864

Mares, F H (ed), *The Memoirs of Robert Carey*, Oxford, 1972

Moore, Sir Francis, *Cases Collected and Reported by Sir Francis Moore*, London, 1663

Morris, John (ed), *The Condition of Catholics under James I: Father Gerard's Narrative of the Gunpowder Plot . . . with his life . . .*, 2nd edn, London, 1872

Murdin, William (ed), *A Collection of State Papers . . .* (at Hatfield House), London, 1759

Murphy, W P D (ed), *The Earl of Hertford's Lieutenancy Papers 1603–1612*, Wiltshire Record Society, vol 23, Devizes, 1969

Nash, T Russell, 'Copy of the Original Death-Warrant of Humphrey Littleton, with Observations on it', *Archaeologia*, XV, 1803, pp 130–9

Nicholls, Mark (ed), 'The Wizard Earl in Star Chamber', *The Historical Journal*, XXX, 1987, pp 173–89

Nichols, John Gough (ed), *The Progresses, processions and magnificent festivities of King James the First*, 4 vols, London, 1828

Oldys, William (ed), *The Harleian Miscellany*, London, 1808–13

Pollen, J H (ed), 'The Memoirs of Father Robert Persons', part 2, Catholic Record Society, Records Series *Miscellanea*, vol 4, London, 1907

Powell, W S (ed), *John Pory, 1572–1636: The Life and Letters of a Man of Many Parts*, 2 vols (vol 2 a microfiche supplement), Chapel Hill NC, 1977

Public Record Office Deputy Keeper's Fourth and Fifth Reports, with Appendices, London, 1843–4

Register of the Privy Council of Scotland, ed David Masson, vols 6 and 7, Edinburgh, 1884–5

Roberts, George (ed), *Diary of Walter Yonge Esq, Justice of the Peace, and*

MP for Honiton, written at Colyton and Axminster, co Devon, from 1604 to 1628, Camden Society, Old Series, vol 41, London, 1848

Roger, N A M (ed), 'Ordnance Records and the Gunpowder Plot', *Bulletin of the Institute of Historical Research*, LIII, 1980, pp 124–5

Rushworth, John, *Historical Collections . . .*, 8 vols, London, 1721

Rutter, Carol Chillington (ed), *Documents of the Rose Playhouse*, Manchester, 1984

Rymer, Thomas (ed), *Foedera, conventiones, literae . . .*, 3rd edn, 10 vols, The Hague, 1739–45

Sawyer, Edmund (ed), *Memorials of Affairs of State . . . Collected (chiefly) from the Original Papers of Sir Ralph Winwood . . .*, 3 vols, London, 1725

Scott, Harold Spencer (ed), 'The Journal of Sir Roger Wilbraham, Solicitor-General in Ireland and master of Requests, for the years 1593–1616', *The Camden Miscellany X*, Camden Society, 3rd Series, vol 4, London, 1902

Sorlien, Robert Parker (ed), *The Diary of John Manningham of the Middle Temple 1602–1603*, Hanover NH, 1976

Spedding, James, and others (eds), *The Works of Francis Bacon*, 14 vols, London, 1857–74 (*The Letters and Life of Sir Francis Bacon* form vols 8–14)

Stow, John, *Annales, or, a Generall Chronicle of England . . .* (edited and continued by Edmond Howes), London, 1631

Stoye, J W (ed), 'An Early Letter of John Chamberlain', *The English Historical Review*, LXII, 1947, pp 522–32

Sully, Maximilien de Bethune, duc de, *Memoires ou Oeconomies Royales d'Estat*, 4 vols in 3, Paris, 1664

Talbot, Clare (ed), *Recusant Records*, Catholic Record Society Miscellanea, London, 1961

A True and Perfect Relation of the Whole Proceedings against the late most barbarous Traitors, Garnet a Iesuite, and his Confederats . . ., London, 1606, (STC 11618–19)

A True and Summarie reporte of the declaration of some part of the Earl of Northumberland's Treasons . . ., London, 1585

Wake, Joan (ed), 'The Death of Francis Tresham', *Northamptonshire Past and Present*, II, 1954, pp 31–41

Wall, Alison (ed), 'An Account of the Essex Revolt, February 1601', *Bulletin of the Institute of Historical Research*, LIV, 1981, pp 131–3

Watson, William, *A Decacordon of Ten Quodlibeticall Questions . . .*, London, 1602

Sir Henry Whithed's Letter-Book, vol 1, prepared by members of the staff of the Hampshire Record Office, Hampshire Record Series, vol 1, Portsmouth, 1976

Willson, David Harris (ed), *The Parliamentary Diary of Robert Bowyer, 1606–1607*, Minneapolis, 1931

C Secondary works

Adair, E R, *The Sources for the History of the Council in the Sixteenth and Seventeenth Centuries*, Port Washington NY, 1971 (reissue of 1924 edition)

The Advocate of Conscience Liberty, or an apology for Toleration rightly stated, [London], 1673

Aikin, Lucy, *Memoirs of the Court of King James the First*, 2nd edn, 2 vols, London, 1822

Anstruther, Godfrey, 'Powder Treason', *Blackfriars*, XXXIII, 1952, pp 450–9

  Vaux of Harrowden: A Recusant Family, Newport, 1953

Batho, G R, 'A Difficult Father-in-Law', *History Today*, VI, 1956, pp 744–51

  'Henry, Ninth Earl of Northumberland and Syon House, Middlesex, 1594–1632', *Transactions of the Ancient Monuments Society*, New Series IV, 1956, pp 95–109

  'The Finances of an Elizabethan Nobleman: Henry Percy, Ninth Earl of Northumberland (1564–1632)', *The Economic History Review*, 2nd Series IX, 1957, pp 433–50

  'The Education of a Stuart Nobleman', *British Journal of Educational Studies*, V number 2, 1957, pp 131–43

  'The Percies and Alnwick Castle, 1557–1632', *Archaeologia Aeliana*, 4th Series XXXV, 1957, pp 48–63

  'The Payment and Mitigation of a Star Chamber Fine', *The Historical Journal*, I, 1958, pp 40–51

  'The Library of the Wizard Earl: Henry Percy, Ninth Earl of Northumberland (1564–1632)', *The Library*, XV, 1960, pp 246–61

Bellamy, John, *The Tudor Law of Treason*, London, 1979

Birch, Thomas (ed), *An Historical View of the Negotiations between the courts of England, France, and Brussels from the year 1592 to 1617*, London, 1749

Black, J B, *The Reign of Elizabeth 1558–1603*, 2nd edn, Oxford, 1959

Bossy, John, 'Henri IV, the Apellants and the Jesuits', *Recusant History*, VIII number 2, 1965, pp 80–122

  'The English Catholic Community 1603–1625', in *The Reign of James VI and I*, ed A G R Smith, London, 1973, 91–105

Brenan, Gerald, *A History of the House of Percy*, 2 vols, London, 1902

Caraman, Philip, *Henry Garnet, 1555–1606, and the Gunpowder Plot*, London, 1964

Cheyney, Edward P, 'The Court of Star Chamber', *American Historical Review*, XVIII, 1913, pp 727–50

Coakley, Thomas M, 'Robert Cecil in Power: Elizabethan Politics in Two Reigns', in *Early Stuart Studies; Essays in Honor of David Harris Willson*, ed H S Reinmuth, Minneapolis, 1970, 64–94

Cokayne, George Edward, *The Complete Peerage . . .*, eds the Hon Vicary Gibbs, H Arthur Doubleday and others, 13 vols in 14, London, 1910–59

Collins, Arthur, *Collins' Peerage of England . . . Greatly augmented, and continued to the present time, by Sir Samuel Egerton Brydges*, 9 vols, London, 1812

Collinson, Patrick, 'The Elizabethan Church and the New Religion', in *The Reign of Elizabeth I*, ed Christopher Haigh, London, 1984, 169–94

Cross, M Claire, *The Puritan Earl: The Life of Henry Hastings, third Earl of Huntingdon, 1536–1595*, London, 1966

De Fonblanque, Edward Barrington, *Annals of the House of Percy*, 2 vols and pedigree, London, 1887

De Luna, B N, *Jonson's Romish Plot: A Study of 'Catiline' and its Historical Context*, Oxford, 1967

De Thou, Jacques Auguste, *Iacobi Augusti Thuani historiarum sui temporis ab anno Domini 1543 vsque ad annum 1607 . . .*, 5 vols in 4, Geneva, 1620(–21)

Dietz, F C, *The Exchequer in Elizabeth's Reign*, Smith College Studies in History vol 8, Northampton Mass, 1923

    Receipts and Issues of the Exchequer temp James I and Charles I, Smith College Studies in History vol 13, Northampton Mass, 1928

    English Public Finance 1558–1641, New York, 1964

Dodd, A H, 'The Spanish Treason, the Gunpowder Plot and the Catholic Refugees', *The English Historical Review*, LIII, 1938, pp 627–50

Durst, Paul, *Intended Treason; What really happened in the Gunpowder Plot*, London, 1970

Edwards, Edward, *The Life of Sir Walter Ralegh . . . Together with his Letters: Now First Collected*, 2 vols, London, 1868

Edwards, Francis, *Guy Fawkes: The Real Story of the Gunpowder Plot?*, London, 1969

    'The Attempt in 1608 on Hugh Owen, Intelligencer for the Archdukes in Flanders', *Recusant History*, XVII, 1984, pp 140–57

Fincham, Kenneth, and Lake, Peter, 'The Ecclesiastical Policy of King James I', *Journal of British Studies*, XXIV, April 1985, pp 169–207

Forster, Ann M C, 'The Real Roger Widdrington', *Recusant History*, XI, pp 196–205

French, Peter J, *John Dee: The World of an Elizabethan Magus*, London, 1984 (paperback edition)

Galloway, B, *The Union of England and Scotland, 1603–8*, Edinburgh, 1986

Gardiner, Samuel Rawson, *History of England from the Accession of James I to the outbreak of the Civil War 1603–1642*, 10 vols, London, 1883–4 (Gardiner's earlier two-volume *History* from 1603 to 1616 includes the 'decree in Star Chamber against the earl of Northumberland' from Harley MS 589 as one of its appendices)

    What Gunpowder Plot Was, London, 1897

Garnett, Henry, *Portrait of Guy Fawkes: An Experiment in Biography*, London, 1962

Gerard, John, *What was the Gunpowder Plot? The Traditional Story tested by Original Evidence*, London, 1897

    The Gunpowder Plot and the Gunpowder Plotters: In Reply to Professor Gardiner, London, 1897

Thomas Winter's Confession and the Gunpowder Plot, London, 1898

Goodman, Godfrey, *The Court of King James the First,* ed John S Brewer, 2 vols, London, 1839

Haigh, Christopher, 'The Church of England, the Catholics and the People', in *The Reign of Elizabeth I,* ed Christopher Haigh, London, 1984, 195–219

Hallam, Henry, *The Constitutional History of England, From the Accession of Henry VII to the Death of George II,* 7th edn, 3 vols, London, 1854

Handbook of British Chronology, eds E B Fryde et al, 3rd edn, London, 1986

Handover, Phyllis M, *The Second Cecil: The Rise to Power, 1563–1604, of Sir Robert Cecil, later first Earl of Salisbury,* London, 1959

Harrison, G B, *A Second Elizabethan Journal: Being a Record of Those Things most Talked about During the Years 1595–1598,* London, 1931
A Jacobean Journal . . . 1603–1606, London, 1941

Haynes, Alan, *Robert Cecil, Earl of Salisbury, 1563–1612: Servant of Two Sovereigns,* London, 1989

A History of Northumberland issued under the direction of the Northumberland County History Committee, 15 vols, Newcastle-upon-Tyne, 1893–1940

Hughes, John, and Kennet, W (eds), *A Complete History of England: with the lives of all the Kings and Queens thereof,* 2nd edn, 3 vols, London, 1719

Humphreys, John, 'The Wyntours of Huddington and the Gunpowder Plot', *Transactions of the Birmingham and Midlands Institute,* XXX, 1904, pp 47–88
'The Habingtons of Hindlip and the Gunpowder Plot', *Transactions of the Birmingham and Midlands Institute,* XXXI, 1905, pp 47–66

Hurstfield, Joel, 'Robert Cecil, Earl of Salisbury: Minister of Elizabeth and James I', *History Today,* VII, 1957, pp 179–89
'The Succession Struggle in Late Elizabethan England', in *Elizabethan Government and Society: Essays Presented to Sir John Neale,* eds S T Bindoff, J Hurstfield, C H Williams, London, 1961, 369–96
'A Retrospect, Gunpowder Plot and the Politics of Dissent', in *Freedom, Corruption and Government in Elizabethan England,* London, 1973, 327–51

Izon, John, 'New Light on the Gunpowder Plot', *History Today,* IV, 1954, pp 245–50

Jardine, David, *Criminal Trials,* 2 vols, London, 1832–5
A Narrative of the Gunpowder Plot, London, 1857

Jensen, J Vernon, 'The Staff of the Jacobean Privy Council', *Huntington Library Quarterly,* XL, 1976, pp 11–44

Lake, Peter, 'Anti-popery: The Structure of a Prejudice', in *Conflict in Early Stuart England: Studies in Religion and Politics 1603–1642,* eds Richard Cust and Ann Hughes, London, 1989, 72–106

La Rocca, John J, '"Who Can't Pray With Me, Can't Love Me": Toleration and the Early Jacobean Recusancy Policy', *Journal of British Studies,* XXIII number 2, 1984, pp 22–36

'James I and his Catholic Subjects, 1606–12: Some Financial Implications', *Recusant History*, XVIII, 1987, pp 251–62

Lee, Maurice (Jnr), *Great Britain's Solomon: James VI and I in his Three Kingdoms*, Champaign Ill, 1990

Lindquist, Eric N, 'The Last Years of the First Earl of Salisbury, 1610–1612', *Albion*, XVIII, 1986, pp 23–41

Loomie, Albert J, *The Spanish Elizabethans: the English Exiles at the Court of Philip II*, London (USA printed), 1965

'Toleration and Diplomacy: The Religious Issue in Anglo-Spanish Relations, 1603–1605', *Transactions of the American Philosophical Society*, New Series LIII part 6, 1963

'Guy Fawkes in Spain: The Spanish Treason in Spanish Documents', *Bulletin of the Institute of Historical Research*, Special Supplement 9, 1971

Lunn, Maurus, 'Chaplains to the English Regiment in Spanish Flanders, 1605–06', *Recusant History*, XI, pp 133–55

McGrath, Patrick, *Papists and Puritans under Elizabeth I*, London, 1967

Malloch, A E, 'Father Henry Garnet's Treatise of Equivocation', *Recusant History*, XV, pp 387–95

Marcham, Frederick George, 'James I of England and the "Little Beagle" Letters', in *Persecution and Liberty: Essays in honor of George Lincoln Burr*, New York, 1931

Markham, Clements, *'The Fighting Veres': Lives of Sir Francis Vere . . . and of Sir Horace Vere*, London, 1888

Milward, P, *Religious Controversies of the Jacobean Age: A Survey of Printed Sources*, London, 1978

Morgan, George Blacker, *The Identification of the Writer of the Anonymous Letter to Lord Monteagle in 1605*, London, 1916

The Great English Treason for Religion known as Gunpowder Plot . . ., 2 vols, Oxford, 1931–2

Munden, R C, 'James I and "the growth of mutual distrust": King, Commons, and Reform, 1603–1604', in *Faction and Parliament: Essays on Early Stuart History*, ed Kevin Sharpe, Oxford, 1978, 43–72

Nicholls, Mark, 'Sir Charles Percy', *Recusant History*, XVIII, 1987, pp 237–50

'Investigating Gunpowder Plot', *Recusant History*, XIX, 1988, pp 124–45

Osborn, Francis, *Traditionall Memoyres on the Raigne of King Iames* (second part of *Historical Memoires on the Reigns of Queen Elizabeth, and King James*), London, 1658

Parkinson, C Northcote, *Gunpowder, Treason and Plot*, London, 1976

Peck, Linda Levy, *Northampton: Patronage and Policy at the Court of James I*, London, 1982

'Problems in Jacobean Administration: Was Henry Howard, Earl of Northampton, a Reformer?', *The Historical Journal*, XIX, 1976, pp 831–58

'Corruption at the Court of James I: The Undermining of Legitimacy', in *After the Reformation*, ed B Malament, Philadelphia, 1980

Pfister, C, 'Les "Economies Royales" de Sully et le Grand Dessein de Henri IV' (part 3), *Revue Historique*, LV, May–Aug 1894, pp 291–302

Ryan, Clarence J, 'The Jacobean Oath of Allegiance and English Lay Catholics', *The Catholic Historical Review*, XXVIII, 1942, pp 159–83

Sanderson, William, *A Compleat History of the lives and reigns of Mary . . . and . . . James . . .*, London, 1656(5)

Shirley, John W, *Thomas Harriot: A Biography*, Oxford, 1983

Sidney, Philip, *A History of the Gunpowder Plot: The Conspiracy and its Agents*, 2nd edn, London, 1905

Simons, Eric N, *The Devil of the Vault: A Life of Guy Fawkes*, London, 1963

Smith, Lacey Baldwin, *Treason in Tudor England: Politics and Paranoia*, London, 1986

Spink, Henry Hawkes, *The Gunpowder Plot and Lord Mounteagle's Letter . . .*, London, 1902

Sprott, S E, 'Sir Edmund Baynham', *Recusant History*, X, pp 96–110

Stafford, Helen G, *James VI of Scotland and the Throne of England*, New York, 1940

Stebbing, William, *Sir Walter Ralegh: A Biography*, Oxford, 1891 (reprinted with a list of authorities in 1899)

Strype, John, *Annals of the Reformation and establishment of Religion, and other various occurrences in the Church of England, during Queen Elizabeth's happy reign*, 4 vols, Oxford, 1824

Swift, Roger, 'Guy Fawkes Celebrations in Victorian Exeter', *History Today*, XXXI, Nov 1981, pp 5–9

Thomas, Keith, *Religion and the Decline of Magic*, London, 1971

Tierney, Mark A (ed), *Dodd's Church History of England . . . from the commencement of the sixteenth century to the revolution in 1688*, 5 vols, London, 1839–43

Toyne, S M, 'Guy Fawkes and the Powder Plot', *History Today*, I, 1951, pp 16–24

Trevor-Roper, H R, 'The Gentry, 1540–1640', *Economic History Review* Supplement number 1, Cambridge, 1953
Historical Essays, London, 1957

Usher, Roland G, *The Reconstruction of the English Church*, 2 vols, New York, 1910

Venn, J, and Venn, J A, *Alumni Cantabrigienses*, Cambridge, 1924

Watts, S J, *From Border to Middle Shire: Northumberland, 1586–1625*, Leicester, 1975

Wiener, Carol Z, 'The Beleaguered Isle: A Study of Elizabethan and Early-Jacobean Anti-Catholicism', *Past and Present*, LI, 1971, pp 27–62

Willaert, L, 'Negociations Politico-Religieuses entre L'Angleterre et les Pays-Bas Catholiques (1598–1625)' (part 4), *Revue D'Histoire Ecclesiastique*, VII, 1906, pp 585–607

Williamson, George C, *George, Third Earl of Cumberland, 1558–1605*, Cambridge, 1920

Williamson, Hugh Ross, *The Gunpowder Plot*, London, 1951

Willson, David Harris, *King James VI and I*, London, 1956

Wood, Anthony À, *Athenae Oxonienses . . . to which are added the Fasti, or Annals of the said University*, ed Philip Bliss, 5 vols, London, 1813–20

Wormald, Jenny, 'James VI and I: Two Kings or One?', *History*, LXVIII, 1983, pp 187–209

'Gunpowder, Treason, and Scots', *Journal of British Studies*, XXIV, 1985, pp 141–68

Yates, Frances Amelia, *A Study of Love's Labour's Lost*, Cambridge, 1936

D   Theses

Batho, G R, 'The Household Accounts of Henry Percy, Ninth Earl of Northumberland (1564–1632)', London MA, 1953

Coakley, Thomas M, 'The Political Position and Domestic Policy of Robert Cecil 1603–1612', Minnesota PhD, 1959

La Rocca, John J, 'English Catholics and the Recusancy Laws 1558–1625: A Study in Religion and Politics', Rutgers PhD, 1977

Munden, R C, 'The Politics of Accession: James I and the Parliament of 1604', East Anglia MPhil, 1974

Nicholls, A M, 'Politics and Percies: The ninth earl of Northumberland, his Brothers, and Gunpowder Plot', Cambridge PhD, 1986

Tighe, William J, 'The Gentlemen Pensioners in Elizabethan Politics and Government', Cambridge PhD, 1984

Index